LOVE

by Cathy Guisewite

**Andrews McMeel
Publishing**

Kansas City

01 02 03 04 05 BAE 10 9 8 7 6 5 4 3 2 1

Library of Congress Catalog Card Number: 2001090618

ISBN: 0-7407-2061-9

Cathy® may be viewed on the Internet at:
www.uexpress.com

Contents

Introduction

"Hello," he whispered. "I love you." He'd never even met me before, but he took me in his arms and told me I was the most beautiful thing he'd ever seen.

He said he'd been waiting his whole life for me . . . that he would love me and take care of me to the end of time.

He was so tall and so handsome. So strong and so gentle. There were tears in his eyes. I felt like I belonged with him forever. It was magic. It was perfect.

I was 30 seconds old, and my introduction to Dad had pretty much just ruined it for the next 45 years for the other 45 billion men on Earth.

Before I'd even had my first meal, the picture of the perfect man had been imprinted on the completely clean slate of my baby brain.

Before diaper number one of day number one of life, my expectations for love were set. My most primal memories of what love is—how effortlessly love arrives, how blissful it feels, how easy and natural and magical it is— were hard-wired by those first perfect moments with Dad.

Growing up, Dad remained the perfect guy. He could fix anything, heal anything, answer anything, do the hard homework problems, stand up to the big kids. He helped me build trains and cars and giant dreams. He hid candy bars in his briefcase and ate the biggest hot fudge sundaes in the world with no guilt.

Dad was wise and funny, charming and thoughtful, sensitive and brilliant. Dad would do anything for me. Dad made me feel important and special and safe. Dad gave me a sense of humor about Mom.

Even to this day, Dad likes to slip me a 20 dollar bill now and then just to make sure I have enough spending money.

And so, with Dad as my ideal, the hunt began.

I dedicate this book to two men: my husband, Chris, for measuring up to the impossible, and my dad, Bill, for giving me a role model of love that was powerful enough to survive a 45-year search.

MY 1975 LIST: HE MUST BE HANDSOME, STRONG AND CHARMING.
MY 1980 LIST: HE MUST BE HANDSOME, STRONG, CHARMING, OPEN, LOVING AND SUPPORTIVE.
MY 1985 LIST: HE MUST BE HANDSOME, STRONG, CHARMING, OPEN, LOVING, SUPPORTIVE, DYNAMIC, DEPENDABLE, SOLID, FLEXIBLE, POWERFUL, GENTLE, SERIOUS, SPONTANEOUS, SEXY, LOYAL, SOPHISTICATED, BOYISH, INDEPENDENT, DEVOTED, TOUGH, TENDER, BRILLIANT, HUMBLE, SUCCESSFUL, WISE AND CUTE.
MY 1988 LIST: HE MUST HAVE A SENSE OF HUMOR.
GUISEWITE

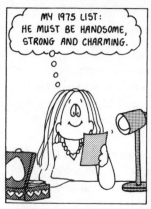

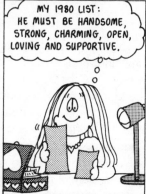

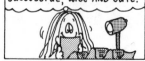

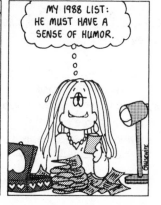

Then and Now

The entire relationship between men and women blew up exactly five seconds before I was ready to get serious about dating.

Every generation claims superiority in what it's had to endure in the search for love. While my generation may not have had it the worst, I will forever argue that we had it the weirdest.

In the 1970s, all the rules for courtship—which had at least provided a focal point for rebellion and/or blame—were "out."

All the rules for appropriate behavior were "out."

"Morals" were "out."

Social chaos, massive inner conflict, and total hostility between the sexes were "in."

No one had a clue.

No woman ever had a clue what was going on with men, and now no woman had a clue what she was or wasn't supposed to do with one.

I was launched onto the dating scene five seconds after men and women became enlightened enough to realize their lives had already been destroyed ("I am Man! Wash my clothes!") or were about to be destroyed ("I am Woman! Wash them yourself!") by the opposite sex.

In a period of a few years, we'd gone from 10 P.M. curfews for "college girls" to coed dorms for "college women." The possible good-night kiss at the well-lit door had become the presumed sleepover.

Parents were horrified.

Women were exhilarated, defiant, defensive, and confused.

Men felt abandoned, unappreciated, hostile, resentful, betrayed . . .and also quite "lucky."

Whether or not a woman had a right to work was actually a dating negotiating point.

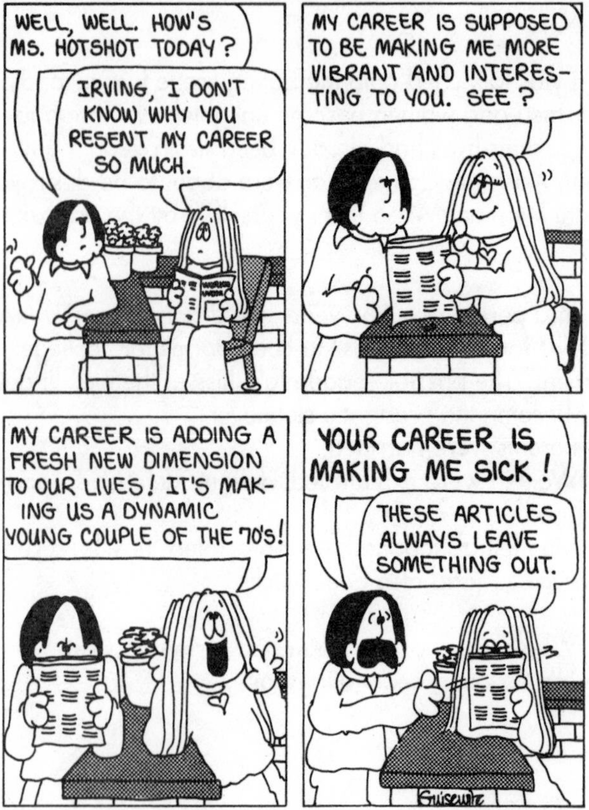
WELL, WELL. HOW'S MS. HOTSHOT TODAY?
IRVING, I DON'T KNOW WHY YOU RESENT MY CAREER SO MUCH.
MY CAREER IS SUPPOSED TO BE MAKING ME MORE VIBRANT AND INTERESTING TO YOU. SEE?
MY CAREER IS ADDING A FRESH NEW DIMENSION TO OUR LIVES! IT'S MAKING US A DYNAMIC YOUNG COUPLE OF THE 70'S!
YOUR CAREER IS MAKING ME SICK!
THESE ARTICLES ALWAYS LEAVE SOMETHING OUT.
Guisewite

A man who opened the door for the wrong woman was dumped for being a "pig."

A woman who insisted on the title "Ms." was dumped for being a "libber."

The men in my dating group were the last men in the history of America who would grow up believing a cheerful woman in a dress would have a nice, hot, homemade meal on the table for them every night at 5:30.

The women in my group were the last women in the history of America who would grow up being taught to "smile and let the man win."

We met as grown-ups on the exact dividing line in history. The culmination of a centuries-long effort for women's rights had hit Main Street. Grandmas were going on strike. Women were burning their underwear.

We faced off: Man hungry for dinner versus woman hungry to start her own billion-dollar food conglomerate.

Love survived all this: an astounding overhaul of how men and women relate; an unbelievable revolution of expectations and attitudes. Everything changed.
Everything completely, utterly, totally changed.

Except a few things that stayed exactly the same.

Romance, 1982:

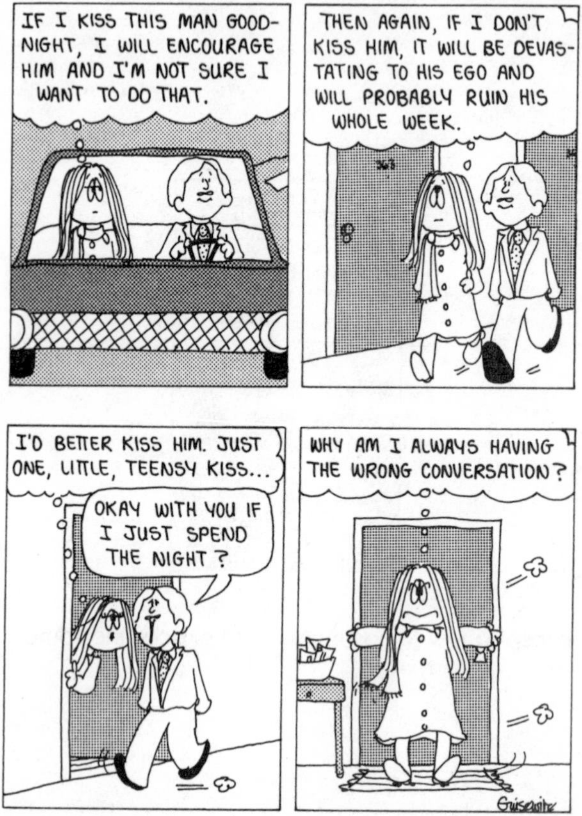

IF I KISS THIS MAN GOOD-NIGHT, I WILL ENCOURAGE HIM AND I'M NOT SURE I WANT TO DO THAT.
THEN AGAIN, IF I DON'T KISS HIM, IT WILL BE DEVASTATING TO HIS EGO AND WILL PROBABLY RUIN HIS WHOLE WEEK.
I'D BETTER KISS HIM. JUST ONE, LITTLE, TEENSY KISS...
OKAY WITH YOU IF I JUST SPEND THE NIGHT?
WHY AM I ALWAYS HAVING THE WRONG CONVERSATION?
Guisewite

Romance, 1998:

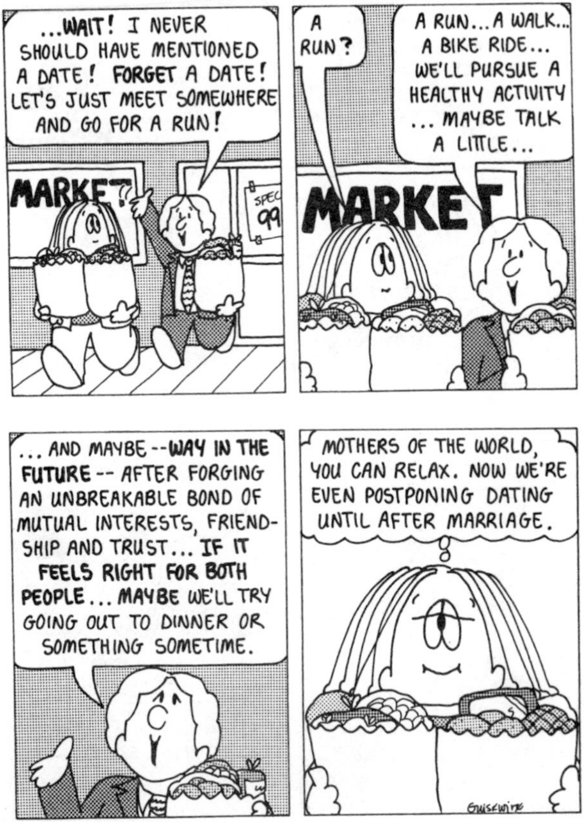
...WAIT! I NEVER SHOULD HAVE MENTIONED A DATE! FORGET A DATE! LET'S JUST MEET SOMEWHERE AND GO FOR A RUN!
MARKET
A RUN?
A RUN... A WALK... A BIKE RIDE... WE'LL PURSUE A HEALTHY ACTIVITY ... MAYBE TALK A LITTLE...
MARKET
... AND MAYBE --WAY IN THE FUTURE-- AFTER FORGING AN UNBREAKABLE BOND OF MUTUAL INTERESTS, FRIENDSHIP AND TRUST... IF IT FEELS RIGHT FOR BOTH PEOPLE... MAYBE WE'LL TRY GOING OUT TO DINNER OR SOMETHING SOMETIME.
MOTHERS OF THE WORLD, YOU CAN RELAX. NOW WE'RE EVEN POSTPONING DATING UNTIL AFTER MARRIAGE.
Guisewite

Communication, 1983:

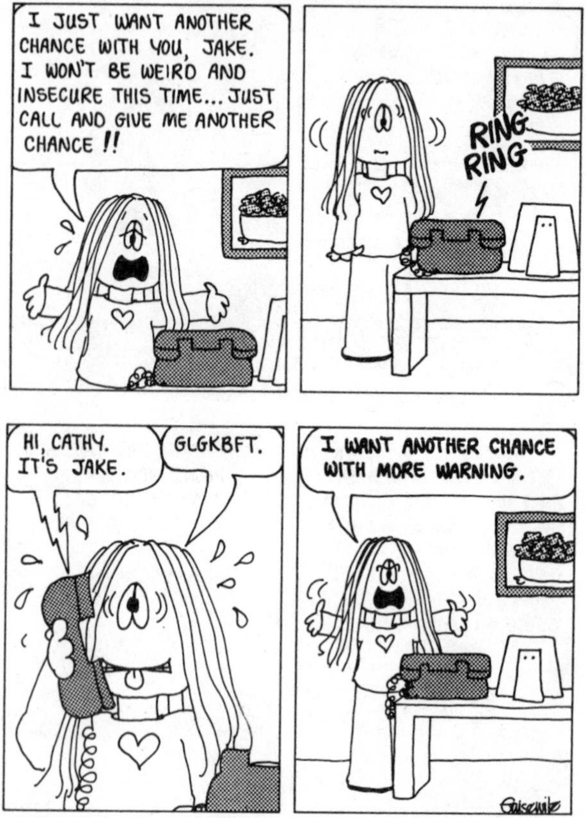
I JUST WANT ANOTHER CHANCE WITH YOU, JAKE. I WON'T BE WEIRD AND INSECURE THIS TIME... JUST CALL AND GIVE ME ANOTHER CHANCE!!
RING RING
HI, CATHY. IT'S JAKE.
GLGKBFT.
I WANT ANOTHER CHANCE WITH MORE WARNING.
Guisewite

Communication, 1997:

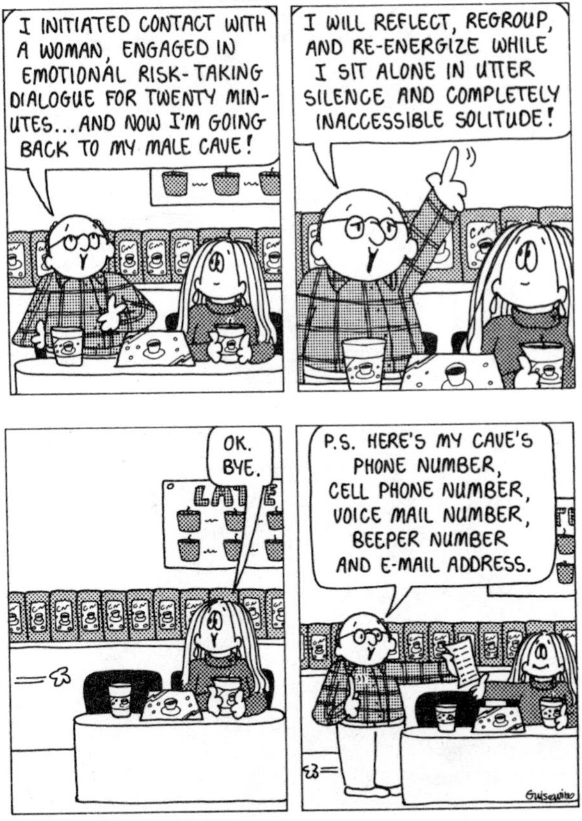
I INITIATED CONTACT WITH A WOMAN, ENGAGED IN EMOTIONAL RISK-TAKING DIALOGUE FOR TWENTY MINUTES... AND NOW I'M GOING BACK TO MY MALE CAVE!
I WILL REFLECT, REGROUP, AND RE-ENERGIZE WHILE I SIT ALONE IN UTTER SILENCE AND COMPLETELY INACCESSIBLE SOLITUDE!
OK. BYE.
P.S. HERE'S MY CAVE'S PHONE NUMBER, CELL PHONE NUMBER, VOICE MAIL NUMBER, BEEPER NUMBER AND E-MAIL ADDRESS.
Guisewite

Chivalry, 1977:

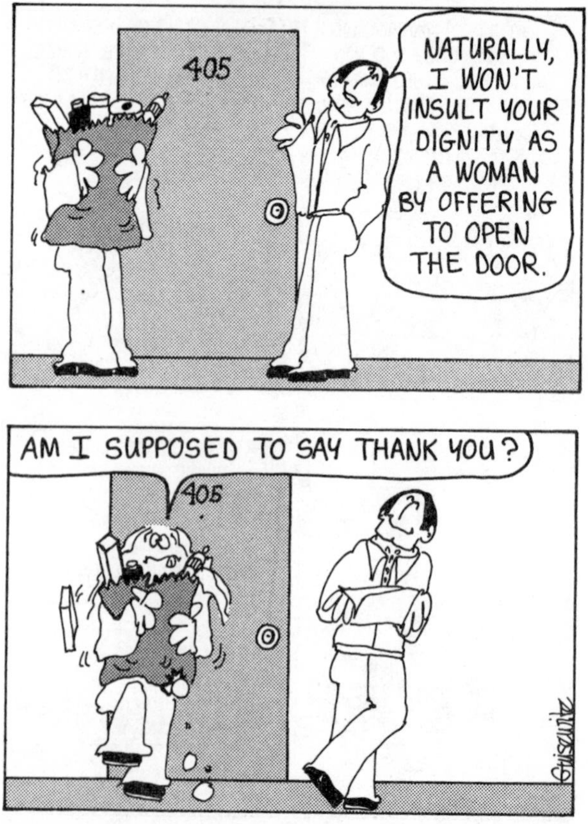

NATURALLY, I WON'T INSULT YOUR DIGNITY AS A WOMAN BY OFFERING TO OPEN THE DOOR.
405
AM I SUPPOSED TO SAY THANK YOU?
405
Guisewite

Chivalry, 1991:

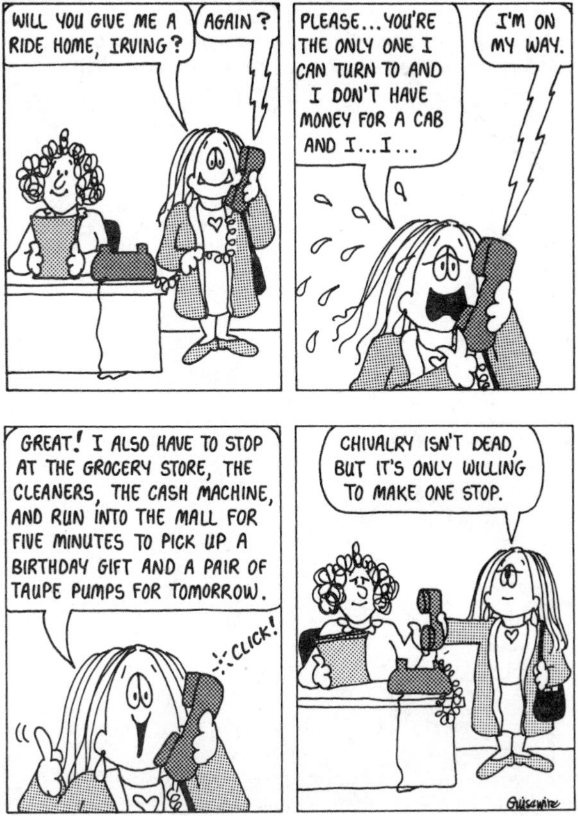
WILL YOU GIVE ME A RIDE HOME, IRVING?
AGAIN?
PLEASE... YOU'RE THE ONLY ONE I CAN TURN TO AND I DON'T HAVE MONEY FOR A CAB AND I... I...
I'M ON MY WAY.
GREAT! I ALSO HAVE TO STOP AT THE GROCERY STORE, THE CLEANERS, THE CASH MACHINE, AND RUN INTO THE MALL FOR FIVE MINUTES TO PICK UP A BIRTHDAY GIFT AND A PAIR OF TAUPE PUMPS FOR TOMORROW.
CLICK!
CHIVALRY ISN'T DEAD, BUT IT'S ONLY WILLING TO MAKE ONE STOP.
Guisewite

The Modern Mom, 1982:

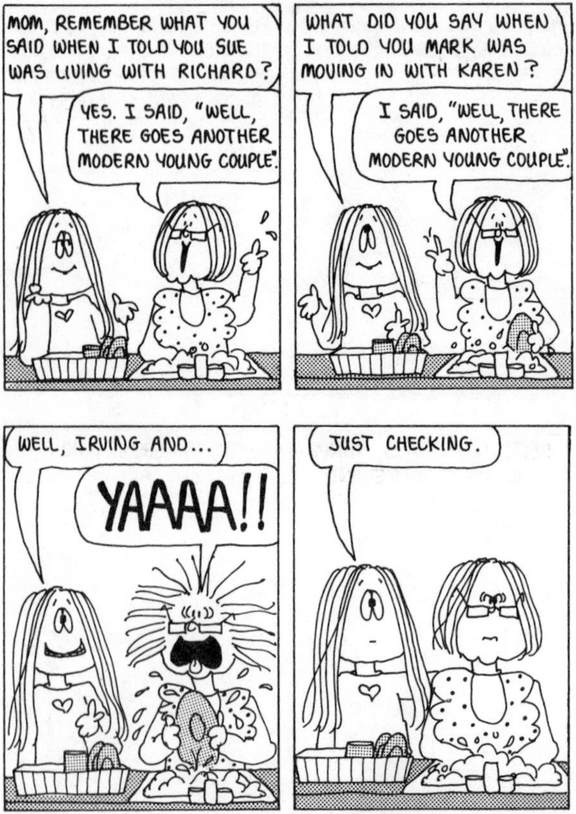
MOM, REMEMBER WHAT YOU SAID WHEN I TOLD YOU SUE WAS LIVING WITH RICHARD?
YES. I SAID, "WELL, THERE GOES ANOTHER MODERN YOUNG COUPLE".
WHAT DID YOU SAY WHEN I TOLD YOU MARK WAS MOVING IN WITH KAREN?
I SAID, "WELL, THERE GOES ANOTHER MODERN YOUNG COUPLE".
WELL, IRVING AND...
YAAAA!!
JUST CHECKING.

The Modern Mom, 1996:

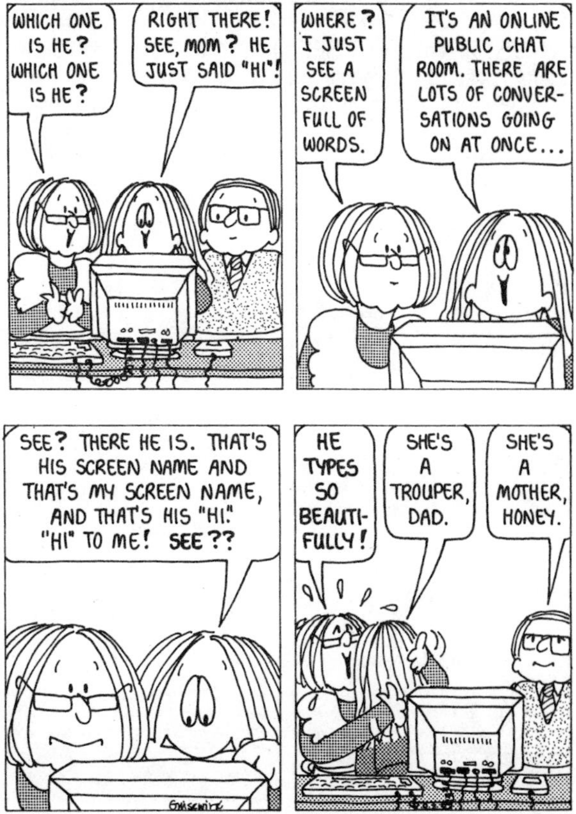
WHICH ONE IS HE? WHICH ONE IS HE?
RIGHT THERE! SEE, MOM? HE JUST SAID "HI"!
WHERE? I JUST SEE A SCREEN FULL OF WORDS.
IT'S AN ONLINE PUBLIC CHAT ROOM. THERE ARE LOTS OF CONVERSATIONS GOING ON AT ONCE...
SEE? THERE HE IS. THAT'S HIS SCREEN NAME AND THAT'S MY SCREEN NAME, AND THAT'S HIS "HI." "HI" TO ME! SEE??
HE TYPES SO BEAUTIFULLY!
SHE'S A TROUPER, DAD.
SHE'S A MOTHER, HONEY.

Saying Good-bye, 1976:

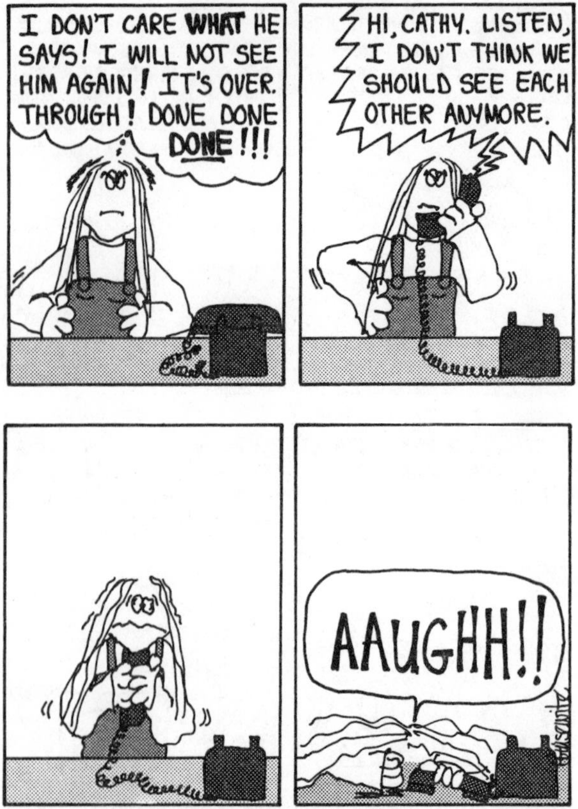
I DON'T CARE WHAT HE SAYS! I WILL NOT SEE HIM AGAIN! IT'S OVER. THROUGH! DONE DONE DONE!!!
HI, CATHY. LISTEN, I DON'T THINK WE SHOULD SEE EACH OTHER ANYMORE.
AAUGHH!!

Saying Good-bye, 1996:

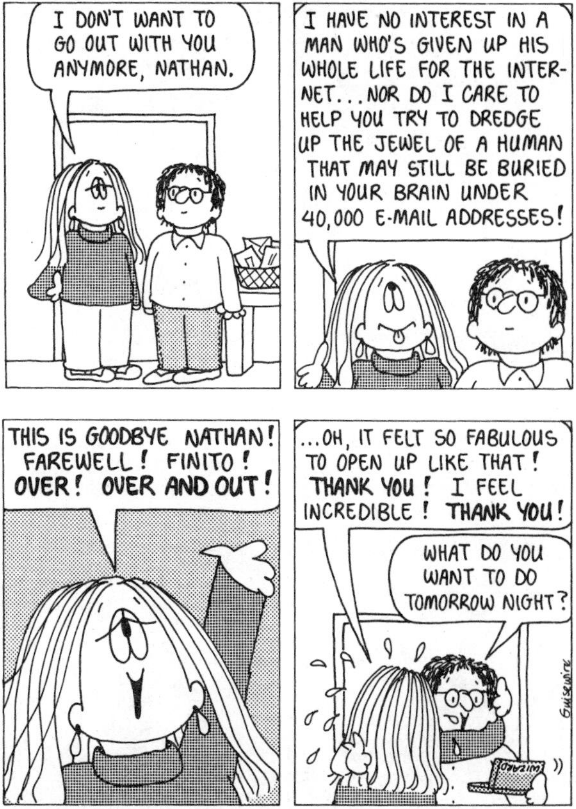
I DON'T WANT TO GO OUT WITH YOU ANYMORE, NATHAN.
I HAVE NO INTEREST IN A MAN WHO'S GIVEN UP HIS WHOLE LIFE FOR THE INTER-NET... NOR DO I CARE TO HELP YOU TRY TO DREDGE UP THE JEWEL OF A HUMAN THAT MAY STILL BE BURIED IN YOUR BRAIN UNDER 40,000 E-MAIL ADDRESSES!
THIS IS GOODBYE NATHAN! FAREWELL! FINITO! OVER! OVER AND OUT!
...OH, IT FELT SO FABULOUS TO OPEN UP LIKE THAT! THANK YOU! I FEEL INCREDIBLE! THANK YOU!
WHAT DO YOU WANT TO DO TOMORROW NIGHT?
WIZARD
GUISEWITE

Emotional Risk Taking, 1985:

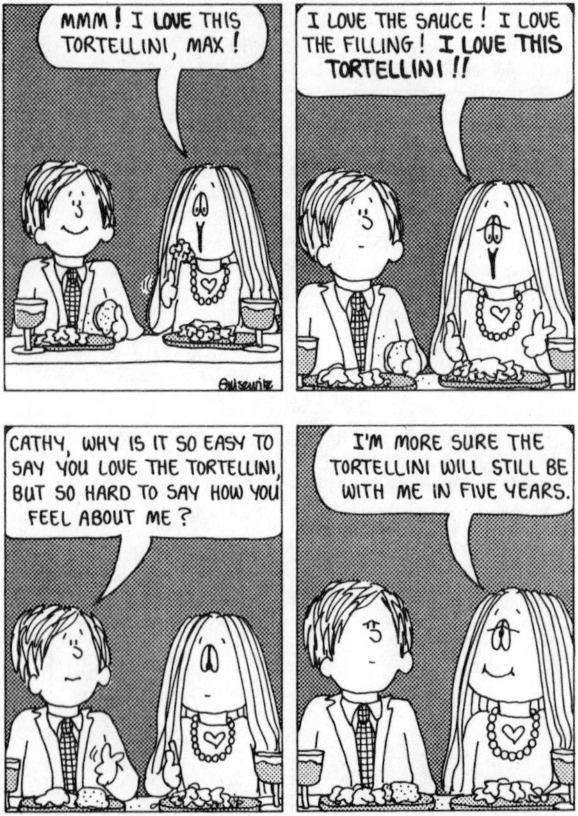
MMM! I LOVE THIS TORTELLINI, MAX!
I LOVE THE SAUCE! I LOVE THE FILLING! I LOVE THIS TORTELLINI!!
CATHY, WHY IS IT SO EASY TO SAY YOU LOVE THE TORTELLINI, BUT SO HARD TO SAY HOW YOU FEEL ABOUT ME?
I'M MORE SURE THE TORTELLINI WILL STILL BE WITH ME IN FIVE YEARS.

Emotional Risk Taking, 2001:

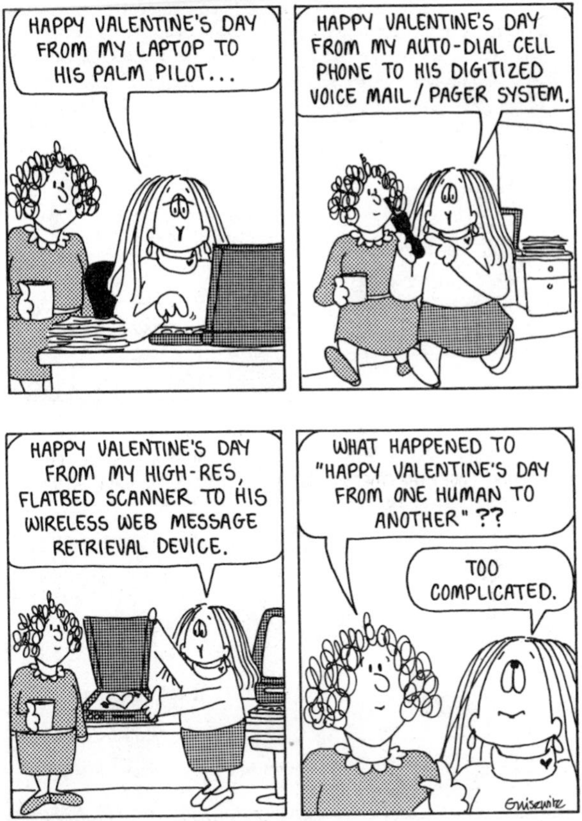

HAPPY VALENTINE'S DAY FROM MY LAPTOP TO HIS PALM PILOT...
HAPPY VALENTINE'S DAY FROM MY AUTO-DIAL CELL PHONE TO HIS DIGITIZED VOICE MAIL / PAGER SYSTEM.
HAPPY VALENTINE'S DAY FROM MY HIGH-RES, FLATBED SCANNER TO HIS WIRELESS WEB MESSAGE RETRIEVAL DEVICE.
WHAT HAPPENED TO "HAPPY VALENTINE'S DAY FROM ONE HUMAN TO ANOTHER"??
TOO COMPLICATED.
Guisewite

Life Questioning, 1981:

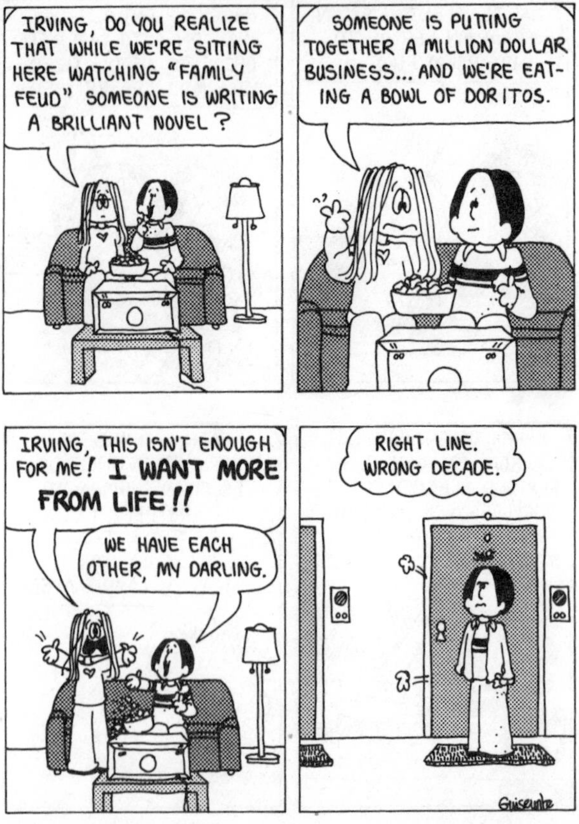
IRVING, DO YOU REALIZE THAT WHILE WE'RE SITTING HERE WATCHING "FAMILY FEUD" SOMEONE IS WRITING A BRILLIANT NOVEL?
SOMEONE IS PUTTING TOGETHER A MILLION DOLLAR BUSINESS... AND WE'RE EATING A BOWL OF DORITOS.
IRVING, THIS ISN'T ENOUGH FOR ME! I WANT MORE FROM LIFE!!
WE HAVE EACH OTHER, MY DARLING.
RIGHT LINE. WRONG DECADE.
Guisewite

Life Questioning, 1995:

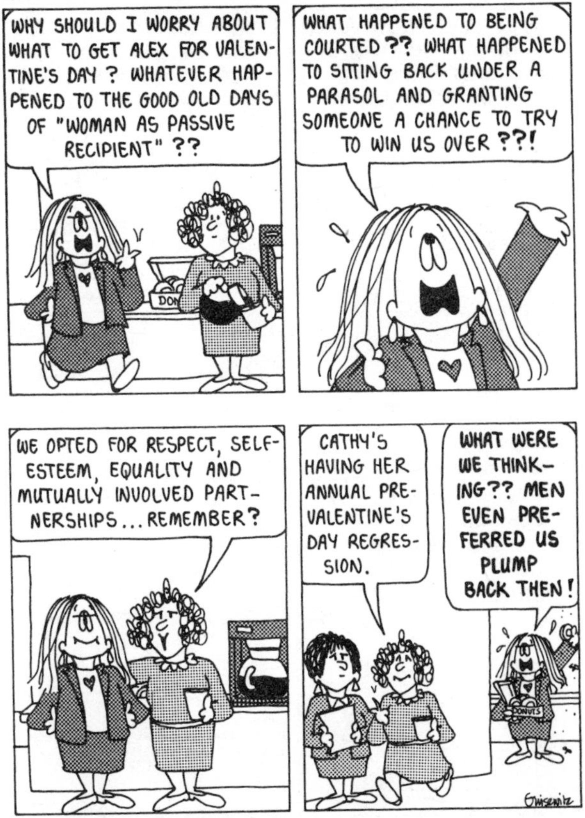

WHY SHOULD I WORRY ABOUT WHAT TO GET ALEX FOR VALEN- TINE'S DAY ? WHATEVER HAP- PENED TO THE GOOD OLD DAYS OF "WOMAN AS PASSIVE RECIPIENT" ??
WHAT HAPPENED TO BEING COURTED ?? WHAT HAPPENED TO SITTING BACK UNDER A PARASOL AND GRANTING SOMEONE A CHANCE TO TRY TO WIN US OVER ??!
WE OPTED FOR RESPECT, SELF- ESTEEM, EQUALITY AND MUTUALLY INVOLVED PART- NERSHIPS... REMEMBER?
CATHY'S HAVING HER ANNUAL PRE- VALENTINE'S DAY REGRES- SION.
WHAT WERE WE THINK- ING?? MEN EVEN PRE- FERRED US PLUMP BACK THEN!
DONUTS
Guisewite

Jealousy, 1980:

YOU'RE JUST PRETENDING YOU'RE NOT JEALOUS OF MARTHA BECAUSE YOU WANT ME TO THINK YOU DON'T CARE.

YOU FIGURE THAT IF YOU SHOW ME YOU CARE, I'LL FEEL THREATENED.

WHEN ACTUALLY BY ACTING LIKE YOU DON'T CARE, YOU'RE SHOWING ME HOW MUCH YOU REALLY DO CARE... AND FRANKLY, CATHY, I DON'T NEED THAT KIND OF PRESSURE!!

WELL! I HANDLED THAT ONE NICELY.

Guisewite

Jealousy, 1990:

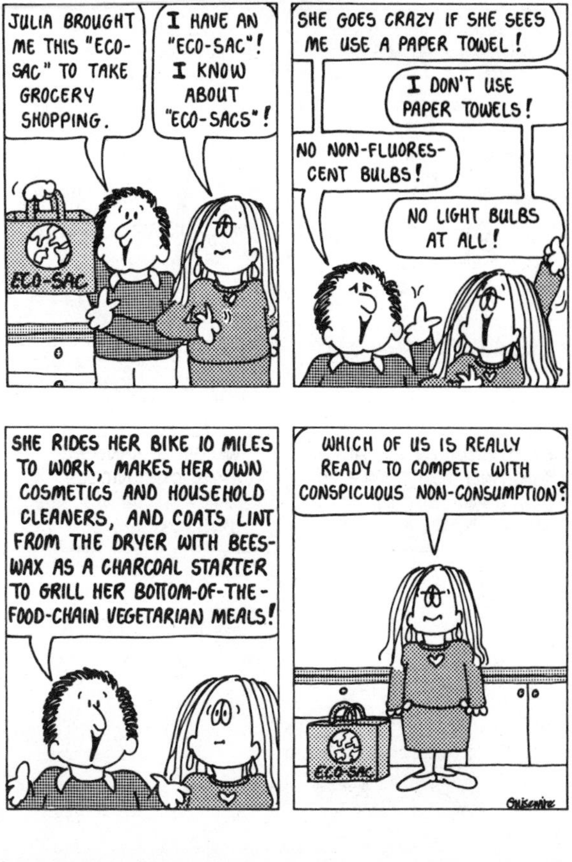

JULIA BROUGHT ME THIS "ECO-SAC" TO TAKE GROCERY SHOPPING.
I HAVE AN "ECO-SAC"! I KNOW ABOUT "ECO-SACS"!
ECO-SAC
SHE GOES CRAZY IF SHE SEES ME USE A PAPER TOWEL!
I DON'T USE PAPER TOWELS!
NO NON-FLUORES-CENT BULBS!
NO LIGHT BULBS AT ALL!
SHE RIDES HER BIKE 10 MILES TO WORK, MAKES HER OWN COSMETICS AND HOUSEHOLD CLEANERS, AND COATS LINT FROM THE DRYER WITH BEES-WAX AS A CHARCOAL STARTER TO GRILL HER BOTTOM-OF-THE-FOOD-CHAIN VEGETARIAN MEALS!
WHICH OF US IS REALLY READY TO COMPETE WITH CONSPICUOUS NON-CONSUMPTION?
ECO-SAC
Guisewite

Guessing, 1981:

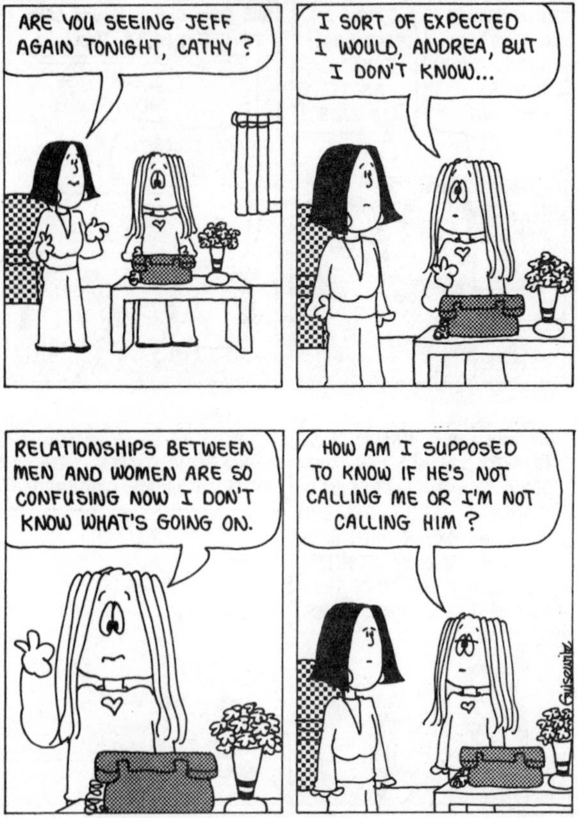
ARE YOU SEEING JEFF AGAIN TONIGHT, CATHY?
I SORT OF EXPECTED I WOULD, ANDREA, BUT I DON'T KNOW...
RELATIONSHIPS BETWEEN MEN AND WOMEN ARE SO CONFUSING NOW I DON'T KNOW WHAT'S GOING ON.
HOW AM I SUPPOSED TO KNOW IF HE'S NOT CALLING ME OR I'M NOT CALLING HIM?
Guisewite

Guessing, 1996:

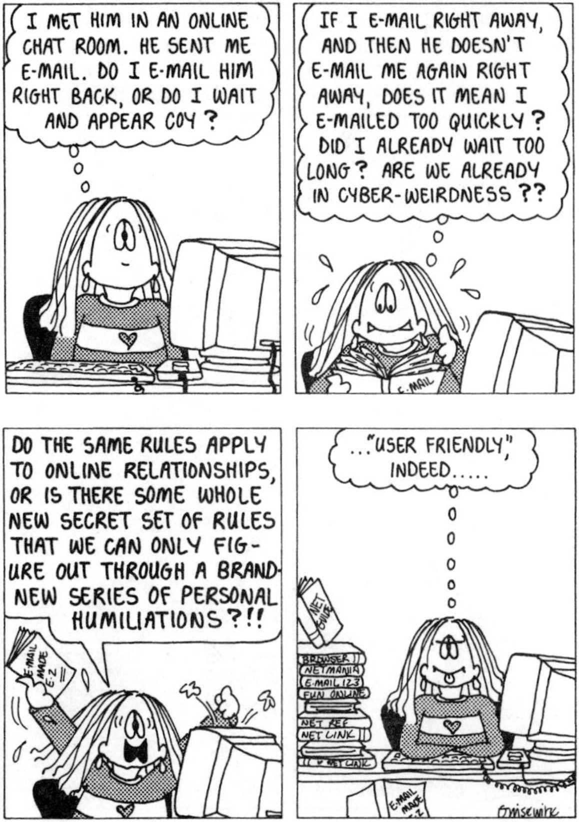
I MET HIM IN AN ONLINE CHAT ROOM. HE SENT ME E-MAIL. DO I E-MAIL HIM RIGHT BACK, OR DO I WAIT AND APPEAR COY ?
IF I E-MAIL RIGHT AWAY, AND THEN HE DOESN'T E-MAIL ME AGAIN RIGHT AWAY, DOES IT MEAN I E-MAILED TOO QUICKLY ? DID I ALREADY WAIT TOO LONG ? ARE WE ALREADY IN CYBER-WEIRDNESS ??
E-MAIL
DO THE SAME RULES APPLY TO ONLINE RELATIONSHIPS, OR IS THERE SOME WHOLE NEW SECRET SET OF RULES THAT WE CAN ONLY FIGURE OUT THROUGH A BRAND-NEW SERIES OF PERSONAL HUMILIATIONS ?!!
E-MAIL MADE E-Z
..."USER FRIENDLY," INDEED.....
NET GUIDE
BROWSER
NETMANIA
E-MAIL 123
FUN ONLINE
NET REF
NET LINK
E-MAIL MADE E-Z
Guisewite

Having It All, 1979:

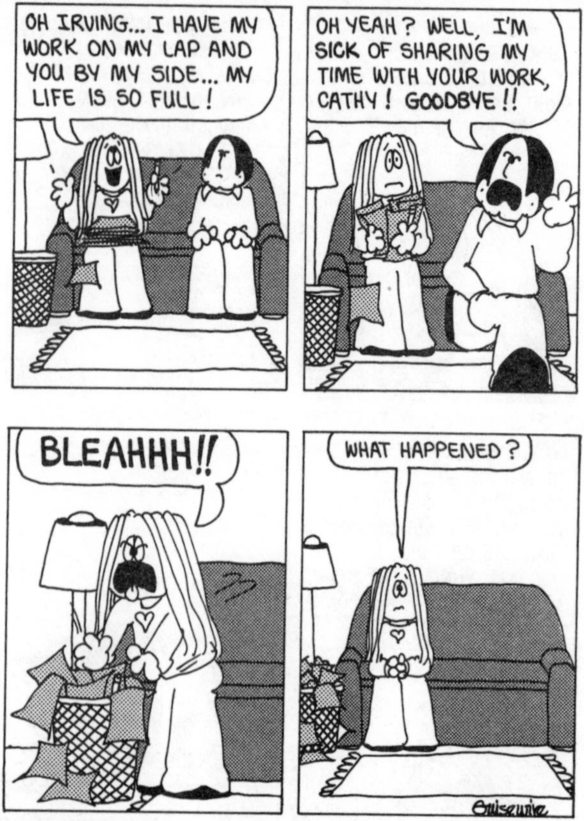
OH IRVING... I HAVE MY WORK ON MY LAP AND YOU BY MY SIDE... MY LIFE IS SO FULL!
OH YEAH? WELL, I'M SICK OF SHARING MY TIME WITH YOUR WORK, CATHY! GOODBYE!!
BLEAHHH!!
WHAT HAPPENED?
Guisewite

Having It All, 1995:

TO DO, 1955:

1. MARRY WELL.

TO DO, 1975:

1. TRANSFORM ROLE OF WOMEN IN SOCIETY.

TO DO, 1995:

1. EARN LIVING.
2. BUY, FURNISH AND MAINTAIN HOME.
3. PAY ALL BILLS.
4. DO ALL LAUNDRY.
5. BUY ALL GROCERIES.
6. COOK ALL MEALS.
7. LOCATE AND MARRY HUSBAND.
8. HAVE AND RAISE CHILDREN.
9. TONE ALL MUSCLES.
10. REBEL AGAINST AGING.
11. SAVE PLANET.
12. BUY AND MAINTAIN AUTOMOBILE.
13. FIGHT AGAINST EVIL.
14. TAKE CHARGE OF LIFE.
15. GO INTO THERAPY TO REGAIN VULNERABILITY.

I AM WOMAN. HEAR ME SNORE.

TO PAY

TO ANSWER

TO DEAL WITH

35

Taking the Initiative, 1980:

HI. I'D LIKE TO SEND THAT MAN A DISH OF MACARONI SALAD.
WHAT ?
SEE THAT CUTE MAN OVER THERE ? TAKE HIM A DISH OF MACARONI SALAD AND PUT IT ON MY BILL !
WHY ARE YOU LOOKING AT ME LIKE THAT ? HAVEN'T YOU EVER SEEN AN ASSERTIVE WOMAN IN ACTION BEFORE ??!
THAT WOMAN OVER THERE WANTS YOU TO HAVE THIS MACARONI SALAD, SIR.
Guisewite

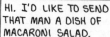

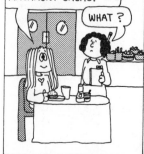

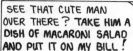

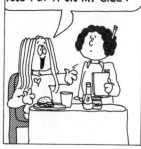

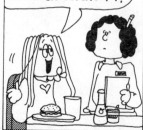

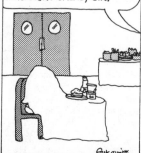

Taking the Initiative, 1983:

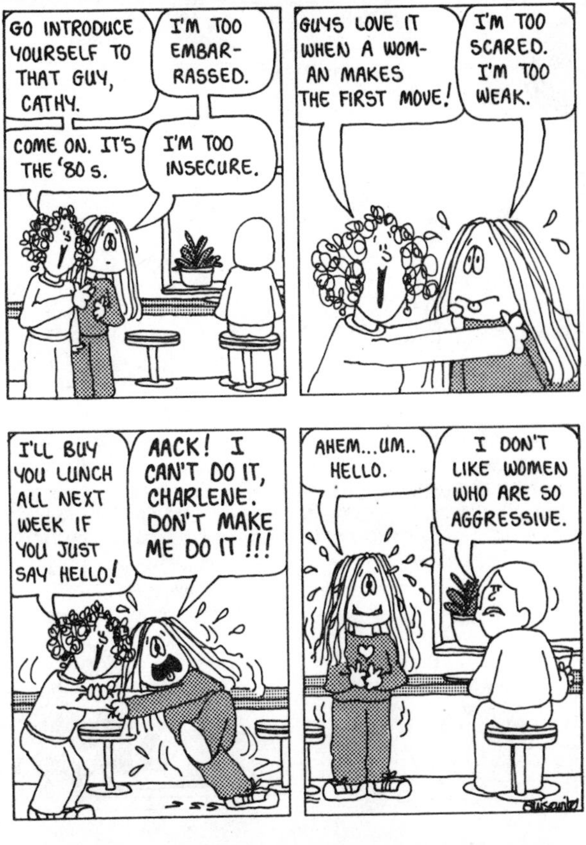
GO INTRODUCE YOURSELF TO THAT GUY, CATHY.
I'M TOO EMBAR-RASSED.
COME ON. IT'S THE '80 S.
I'M TOO INSECURE.
GUYS LOVE IT WHEN A WOM-AN MAKES THE FIRST MOVE!
I'M TOO SCARED. I'M TOO WEAK.
I'LL BUY YOU LUNCH ALL NEXT WEEK IF YOU JUST SAY HELLO!
AACK! I CAN'T DO IT, CHARLENE. DON'T MAKE ME DO IT !!!
AHEM...UM.. HELLO.
I DON'T LIKE WOMEN WHO ARE SO AGGRESSIVE.

Taking the Initiative, 1992:

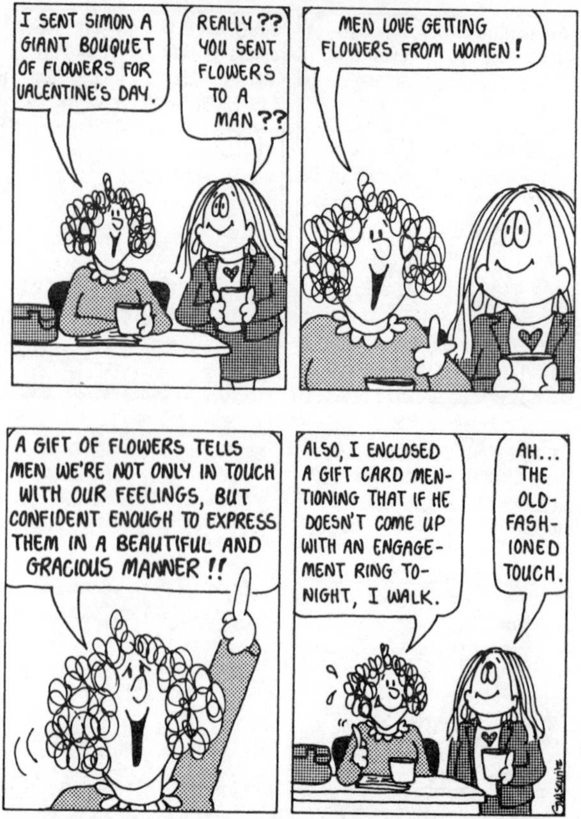
I SENT SIMON A GIANT BOUQUET OF FLOWERS FOR VALENTINE'S DAY.
REALLY?? YOU SENT FLOWERS TO A MAN??
MEN LOVE GETTING FLOWERS FROM WOMEN!
A GIFT OF FLOWERS TELLS MEN WE'RE NOT ONLY IN TOUCH WITH OUR FEELINGS, BUT CONFIDENT ENOUGH TO EXPRESS THEM IN A BEAUTIFUL AND GRACIOUS MANNER!!
ALSO, I ENCLOSED A GIFT CARD MENTIONING THAT IF HE DOESN'T COME UP WITH AN ENGAGEMENT RING TONIGHT, I WALK.
AH... THE OLD-FASHIONED TOUCH.

Taking the Initiative, 1999:

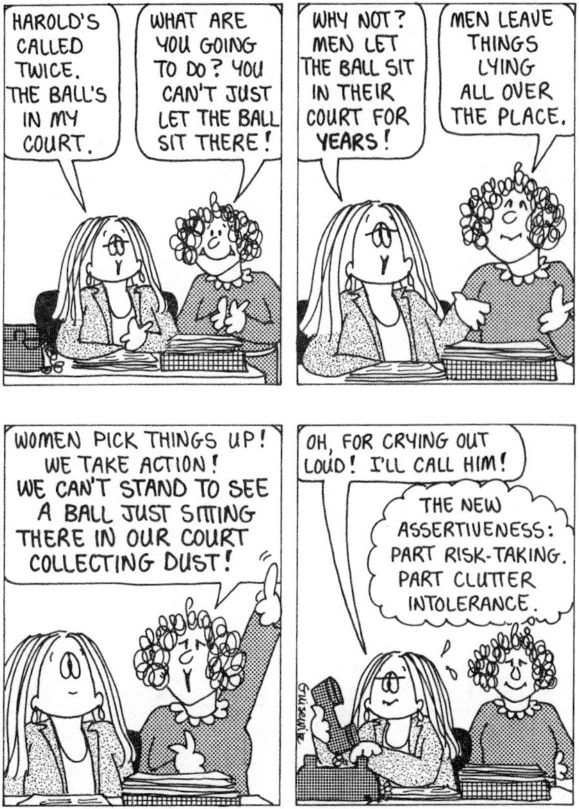
HAROLD'S CALLED TWICE. THE BALL'S IN MY COURT.
WHAT ARE YOU GOING TO DO? YOU CAN'T JUST LET THE BALL SIT THERE!
WHY NOT? MEN LET THE BALL SIT IN THEIR COURT FOR YEARS!
MEN LEAVE THINGS LYING ALL OVER THE PLACE.
WOMEN PICK THINGS UP! WE TAKE ACTION! WE CAN'T STAND TO SEE A BALL JUST SITTING THERE IN OUR COURT COLLECTING DUST!
OH, FOR CRYING OUT LOUD! I'LL CALL HIM!
THE NEW ASSERTIVENESS: PART RISK-TAKING. PART CLUTTER INTOLERANCE.

Taking the Initiative, 2000:

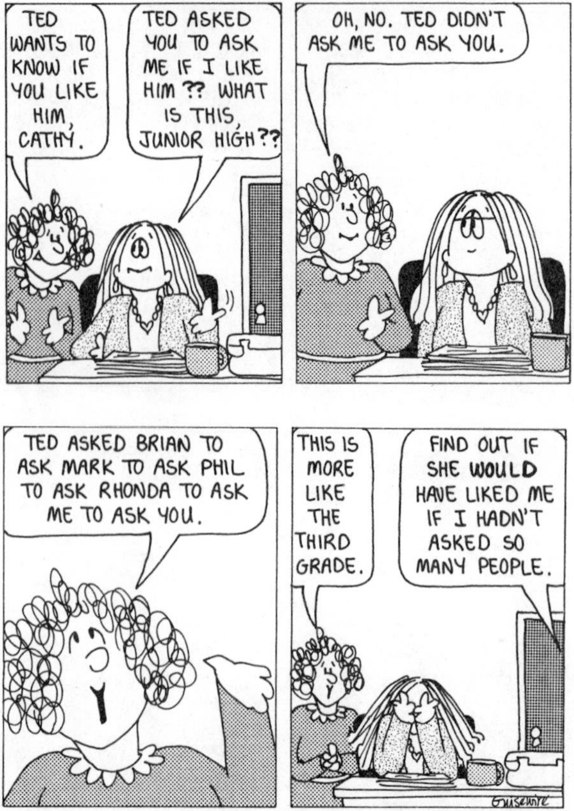
TED WANTS TO KNOW IF YOU LIKE HIM, CATHY.
TED ASKED YOU TO ASK ME IF I LIKE HIM?? WHAT IS THIS, JUNIOR HIGH??
OH, NO. TED DIDN'T ASK ME TO ASK YOU.
TED ASKED BRIAN TO ASK MARK TO ASK PHIL TO ASK RHONDA TO ASK ME TO ASK YOU.
THIS IS MORE LIKE THE THIRD GRADE.
FIND OUT IF SHE WOULD HAVE LIKED ME IF I HADN'T ASKED SO MANY PEOPLE.
Guisewite

Investing in Love, 1969–1999:

1981: WANTED TO MEET SOMEONE NEW, SO ENROLLED IN ADULT ED. COURSE.
COST: $65.00

1987: WANTED TO MEET SOMEONE NEW, SO SIGNED UP FOR DATING SERVICE.
COST: $300.00

1990: WANTED TO MEET SOMEONE NEW, SO JOINED A GYM.
COST: $500.00

1996: WANTED TO MEET SOMEONE NEW, SO BEGAN SHOPPING FOR COMPUTER, MONITOR, MODEM AND SOFTWARE TO CONNECT TO ONLINE ROMANCE CHAT ROOM.
COST: $2,400.00

SOMEDAY MY PRINCE WILL COME, AND WHEN HE DOES, HE'D BETTER BE CARRYING A GREAT BIG BAG OF MONEY.

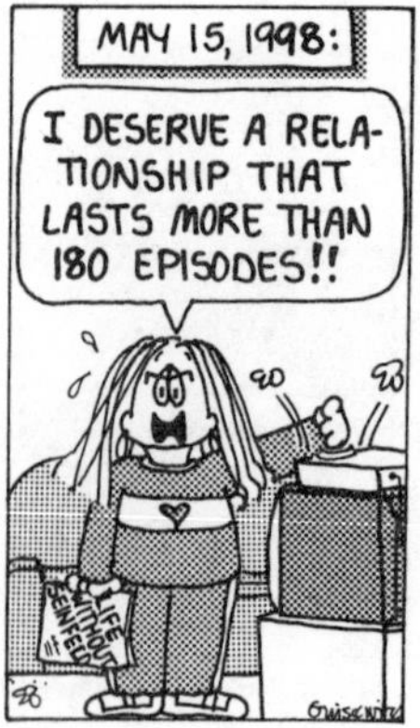
MAY 15, 1998:
I DESERVE A RELATIONSHIP THAT LASTS MORE THAN 180 EPISODES!!
LIFE WITHOUT SEINFELD
Guisewite

Where the Boys Are

No one ever talks about the "joy of looking."

People talk about the joy of dating, the joy of falling in love, the joy of getting married. In fact, one of the main joys of all of the above is that you never have to experience the "joy of looking" again.

It was bad enough back in the good old days when people had to actually leave their homes for things like food, clothing, movies, and jobs. At least the chance of seeing and rejecting a member of the opposite sex in line at the bank or the grocery store existed.

Now it's possible to do everything—including meeting someone, falling in love, getting disgusted, and dumping each other—from the computer while wearing pj's at the kitchen counter. Lots of people's only "human" contact is with the 1-800-hotline operator, and they're usually not exactly calling to flirt.

I live in Los Angeles where, even if people do leave our homes, we have to look good only from the neck up since we're seen only in our cars.

Food is either sent directly to the home or grabbed at the take-out window. The only people who sit down in restaurants long enough to meet someone have already met someone and are eating dinner with him.

The only people who are all alone are talking on the phone to someone else.

Nobody else even pauses unless there's an actual car collision, and then it's just to toss a business card with the insurance agent's cell phone number through the window.

Coffee places are packed, but they're packed either with people who are already couples or with little unapproachable groups.

Even the people who sit down alone immediately build little anti-conversation fortresses in front of themselves: books, laptops, notebooks, newspapers, magazines, briefcases, and/or CD players with headphones clamped over their ears.

Someone brave enough to just sit there—to just confidently occupy the space . . . alone, open, smiling, accessible . . . the one person who is actually approachable in the entire place—looks way too weird to meet.

Young people don't even seem to try. They just travel in packs of singles until someone apparently gives a signal, and everyone picks a partner and gets married.

Older singles aren't so lucky. The pack is gone. Everyone in the pack got married a long time ago. The children of the ex-pack members are starting to date.

Fix-ups start to look good. Except now that no one ever leaves the house, no one ever meets anyone to fix anyone else up with.

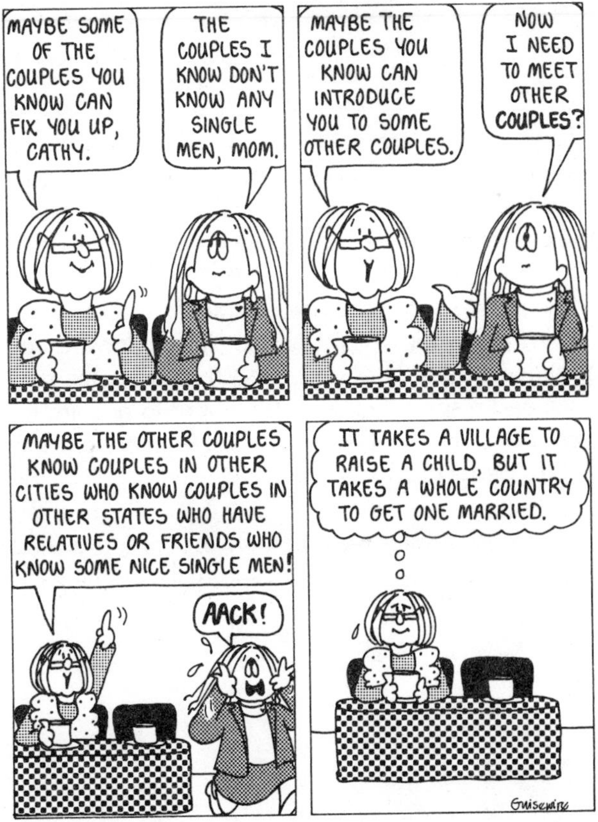
MAYBE SOME OF THE COUPLES YOU KNOW CAN FIX YOU UP, CATHY.
THE COUPLES I KNOW DON'T KNOW ANY SINGLE MEN, MOM.
MAYBE THE COUPLES YOU KNOW CAN INTRODUCE YOU TO SOME OTHER COUPLES.
NOW I NEED TO MEET OTHER COUPLES?
MAYBE THE OTHER COUPLES KNOW COUPLES IN OTHER CITIES WHO KNOW COUPLES IN OTHER STATES WHO HAVE RELATIVES OR FRIENDS WHO KNOW SOME NICE SINGLE MEN!
AACK!
IT TAKES A VILLAGE TO RAISE A CHILD, BUT IT TAKES A WHOLE COUNTRY TO GET ONE MARRIED.

Single people are sent out on blind dates with other single people with the one and only shred of common ground being that they are both still single. The older you get, the fewer qualities people even try to match.

"He's perfect for you! He's single!"
"But what about the list of qualities I'm looking for that I've refined over the last decade? What about the self-confidence and respect I've worked so hard to acquire that empower me to demand what I need from a life partner?"
"He's perfect for you! He's single!"

A lifelong quest for a soul mate reduced to a simple human inclination: Everyone tries to make a sandwich out of the last two pieces of bread.

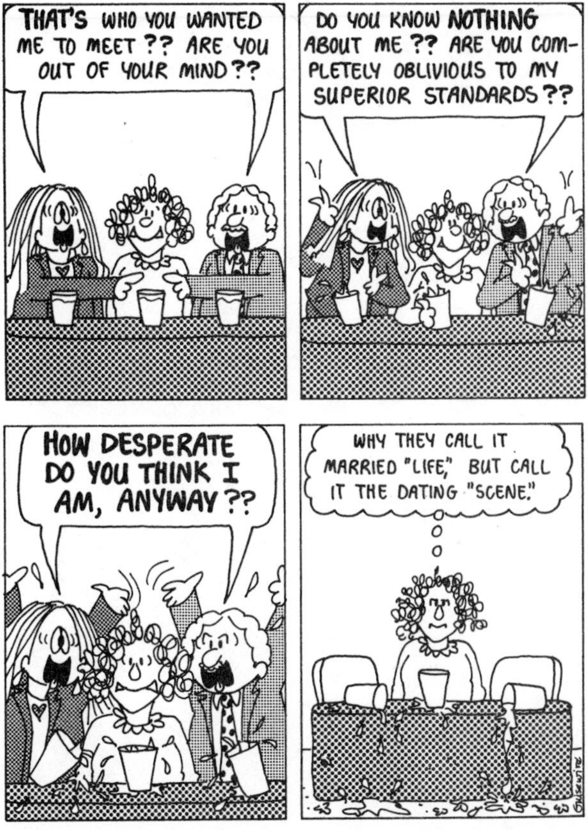
THAT'S WHO YOU WANTED ME TO MEET ?? ARE YOU OUT OF YOUR MIND ??
DO YOU KNOW NOTHING ABOUT ME ?? ARE YOU COMPLETELY OBLIVIOUS TO MY SUPERIOR STANDARDS ??
HOW DESPERATE DO YOU THINK I AM, ANYWAY ??
WHY THEY CALL IT MARRIED "LIFE," BUT CALL IT THE DATING "SCENE."

Just in case modern dating makes anyone nostalgic for the good old days, here are some of the places we used to look for love.

The Singles Bar, 1978:

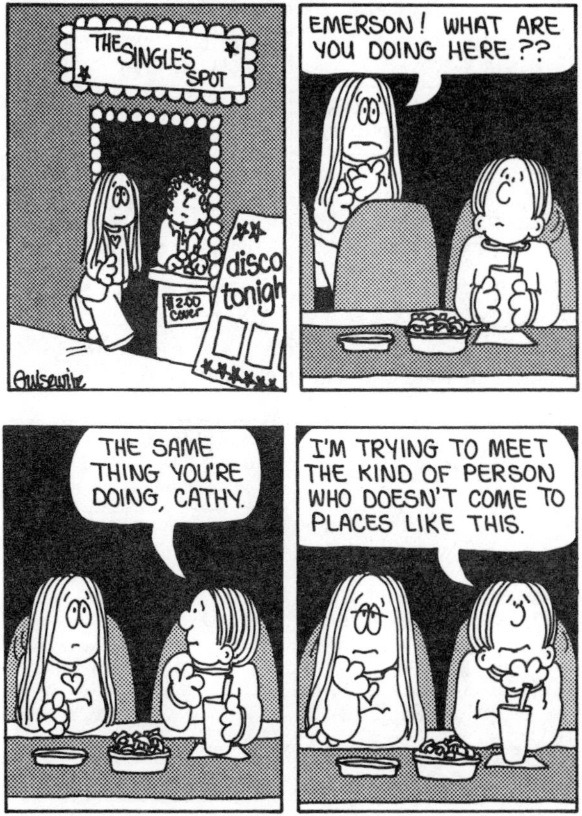
THE SINGLE'S SPOT
disco tonigh
$2.00 cover
EMERSON! WHAT ARE YOU DOING HERE??
THE SAME THING YOU'RE DOING, CATHY.
I'M TRYING TO MEET THE KIND OF PERSON WHO DOESN'T COME TO PLACES LIKE THIS.

The Singles Bar, 1980:

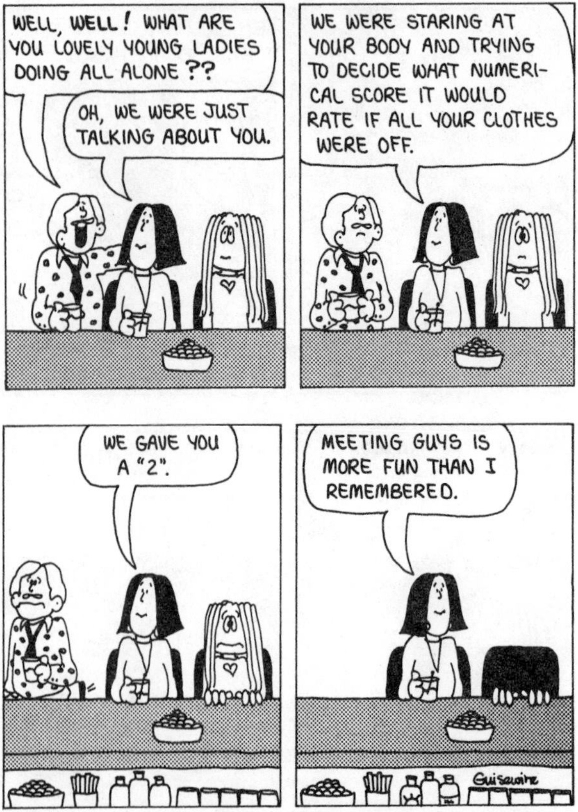
WELL, WELL! WHAT ARE YOU LOVELY YOUNG LADIES DOING ALL ALONE??
OH, WE WERE JUST TALKING ABOUT YOU.
WE WERE STARING AT YOUR BODY AND TRYING TO DECIDE WHAT NUMERICAL SCORE IT WOULD RATE IF ALL YOUR CLOTHES WERE OFF.
WE GAVE YOU A "2".
MEETING GUYS IS MORE FUN THAN I REMEMBERED.
Guisewite

The Office, 1982:

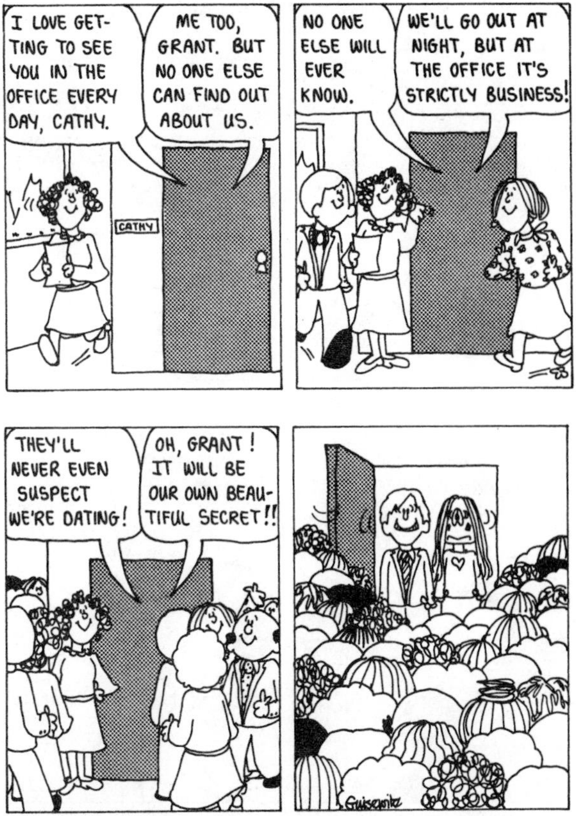
I LOVE GETTING TO SEE YOU IN THE OFFICE EVERY DAY, CATHY.
ME TOO, GRANT. BUT NO ONE ELSE CAN FIND OUT ABOUT US.
CATHY
NO ONE ELSE WILL EVER KNOW.
WE'LL GO OUT AT NIGHT, BUT AT THE OFFICE IT'S STRICTLY BUSINESS!
THEY'LL NEVER EVEN SUSPECT WE'RE DATING!
OH, GRANT! IT WILL BE OUR OWN BEAUTIFUL SECRET!!
Guisewite

The Home, 1983:

WHERE ARE THEY?! WHERE ARE ALL THE SINGLE MEN?!!

STANDING ON YOUR BALCONY SCREAMING ISN'T GOING TO HELP, CATHY.

YOU'LL ONLY MEET SOMEONE NEW WHEN YOU JUST RELAX AND DO THE THINGS YOU NORMALLY DO.

THAT **IS** WHAT I NORMALLY DO.

The Singles Bar, 1983:

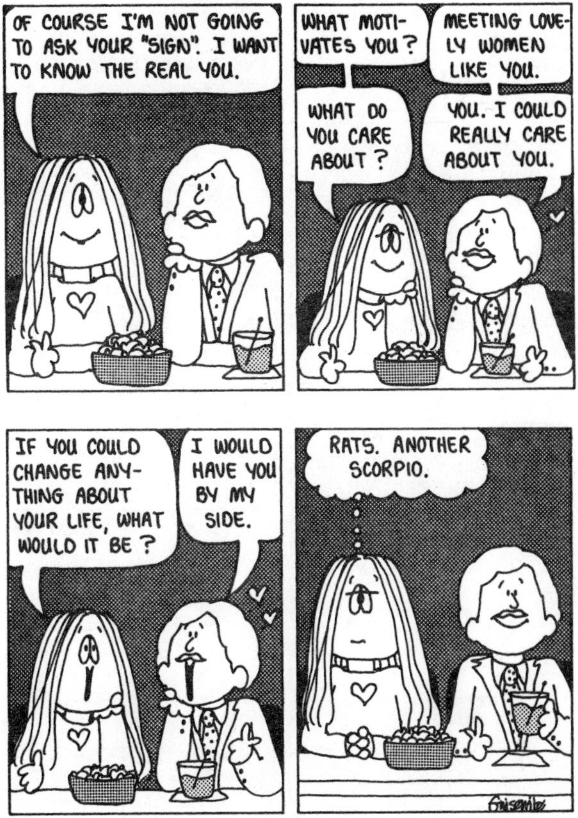
OF COURSE I'M NOT GOING TO ASK YOUR "SIGN". I WANT TO KNOW THE REAL YOU.
WHAT MOTI-VATES YOU?
MEETING LOVE-LY WOMEN LIKE YOU.
WHAT DO YOU CARE ABOUT?
YOU. I COULD REALLY CARE ABOUT YOU.
IF YOU COULD CHANGE ANY-THING ABOUT YOUR LIFE, WHAT WOULD IT BE?
I WOULD HAVE YOU BY MY SIDE.
RATS. ANOTHER SCORPIO.
Guisewite

The Personal Ad, 1984:

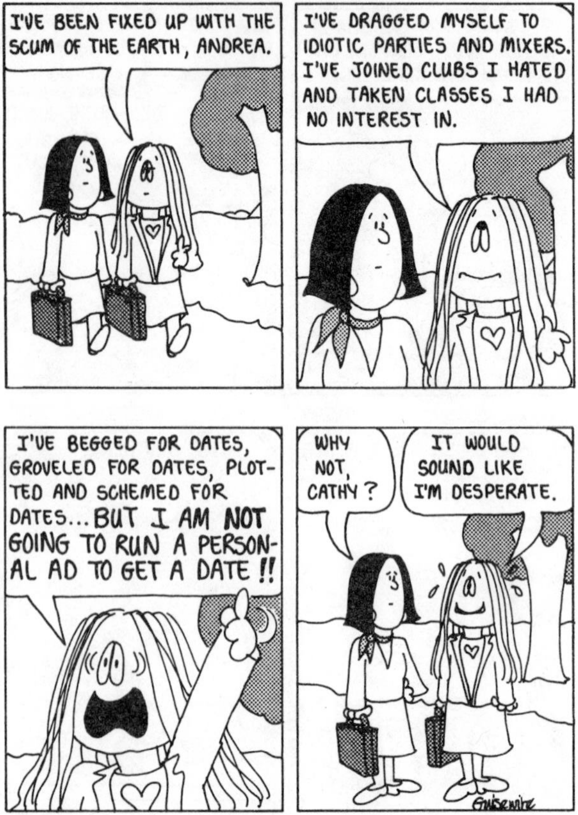
I'VE BEEN FIXED UP WITH THE SCUM OF THE EARTH, ANDREA.
I'VE DRAGGED MYSELF TO IDIOTIC PARTIES AND MIXERS. I'VE JOINED CLUBS I HATED AND TAKEN CLASSES I HAD NO INTEREST IN.
I'VE BEGGED FOR DATES, GROVELED FOR DATES, PLOTTED AND SCHEMED FOR DATES... BUT I AM NOT GOING TO RUN A PERSONAL AD TO GET A DATE !!
WHY NOT, CATHY ?
IT WOULD SOUND LIKE I'M DESPERATE.
Guisewite

The Gym, 1985:

YOU SEEM A LITTLE TENSE. WANT A MASSAGE?

KEEP YOUR HANDS AND YOUR LECHEROUS EYEBALLS TO YOURSELF.

AEROBICS

I DID NOT LIVE THROUGH THE LAST TWO DECADES TO BE GAWKED AT BY SOME PIG IN A SWEATSUIT! I AM A HUMAN BEING, NOT AN OBJECT!

AERO

TOO BAD. HE HAD SUCH A CUTE BUTT.

AEROBICS

The Singles Bar, 1985:

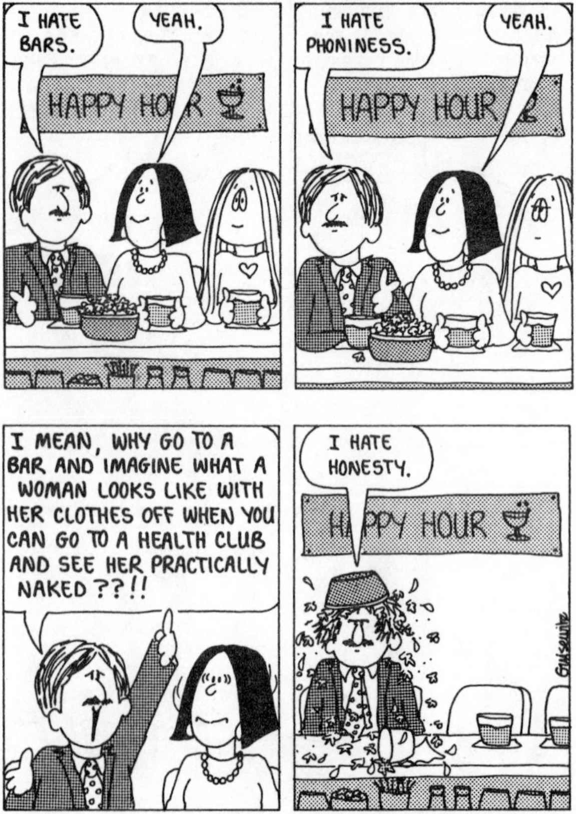
I HATE BARS.
YEAH.
I HATE PHONINESS.
YEAH.
HAPPY HOUR
I MEAN, WHY GO TO A BAR AND IMAGINE WHAT A WOMAN LOOKS LIKE WITH HER CLOTHES OFF WHEN YOU CAN GO TO A HEALTH CLUB AND SEE HER PRACTICALLY NAKED??!!
I HATE HONESTY.
Guisewite

The Juice Bar, 1987:

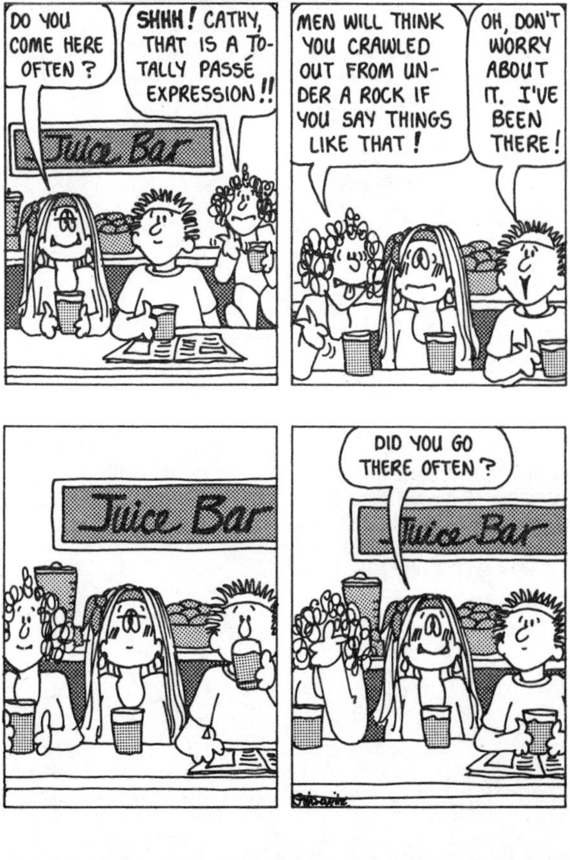

DO YOU COME HERE OFTEN?
SHHH! CATHY, THAT IS A TOTALLY PASSÉ EXPRESSION!!
Juice Bar
MEN WILL THINK YOU CRAWLED OUT FROM UNDER A ROCK IF YOU SAY THINGS LIKE THAT!
OH, DON'T WORRY ABOUT IT. I'VE BEEN THERE!
Juice Bar
DID YOU GO THERE OFTEN?
Juice Bar

"Out," 1987:

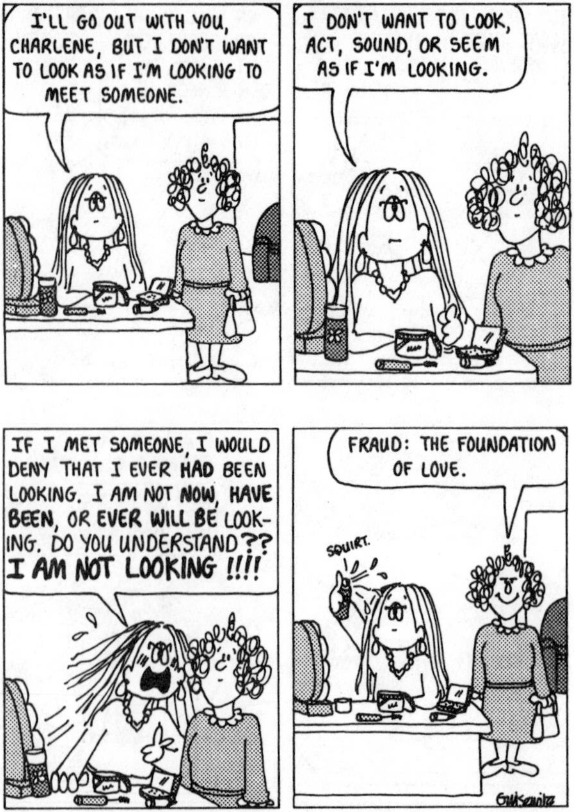
I'LL GO OUT WITH YOU, CHARLENE, BUT I DON'T WANT TO LOOK AS IF I'M LOOKING TO MEET SOMEONE.
I DON'T WANT TO LOOK, ACT, SOUND, OR SEEM AS IF I'M LOOKING.
IF I MET SOMEONE, I WOULD DENY THAT I EVER HAD BEEN LOOKING. I AM NOT NOW, HAVE BEEN, OR EVER WILL BE LOOKING. DO YOU UNDERSTAND?? I AM NOT LOOKING !!!!
FRAUD: THE FOUNDATION OF LOVE.
SQUIRT.
Guisewite

The Gym, 1987:

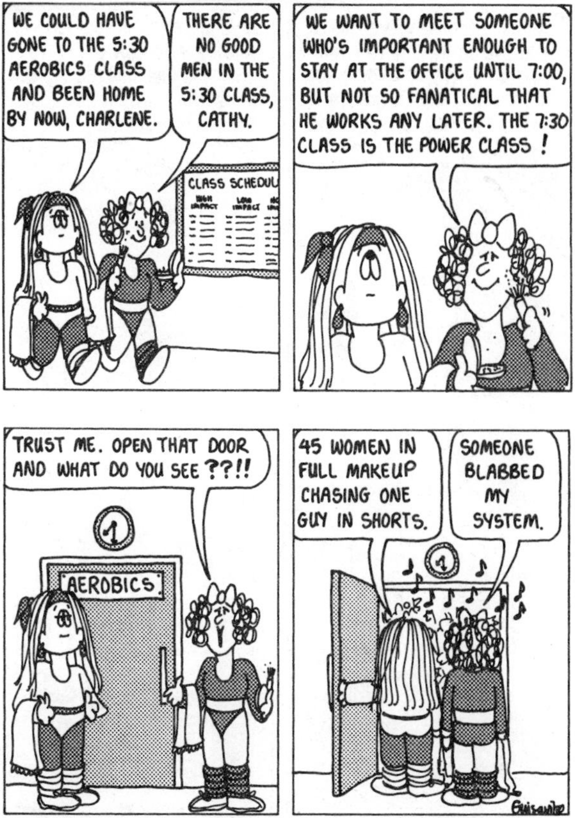

WE COULD HAVE GONE TO THE 5:30 AEROBICS CLASS AND BEEN HOME BY NOW, CHARLENE.
THERE ARE NO GOOD MEN IN THE 5:30 CLASS, CATHY.
CLASS SCHEDUL
WE WANT TO MEET SOMEONE WHO'S IMPORTANT ENOUGH TO STAY AT THE OFFICE UNTIL 7:00, BUT NOT SO FANATICAL THAT HE WORKS ANY LATER. THE 7:30 CLASS IS THE POWER CLASS !
TRUST ME. OPEN THAT DOOR AND WHAT DO YOU SEE ??!!
AEROBICS
45 WOMEN IN FULL MAKEUP CHASING ONE GUY IN SHORTS.
SOMEONE BLABBED MY SYSTEM.

The Party, 1987:

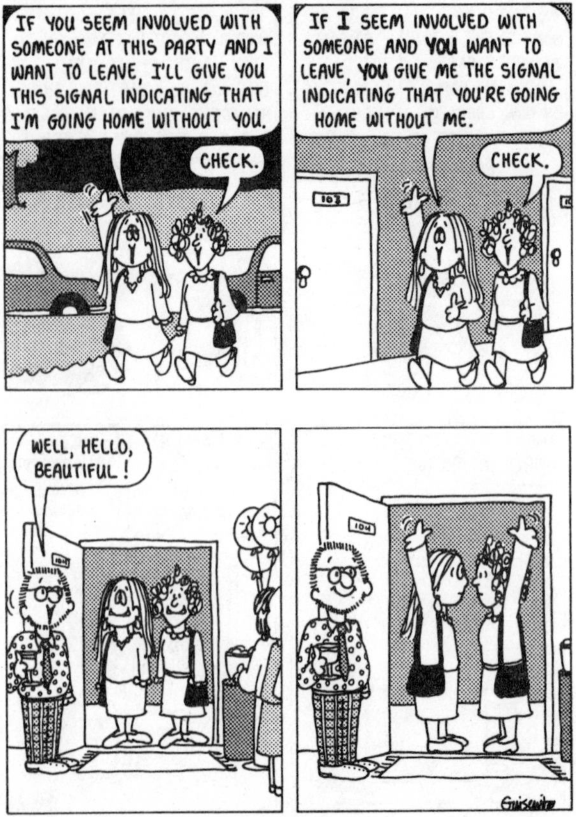
IF YOU SEEM INVOLVED WITH SOMEONE AT THIS PARTY AND I WANT TO LEAVE, I'LL GIVE YOU THIS SIGNAL INDICATING THAT I'M GOING HOME WITHOUT YOU.
CHECK.
IF I SEEM INVOLVED WITH SOMEONE AND YOU WANT TO LEAVE, YOU GIVE ME THE SIGNAL INDICATING THAT YOU'RE GOING HOME WITHOUT ME.
CHECK.
WELL, HELLO, BEAUTIFUL!

The Frozen Food Section, 1987:

The Cafe, 1989:

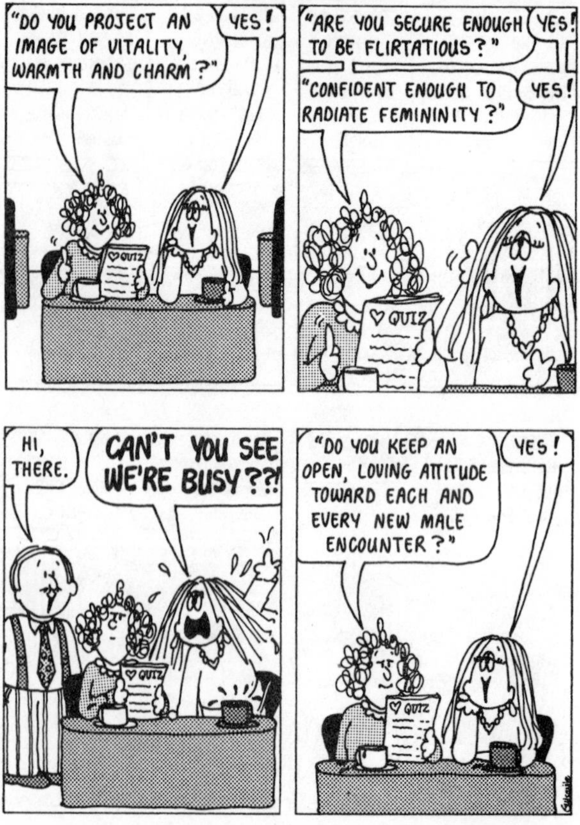

"DO YOU PROJECT AN IMAGE OF VITALITY, WARMTH AND CHARM?"
YES!
"ARE YOU SECURE ENOUGH TO BE FLIRTATIOUS?"
YES!
"CONFIDENT ENOUGH TO RADIATE FEMININITY?"
YES!
HI, THERE.
CAN'T YOU SEE WE'RE BUSY??!
"DO YOU KEEP AN OPEN, LOVING ATTITUDE TOWARD EACH AND EVERY NEW MALE ENCOUNTER?"
YES!

The Sushi Bar, 1989:

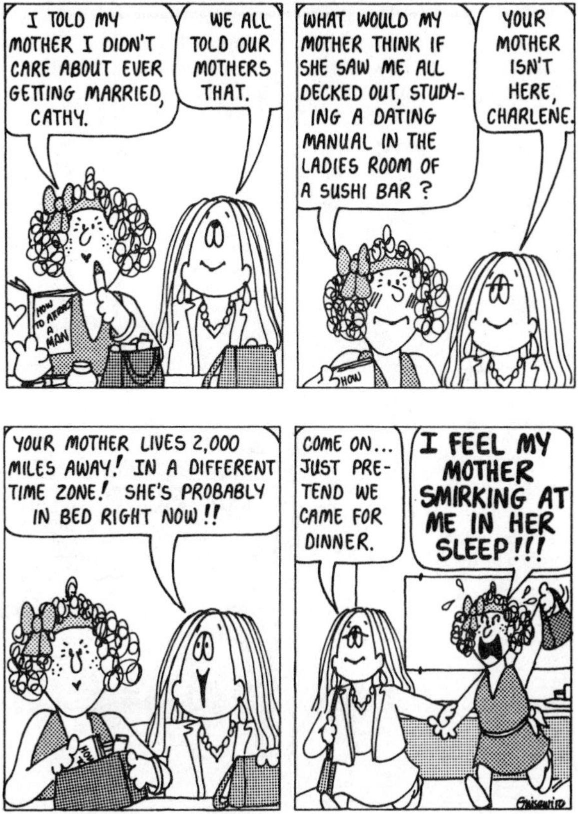

I TOLD MY MOTHER I DIDN'T CARE ABOUT EVER GETTING MARRIED, CATHY.
WE ALL TOLD OUR MOTHERS THAT.
HOW TO ATTRACT A MAN
WHAT WOULD MY MOTHER THINK IF SHE SAW ME ALL DECKED OUT, STUDYING A DATING MANUAL IN THE LADIES ROOM OF A SUSHI BAR?
YOUR MOTHER ISN'T HERE, CHARLENE.
HOW
YOUR MOTHER LIVES 2,000 MILES AWAY! IN A DIFFERENT TIME ZONE! SHE'S PROBABLY IN BED RIGHT NOW!!
COME ON... JUST PRETEND WE CAME FOR DINNER.
I FEEL MY MOTHER SMIRKING AT ME IN HER SLEEP!!!

The Blind Date, 1989:

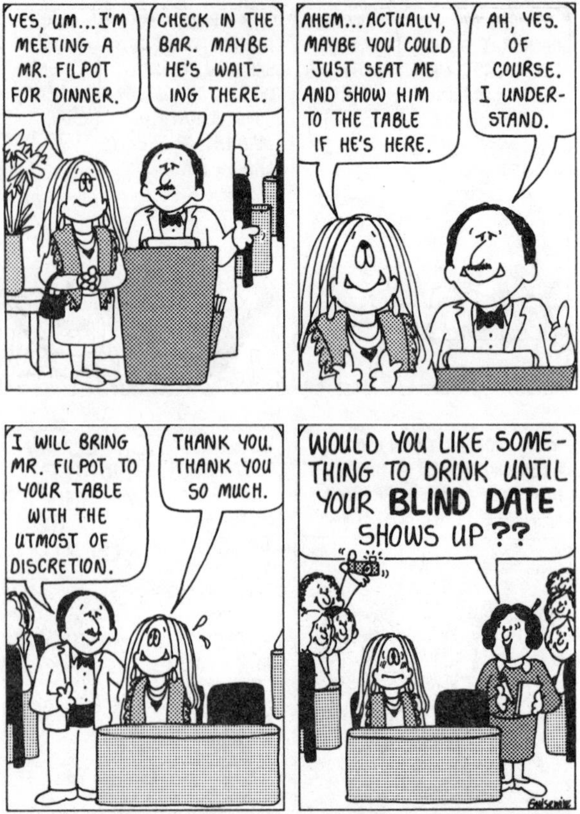
YES, UM...I'M MEETING A MR. FILPOT FOR DINNER.
CHECK IN THE BAR. MAYBE HE'S WAIT-ING THERE.
AHEM...ACTUALLY, MAYBE YOU COULD JUST SEAT ME AND SHOW HIM TO THE TABLE IF HE'S HERE.
AH, YES. OF COURSE. I UNDER-STAND.
I WILL BRING MR. FILPOT TO YOUR TABLE WITH THE UTMOST OF DISCRETION.
THANK YOU. THANK YOU SO MUCH.
WOULD YOU LIKE SOME-THING TO DRINK UNTIL YOUR **BLIND DATE** SHOWS UP??

The Drive-By, 1989:

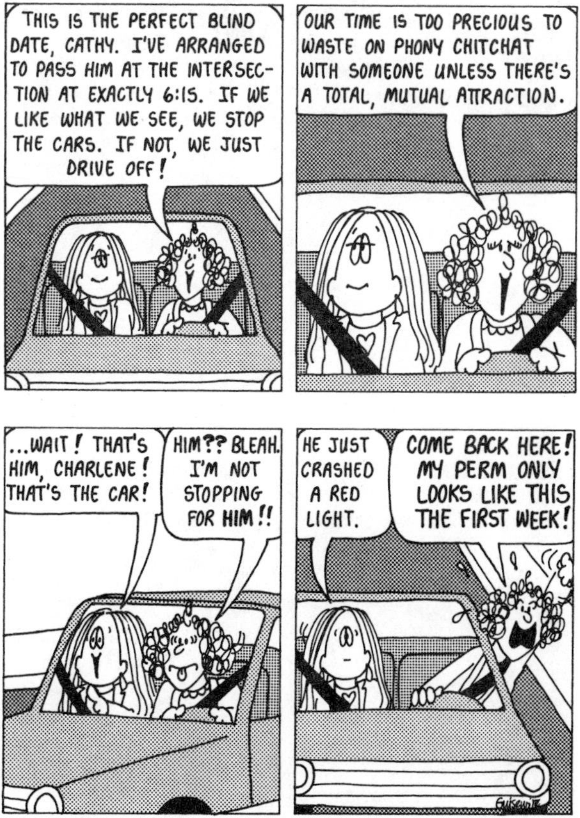

THIS IS THE PERFECT BLIND DATE, CATHY. I'VE ARRANGED TO PASS HIM AT THE INTERSECTION AT EXACTLY 6:15. IF WE LIKE WHAT WE SEE, WE STOP THE CARS. IF NOT, WE JUST DRIVE OFF!
OUR TIME IS TOO PRECIOUS TO WASTE ON PHONY CHITCHAT WITH SOMEONE UNLESS THERE'S A TOTAL, MUTUAL ATTRACTION.
...WAIT! THAT'S HIM, CHARLENE! THAT'S THE CAR!
HIM?? BLEAH. I'M NOT STOPPING FOR HIM!!
HE JUST CRASHED A RED LIGHT.
COME BACK HERE! MY PERM ONLY LOOKS LIKE THIS THE FIRST WEEK!

The Fax, 1989:

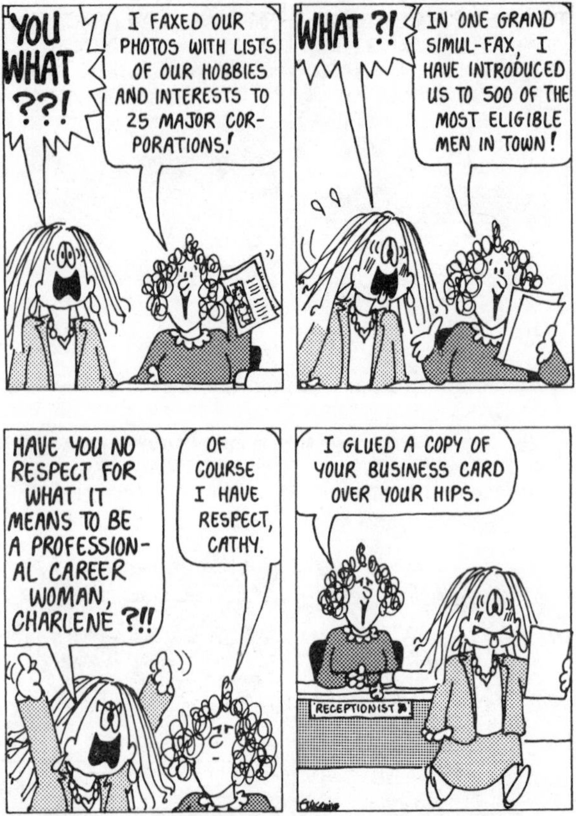
YOU WHAT ??!
I FAXED OUR PHOTOS WITH LISTS OF OUR HOBBIES AND INTERESTS TO 25 MAJOR CORPORATIONS!
WHAT ?!
IN ONE GRAND SIMUL-FAX, I HAVE INTRODUCED US TO 500 OF THE MOST ELIGIBLE MEN IN TOWN!
HAVE YOU NO RESPECT FOR WHAT IT MEANS TO BE A PROFESSIONAL CAREER WOMAN, CHARLENE ?!!
OF COURSE I HAVE RESPECT, CATHY.
I GLUED A COPY OF YOUR BUSINESS CARD OVER YOUR HIPS.
RECEPTIONIST

The Bachelor Auction, 1990:

THE $200-A-PLATE "SAVE OUR OCEANS" FUND-RAISING BANQUET... 75 MEN LEFT WITH 75 OTHER WOMEN.

SAVE OUR OCEANS

THE $350-A-POP "PROTECT THE RAIN FORESTS" FUND-RAISING TANGO-FEST... 120 MEN LEFT WITH 120 OTHER WOMEN.

PROTECT THE RAIN FORESTS

...AND NOW THE $175-A-TICKET MULTI-CHARITY "BACHELOR AUCTION" ...400 MEN, POISED TO LEAVE WITH 400 OTHER WOMEN.

...AT LEAST WE'RE HELPING MAKE THE WORLD A BETTER PLACE FOR OTHER WOMEN TO GET A DATE.

BACHELOR AUCTION

The Plane, 1990:

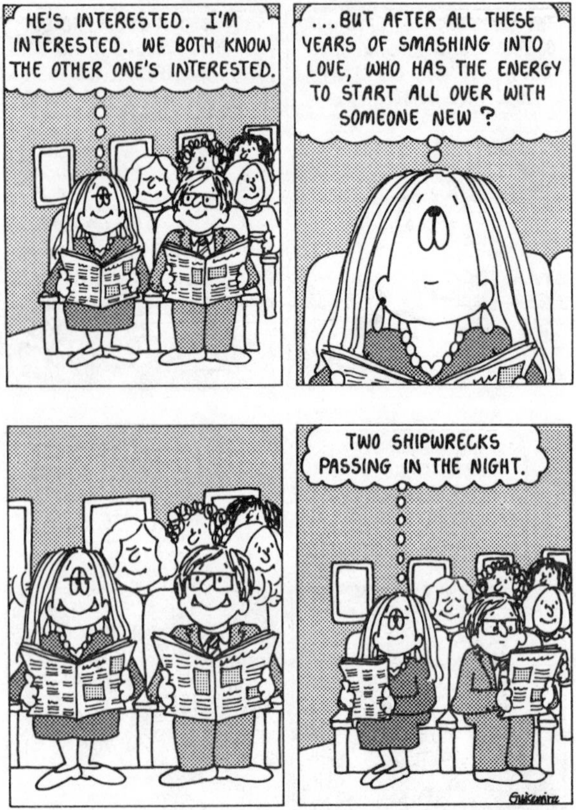
HE'S INTERESTED. I'M INTERESTED. WE BOTH KNOW THE OTHER ONE'S INTERESTED.
...BUT AFTER ALL THESE YEARS OF SMASHING INTO LOVE, WHO HAS THE ENERGY TO START ALL OVER WITH SOMEONE NEW?
TWO SHIPWRECKS PASSING IN THE NIGHT.
Guisewite

The Video Date, 1991:

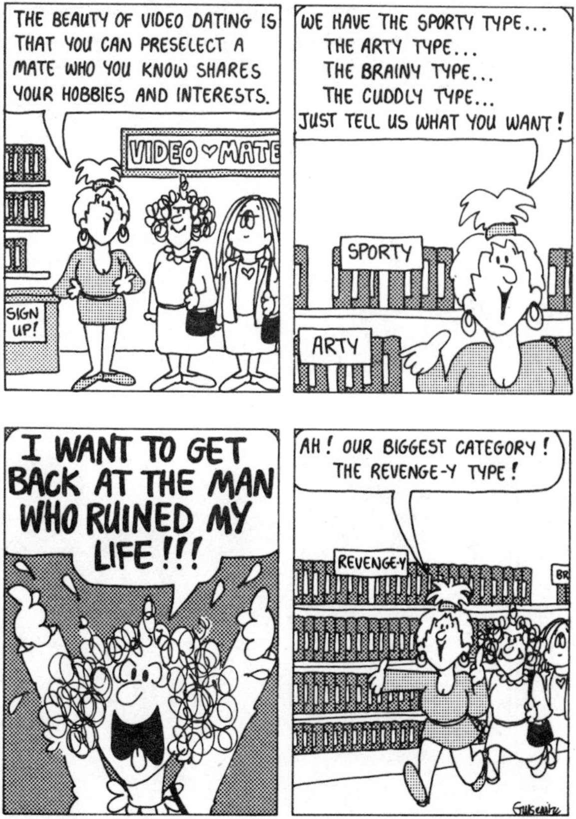
THE BEAUTY OF VIDEO DATING IS THAT YOU CAN PRESELECT A MATE WHO YOU KNOW SHARES YOUR HOBBIES AND INTERESTS.
VIDEO ♥ MATE
SIGN UP!
WE HAVE THE SPORTY TYPE... THE ARTY TYPE... THE BRAINY TYPE... THE CUDDLY TYPE... JUST TELL US WHAT YOU WANT!
SPORTY
ARTY
I WANT TO GET BACK AT THE MAN WHO RUINED MY LIFE!!!
AH! OUR BIGGEST CATEGORY! THE REVENGE-Y TYPE!
REVENGE-Y
Guisewite

The Holiday Party, 1992:

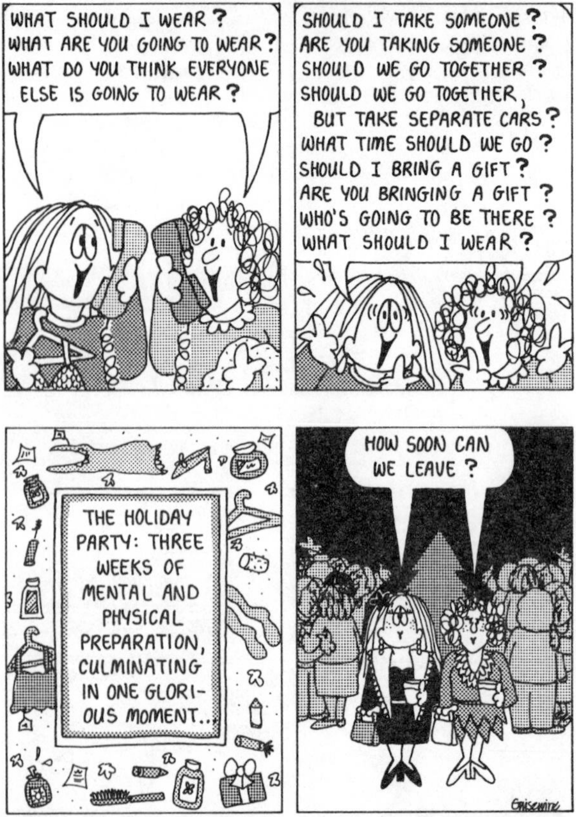
WHAT SHOULD I WEAR? WHAT ARE YOU GOING TO WEAR? WHAT DO YOU THINK EVERYONE ELSE IS GOING TO WEAR?
SHOULD I TAKE SOMEONE? ARE YOU TAKING SOMEONE? SHOULD WE GO TOGETHER? SHOULD WE GO TOGETHER, BUT TAKE SEPARATE CARS? WHAT TIME SHOULD WE GO? SHOULD I BRING A GIFT? ARE YOU BRINGING A GIFT? WHO'S GOING TO BE THERE? WHAT SHOULD I WEAR?
THE HOLIDAY PARTY: THREE WEEKS OF MENTAL AND PHYSICAL PREPARATION, CULMINATING IN ONE GLORIOUS MOMENT...
HOW SOON CAN WE LEAVE?
Guisewite

The Produce Aisle, 1993:

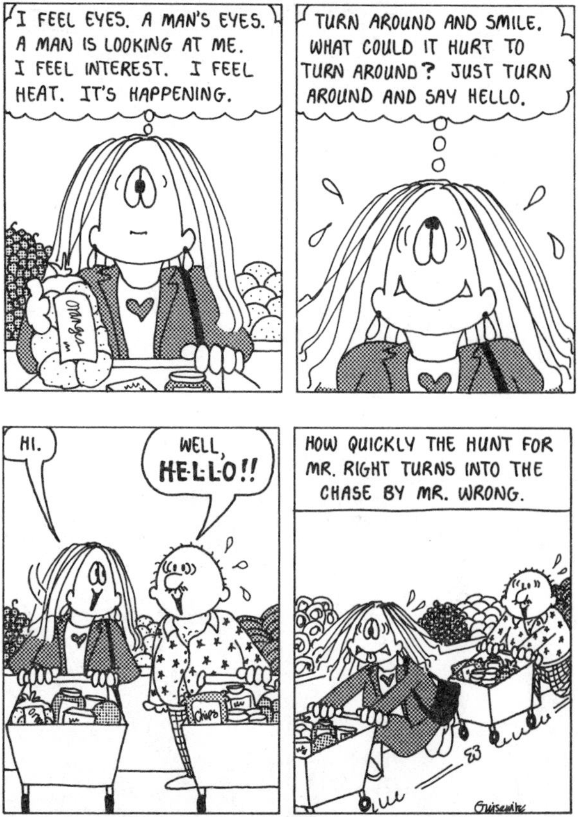
I FEEL EYES. A MAN'S EYES. A MAN IS LOOKING AT ME. I FEEL INTEREST. I FEEL HEAT. IT'S HAPPENING.
oranges
TURN AROUND AND SMILE. WHAT COULD IT HURT TO TURN AROUND? JUST TURN AROUND AND SAY HELLO.
HI.
WELL, HE-L-L-O!!
Chips
HOW QUICKLY THE HUNT FOR MR. RIGHT TURNS INTO THE CHASE BY MR. WRONG.
Guisewite

The Tour Group, 1993:

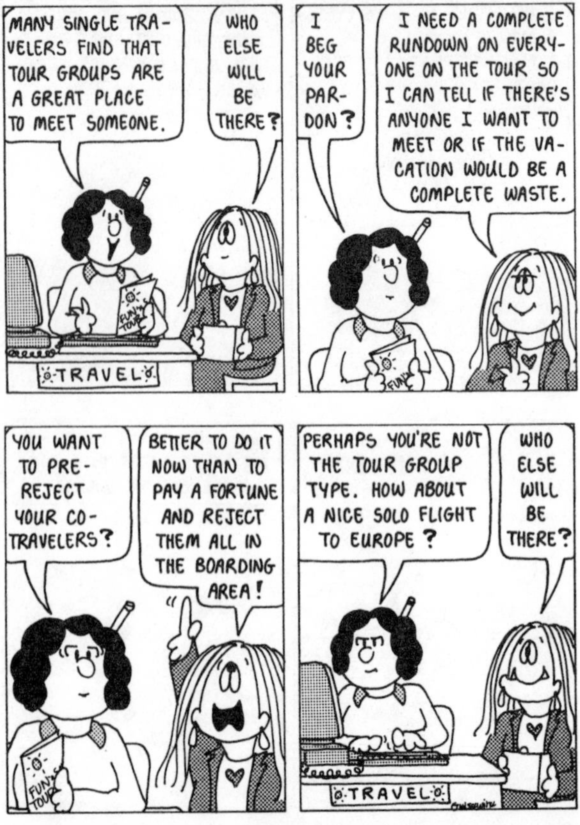
MANY SINGLE TRAVELERS FIND THAT TOUR GROUPS ARE A GREAT PLACE TO MEET SOMEONE.
WHO ELSE WILL BE THERE?
FUN TOUR
TRAVEL
I BEG YOUR PARDON?
I NEED A COMPLETE RUNDOWN ON EVERYONE ON THE TOUR SO I CAN TELL IF THERE'S ANYONE I WANT TO MEET OR IF THE VACATION WOULD BE A COMPLETE WASTE.
YOU WANT TO PRE-REJECT YOUR CO-TRAVELERS?
BETTER TO DO IT NOW THAN TO PAY A FORTUNE AND REJECT THEM ALL IN THE BOARDING AREA!
FUN TOUR
PERHAPS YOU'RE NOT THE TOUR GROUP TYPE. HOW ABOUT A NICE SOLO FLIGHT TO EUROPE?
WHO ELSE WILL BE THERE?
TRAVEL

The Gym, 1994:

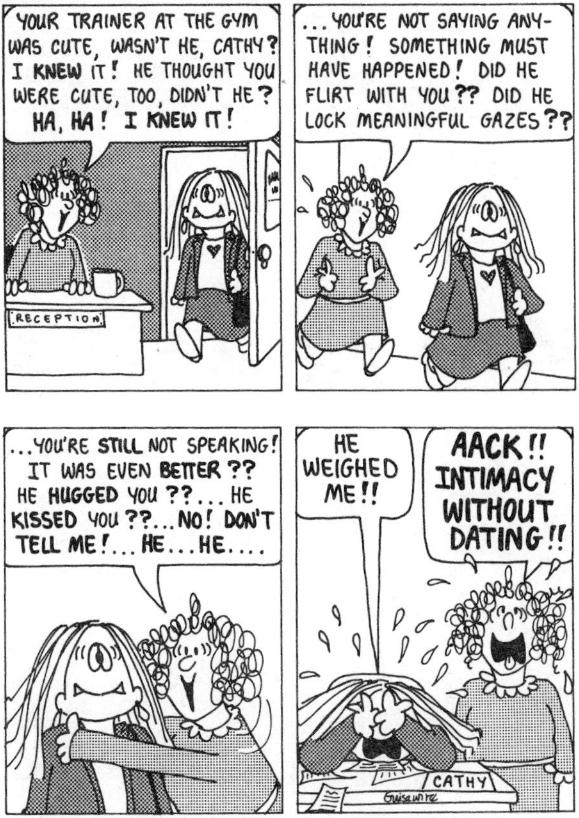

YOUR TRAINER AT THE GYM WAS CUTE, WASN'T HE, CATHY? I KNEW IT! HE THOUGHT YOU WERE CUTE, TOO, DIDN'T HE? HA, HA! I KNEW IT!
RECEPTION
...YOU'RE NOT SAYING ANYTHING! SOMETHING MUST HAVE HAPPENED! DID HE FLIRT WITH YOU?? DID HE LOCK MEANINGFUL GAZES??
...YOU'RE STILL NOT SPEAKING! IT WAS EVEN BETTER?? HE HUGGED YOU??... HE KISSED YOU??...NO! DON'T TELL ME!... HE... HE....
HE WEIGHED ME!!
AACK!! INTIMACY WITHOUT DATING!!
CATHY

The Living Room, 1995:

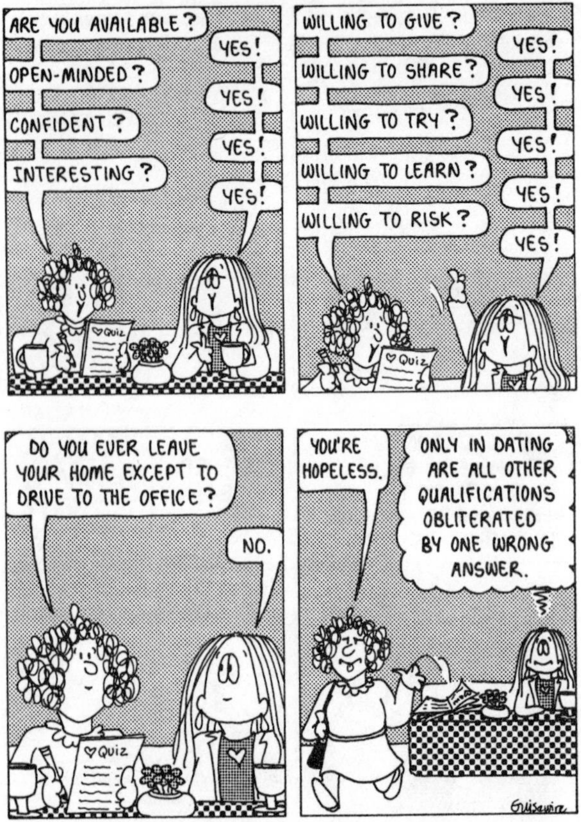
ARE YOU AVAILABLE?
YES!
OPEN-MINDED?
YES!
CONFIDENT?
YES!
INTERESTING?
YES!
♡QUIZ
WILLING TO GIVE?
YES!
WILLING TO SHARE?
YES!
WILLING TO TRY?
YES!
WILLING TO LEARN?
YES!
WILLING TO RISK?
YES!
♡QUIZ
DO YOU EVER LEAVE YOUR HOME EXCEPT TO DRIVE TO THE OFFICE?
NO.
♡QUIZ
YOU'RE HOPELESS.
ONLY IN DATING ARE ALL OTHER QUALIFICATIONS OBLITERATED BY ONE WRONG ANSWER.
Guisewite

The Men's Department, 1995:

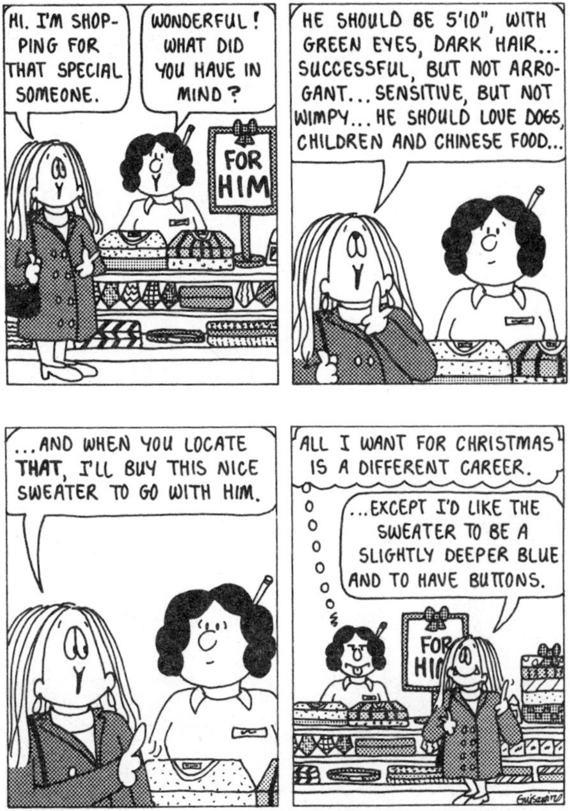
HI. I'M SHOPPING FOR THAT SPECIAL SOMEONE.
WONDERFUL! WHAT DID YOU HAVE IN MIND?
FOR HIM
HE SHOULD BE 5'10", WITH GREEN EYES, DARK HAIR... SUCCESSFUL, BUT NOT ARROGANT... SENSITIVE, BUT NOT WIMPY... HE SHOULD LOVE DOGS, CHILDREN AND CHINESE FOOD...
...AND WHEN YOU LOCATE **THAT**, I'LL BUY THIS NICE SWEATER TO GO WITH HIM.
ALL I WANT FOR CHRISTMAS IS A DIFFERENT CAREER.
...EXCEPT I'D LIKE THE SWEATER TO BE A SLIGHTLY DEEPER BLUE AND TO HAVE BUTTONS.
Guisewite

The Internet, 1996:

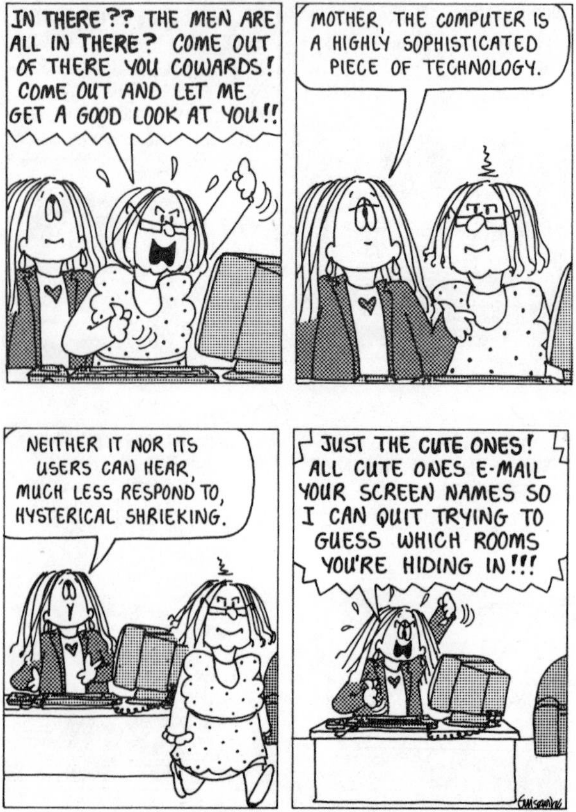
IN THERE?? THE MEN ARE ALL IN THERE? COME OUT OF THERE YOU COWARDS! COME OUT AND LET ME GET A GOOD LOOK AT YOU!!
MOTHER, THE COMPUTER IS A HIGHLY SOPHISTICATED PIECE OF TECHNOLOGY.
NEITHER IT NOR ITS USERS CAN HEAR, MUCH LESS RESPOND TO, HYSTERICAL SHRIEKING.
JUST THE CUTE ONES! ALL CUTE ONES E-MAIL YOUR SCREEN NAMES SO I CAN QUIT TRYING TO GUESS WHICH ROOMS YOU'RE HIDING IN!!!

The Blank Date, 1996:

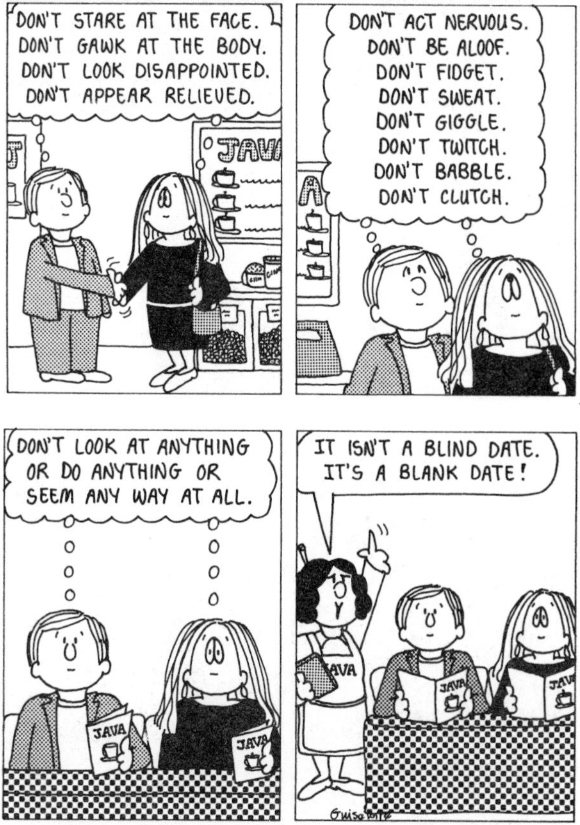
DON'T STARE AT THE FACE. DON'T GAWK AT THE BODY. DON'T LOOK DISAPPOINTED. DON'T APPEAR RELIEVED.
JAVA
DON'T ACT NERVOUS. DON'T BE ALOOF. DON'T FIDGET. DON'T SWEAT. DON'T GIGGLE. DON'T TWITCH. DON'T BABBLE. DON'T CLUTCH.
DON'T LOOK AT ANYTHING OR DO ANYTHING OR SEEM ANY WAY AT ALL.
JAVA
JAVA
IT ISN'T A BLIND DATE. IT'S A BLANK DATE!
JAVA
JAVA
Guisewite

The Ice Cream Aisle, 1996:

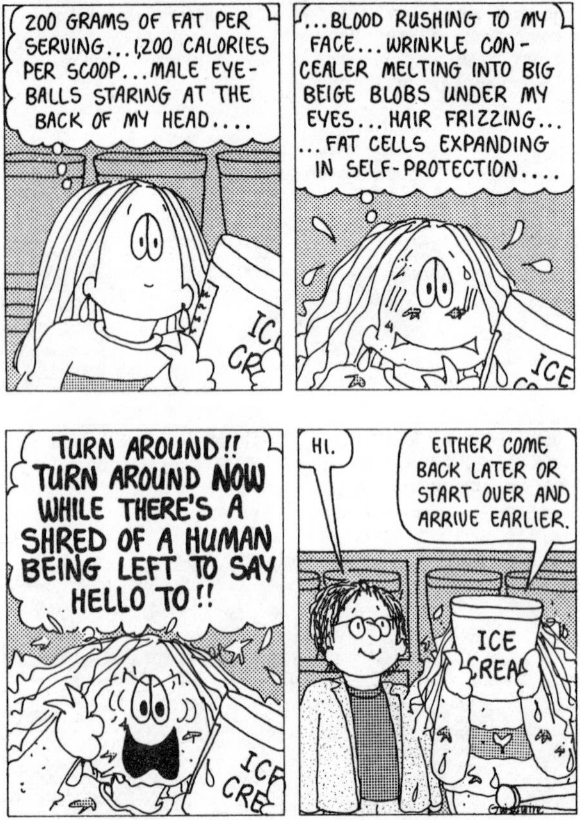
200 GRAMS OF FAT PER SERVING... 1,200 CALORIES PER SCOOP... MALE EYE-BALLS STARING AT THE BACK OF MY HEAD....
ICE CRE
...BLOOD RUSHING TO MY FACE... WRINKLE CON-CEALER MELTING INTO BIG BEIGE BLOBS UNDER MY EYES... HAIR FRIZZING... ...FAT CELLS EXPANDING IN SELF-PROTECTION....
ICE
TURN AROUND!! TURN AROUND NOW WHILE THERE'S A SHRED OF A HUMAN BEING LEFT TO SAY HELLO TO!!
ICE CRE
HI.
EITHER COME BACK LATER OR START OVER AND ARRIVE EARLIER.
ICE CREA

The Fast Food Restaurant, 1997:

The Coffee Shop, 1997:

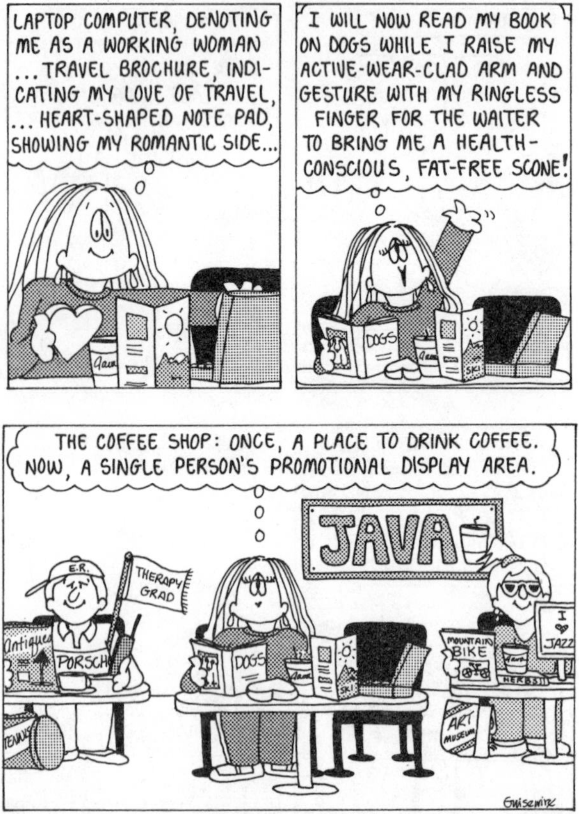
LAPTOP COMPUTER, DENOTING ME AS A WORKING WOMAN ... TRAVEL BROCHURE, INDICATING MY LOVE OF TRAVEL, ... HEART-SHAPED NOTE PAD, SHOWING MY ROMANTIC SIDE...
I WILL NOW READ MY BOOK ON DOGS WHILE I RAISE MY ACTIVE-WEAR-CLAD ARM AND GESTURE WITH MY RINGLESS FINGER FOR THE WAITER TO BRING ME A HEALTH-CONSCIOUS, FAT-FREE SCONE!
DOGS
SKI
THE COFFEE SHOP: ONCE, A PLACE TO DRINK COFFEE. NOW, A SINGLE PERSON'S PROMOTIONAL DISPLAY AREA.
JAVA
E.R.
THERAPY GRAD
Antiques
PORSCH
TENNIS
DOGS
SKI
MOUNTAIN BIKE
HERBS
I ♥ JAZZ
ART MUSEUM
Guisewite

The Business Party, 1997:

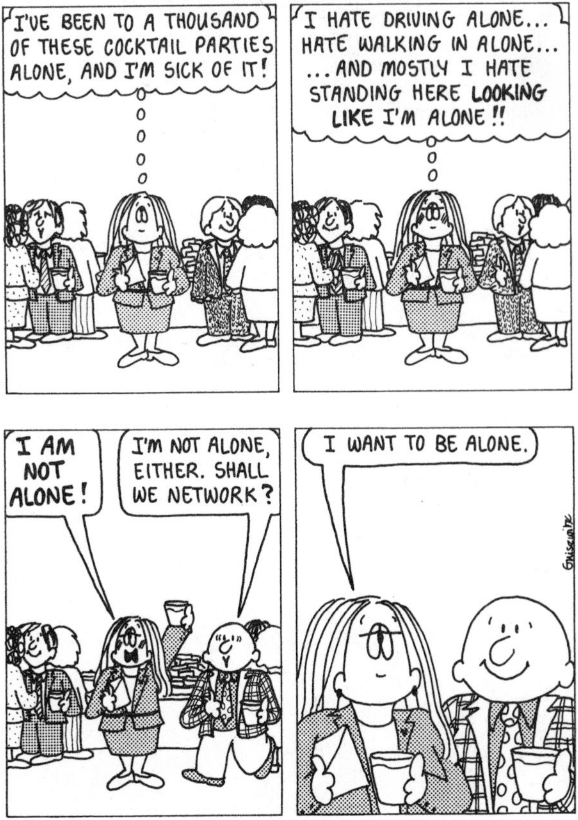
I'VE BEEN TO A THOUSAND OF THESE COCKTAIL PARTIES ALONE, AND I'M SICK OF IT!
I HATE DRIVING ALONE... HATE WALKING IN ALONE... ...AND MOSTLY I HATE STANDING HERE LOOKING LIKE I'M ALONE!!
I AM NOT ALONE!
I'M NOT ALONE, EITHER. SHALL WE NETWORK?
I WANT TO BE ALONE.
Guisewite

The Produce Aisle, 1998:

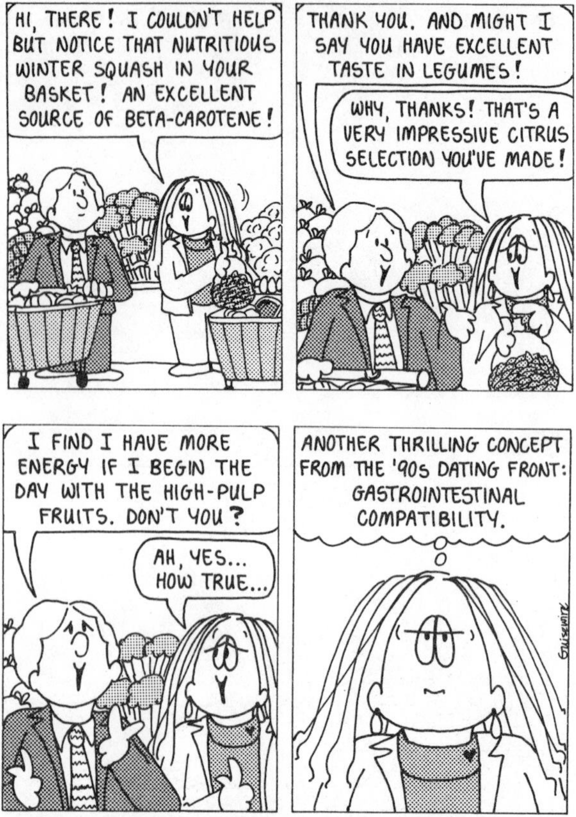
HI, THERE! I COULDN'T HELP BUT NOTICE THAT NUTRITIOUS WINTER SQUASH IN YOUR BASKET! AN EXCELLENT SOURCE OF BETA-CAROTENE!
THANK YOU. AND MIGHT I SAY YOU HAVE EXCELLENT TASTE IN LEGUMES!
WHY, THANKS! THAT'S A VERY IMPRESSIVE CITRUS SELECTION YOU'VE MADE!
I FIND I HAVE MORE ENERGY IF I BEGIN THE DAY WITH THE HIGH-PULP FRUITS. DON'T YOU?
AH, YES... HOW TRUE...
ANOTHER THRILLING CONCEPT FROM THE '90s DATING FRONT: GASTROINTESTINAL COMPATIBILITY.

The Dog Park, 1998:

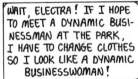

WAIT, ELECTRA! IF I HOPE TO MEET A DYNAMIC BUSINESSMAN AT THE PARK, I HAVE TO CHANGE CLOTHES SO I LOOK LIKE A DYNAMIC BUSINESSWOMAN!

I NEED AN "I'M-YOUNG-AND-HIP" SHEATH DRESS... A "TAKE CHARGE" JACKET ...SOME "OOPS-I-JUST-CAME-FROM-A-BIG-MEETING-AND-DIDN'T-HAVE-TIME-TO-CHANGE-MY-FABULOUS-SHOES" SHOES!

SADLY, THE SUBTLE PERFECTIONS OF WOMEN'S COSTUMES ARE NOTICED ONLY BY OTHER WOMEN WEARING COSTUMES.

YOUR "SEE ME SOAR" STILETTOS ARE SINKING INTO THE DIRT.

THERE'S A MOSQUITO STUCK TO YOUR FAKE TAN.

The Dog Walk, 1998:

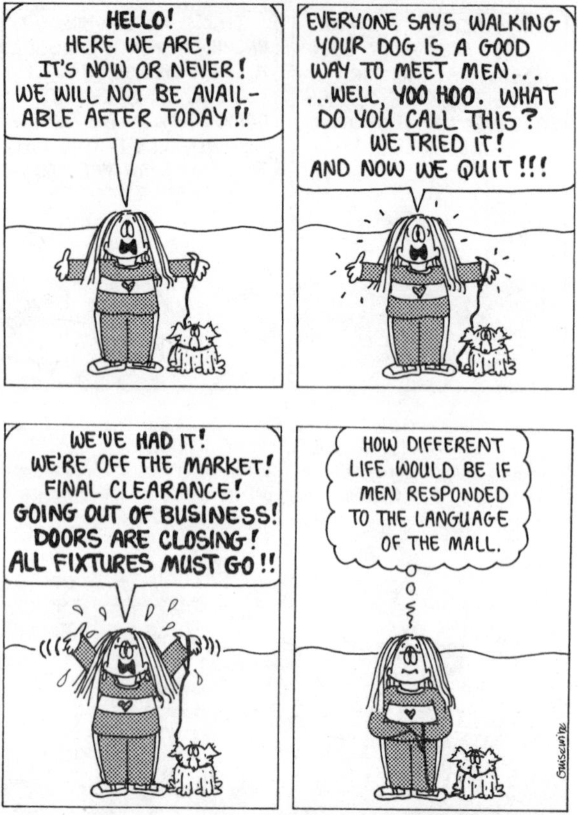
HELLO! HERE WE ARE! IT'S NOW OR NEVER! WE WILL NOT BE AVAIL-ABLE AFTER TODAY!!
EVERYONE SAYS WALKING YOUR DOG IS A GOOD WAY TO MEET MEN... ...WELL, YOO HOO. WHAT DO YOU CALL THIS? WE TRIED IT! AND NOW WE QUIT!!!
WE'VE HAD IT! WE'RE OFF THE MARKET! FINAL CLEARANCE! GOING OUT OF BUSINESS! DOORS ARE CLOSING! ALL FIXTURES MUST GO!!
HOW DIFFERENT LIFE WOULD BE IF MEN RESPONDED TO THE LANGUAGE OF THE MALL.
GUISEWITE

The Office, 1999:

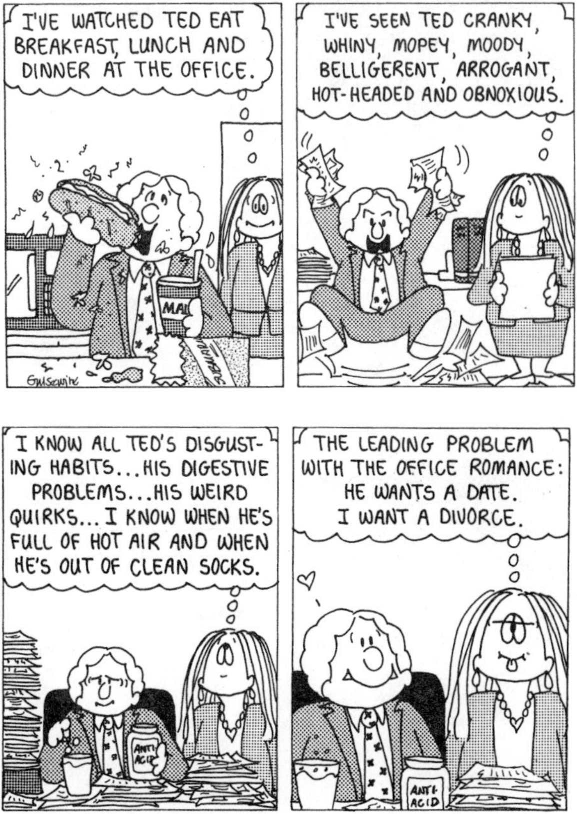
I'VE WATCHED TED EAT BREAKFAST, LUNCH AND DINNER AT THE OFFICE.
I'VE SEEN TED CRANKY, WHINY, MOPEY, MOODY, BELLIGERENT, ARROGANT, HOT-HEADED AND OBNOXIOUS.
I KNOW ALL TED'S DISGUSTING HABITS... HIS DIGESTIVE PROBLEMS... HIS WEIRD QUIRKS... I KNOW WHEN HE'S FULL OF HOT AIR AND WHEN HE'S OUT OF CLEAN SOCKS.
THE LEADING PROBLEM WITH THE OFFICE ROMANCE: HE WANTS A DATE. I WANT A DIVORCE.
ANTI-ACID
ANTI-ACID

The Take-Out Window, 1999:

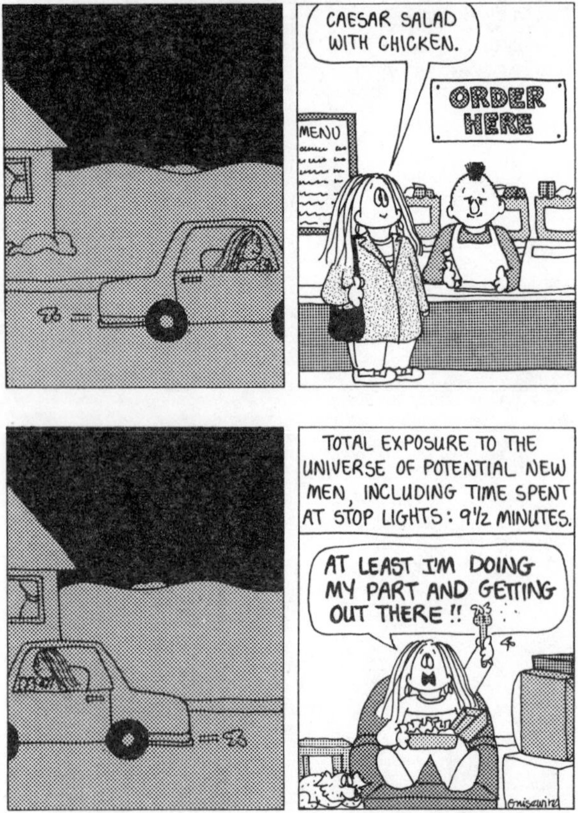
CAESAR SALAD WITH CHICKEN.
MENU
ORDER HERE
TOTAL EXPOSURE TO THE UNIVERSE OF POTENTIAL NEW MEN, INCLUDING TIME SPENT AT STOP LIGHTS: 9½ MINUTES.
AT LEAST I'M DOING MY PART AND GETTING OUT THERE!!

The Video Store, 1999:

600 KINDS OF SHAMPOO...
800 KINDS OF CEREAL...
500 KINDS OF SOAP...

400 KINDS OF JUICE...
1,000 KINDS OF WATER...
700 KINDS OF BREAD...
900 KINDS OF SNEAKERS...
6,000 KINDS OF PANTYHOSE...
10,000 DIFFERENT LIPSTICKS...

ONE AVAILABLE SINGLE MAN ON THE PLANET.

OPTIONS, SCHMOPTIONS.

Aimless Wandering, 2000:

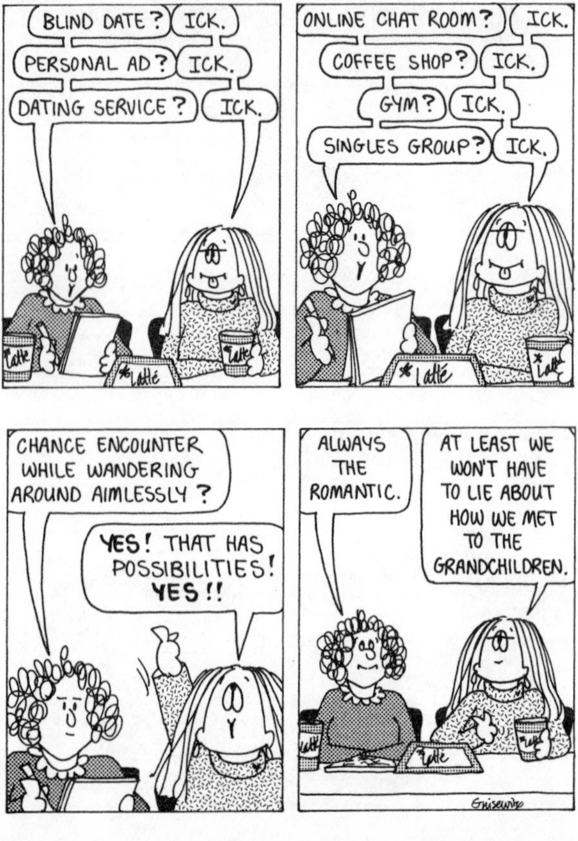
BLIND DATE? ICK.
PERSONAL AD? ICK.
DATING SERVICE? ICK.
Latte
Latté
Latte
ONLINE CHAT ROOM? ICK.
COFFEE SHOP? ICK.
GYM? ICK.
SINGLES GROUP? ICK.
Latté
Latte
CHANCE ENCOUNTER WHILE WANDERING AROUND AIMLESSLY?
YES! THAT HAS POSSIBILITIES! YES!!
ALWAYS THE ROMANTIC.
AT LEAST WE WON'T HAVE TO LIE ABOUT HOW WE MET TO THE GRANDCHILDREN.
Guisewite

The Office, 2001:

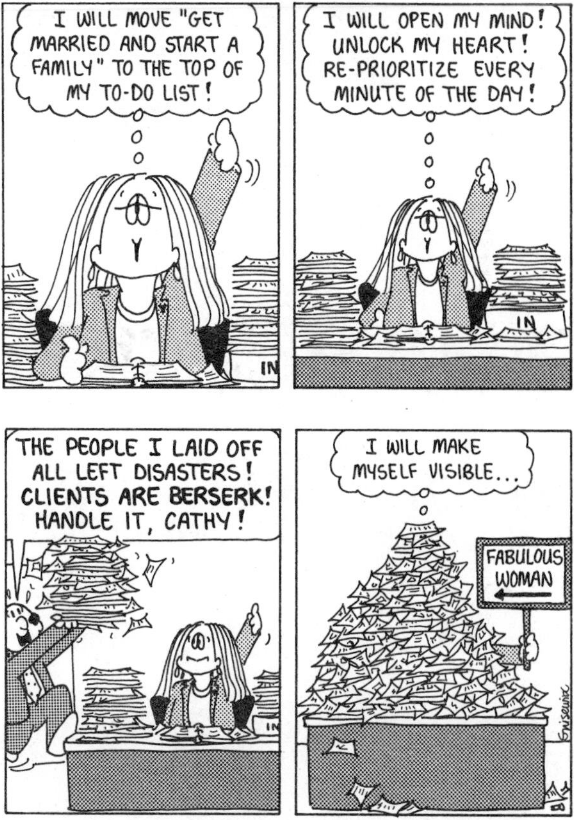
I WILL MOVE "GET MARRIED AND START A FAMILY" TO THE TOP OF MY TO-DO LIST!
IN
I WILL OPEN MY MIND! UNLOCK MY HEART! RE-PRIORITIZE EVERY MINUTE OF THE DAY!
IN
THE PEOPLE I LAID OFF ALL LEFT DISASTERS! CLIENTS ARE BERSERK! HANDLE IT, CATHY!
IN
I WILL MAKE MYSELF VISIBLE...
FABULOUS WOMAN
Guisewite

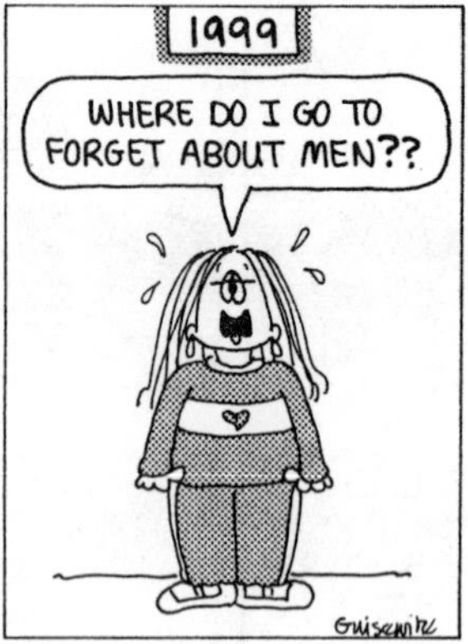
1999
WHERE DO I GO TO FORGET ABOUT MEN??
Guisewite

Picky, Picky, Picky

By the time I was 30, I could reject a man from across the room without ever even saying hello.

Bad socks. Clunky shoes. Goofy eyebrows. Insincere shirt. Annoying neck.

It was a perfect companion to my other skill, which was that I could fall in love with a man from across the room without ever even saying hello.

Cute glasses. Great chin. We'll name our children Anna and Billy and live in a yellow house with lilac bushes in the yard.

Men hunt. Women shop. Trained by a lifetime of hurling through 400,000-acre malls trying to find one thing that fits us, we learned to either invest the next five years in trying to make it work or to take a pass immediately.

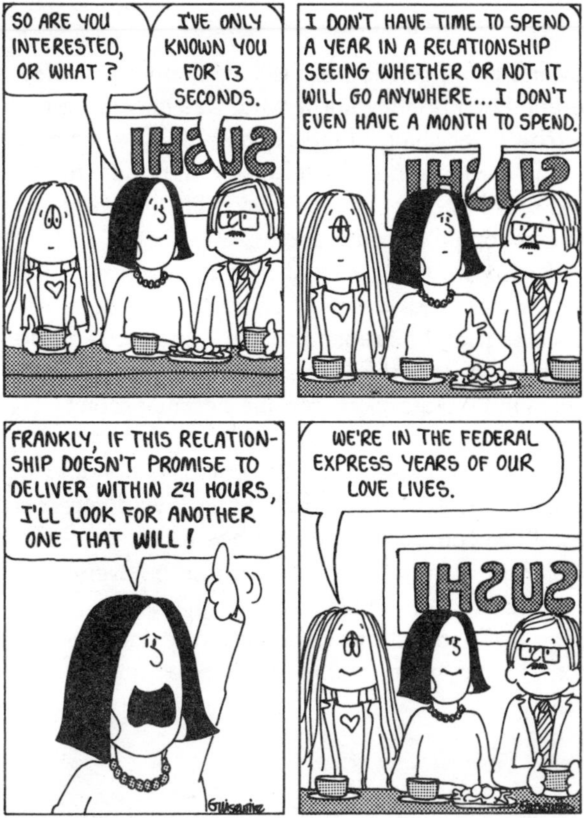
SO ARE YOU INTERESTED, OR WHAT?
I'VE ONLY KNOWN YOU FOR 13 SECONDS.
SUSHI
I DON'T HAVE TIME TO SPEND A YEAR IN A RELATIONSHIP SEEING WHETHER OR NOT IT WILL GO ANYWHERE... I DON'T EVEN HAVE A MONTH TO SPEND.
SUSHI
FRANKLY, IF THIS RELATIONSHIP DOESN'T PROMISE TO DELIVER WITHIN 24 HOURS, I'LL LOOK FOR ANOTHER ONE THAT WILL!
WE'RE IN THE FEDERAL EXPRESS YEARS OF OUR LOVE LIVES.
SUSHI
Guisewite

Men's entire relationship to love and the universe is different, because they know what size they're going to be tomorrow. Everything in their closets fits. The same clothes that fit in the morning will fit in the afternoon. This gives men a sense of order and predictability that most women can't even begin to comprehend.

Women are in a constant state of transition. Clothes that fit before breakfast can't be worn after 2 P.M. An ill-timed stop at the drinking fountain can make an evening gown suddenly become one size too small between the ladies' room and the banquet room.

Even if our bodies weren't constantly changing sizes, our clothes aren't even made to fit us. Five different size nines fit five completely different bodies. A "medium" is everything from a petite to an extra large. Everything has to be tried on. Everything has to be altered.

The dress sort of fits, but needs to be taken up at the bottom, let out in the middle, and nipped in under the arms.

The pants could be great if I hem them up three inches, move the button over, and lose four pounds from the waist down.

The sweater just needs to be dyed a different shade of green and have the buttons switched so it can match this skirt, which would be perfect if it were an inch longer and had a belt, scarf, and chunky open-toed mules in the exact muted shade of mauve as the little hydrangea leaf in the print.

Every single piece of clothing has to be bought with the human fluctuation factor figured in. Will pants bought before lunch on Tuesday have anything to do with my Friday evening shape?

If I'm going to need to be able to be seen without my coat on after a two-and-a-half-hour movie, during which I plan to have popcorn and a 16-ounce diet soda, how much can I eat for breakfast that day without blowing the whole look?

This is what women bring to love.

This is what's in our eyes when we walk into a room and look around. Who could work with a few alterations? Who could work if I make a few alterations to myself? Who would be a fabulous match if I did a complete overhaul of him and me?

Women don't set out to change men. It's just that everything about our lives has trained us to expect that we'll have to change something to make it fit. It's only natural to look at a man who looks sort of appealing and assume we can alter and accessorize him to go with our lives.

It would all seem so tacky and superficial if it weren't these exact same tendencies that inspire some of our deepest loyalty and longest relationships:

The commitment to a version of him that no one, including him, has ever seen . . .

The belief that with time and attention we can bring out the sensitive artist we caught a glimpse of under the aloof football fanatic shell . . .

Our undying faith in what we know the two of us could be . . .

We're trained by the mall to grab a really lovely blouse when we see one and create a relationship for it later. We're trained by the mall to walk right past 60,000 mediocre tank tops without stopping to say "Hello."

Eternal devotion or auto-elimination.

We know the effort we'll put into a relationship. Women aren't that picky. We're just out of time.

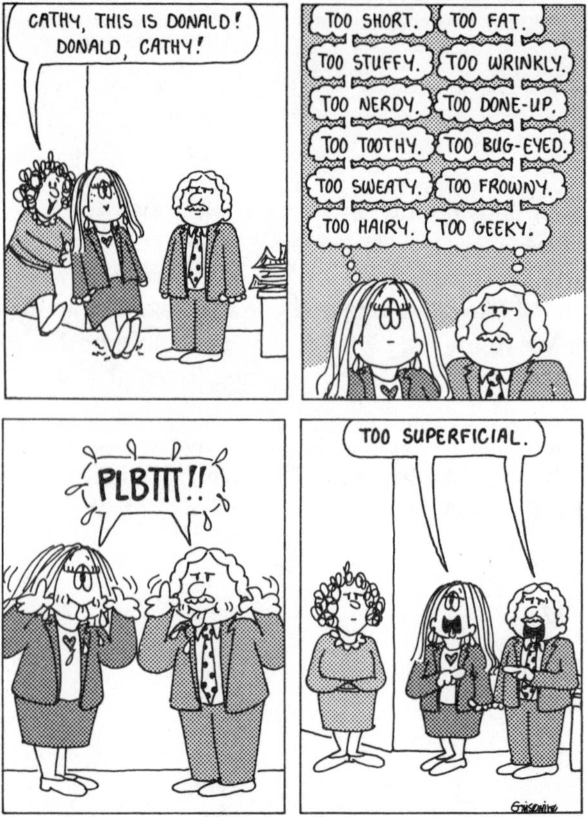
CATHY, THIS IS DONALD! DONALD, CATHY!
TOO SHORT.
TOO FAT.
TOO STUFFY.
TOO WRINKLY.
TOO NERDY.
TOO DONE-UP.
TOO TOOTHY.
TOO BUG-EYED.
TOO SWEATY.
TOO FROWNY.
TOO HAIRY.
TOO GEEKY.
PLBTTT!!
TOO SUPERFICIAL.

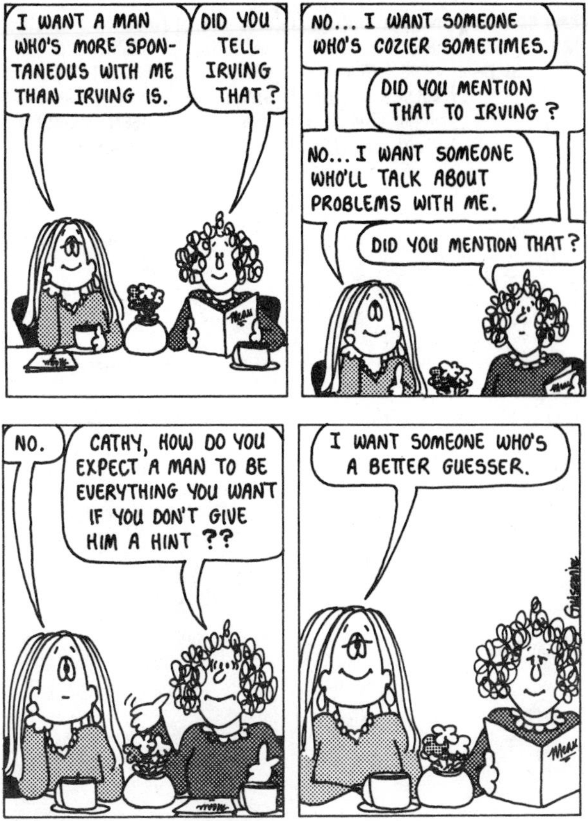
I WANT A MAN WHO'S MORE SPON-TANEOUS WITH ME THAN IRVING IS.
DID YOU TELL IRVING THAT?
NO... I WANT SOMEONE WHO'S COZIER SOMETIMES.
DID YOU MENTION THAT TO IRVING?
NO... I WANT SOMEONE WHO'LL TALK ABOUT PROBLEMS WITH ME.
DID YOU MENTION THAT?
NO.
CATHY, HOW DO YOU EXPECT A MAN TO BE EVERYTHING YOU WANT IF YOU DON'T GIVE HIM A HINT??
I WANT SOMEONE WHO'S A BETTER GUESSER.
Guisewite

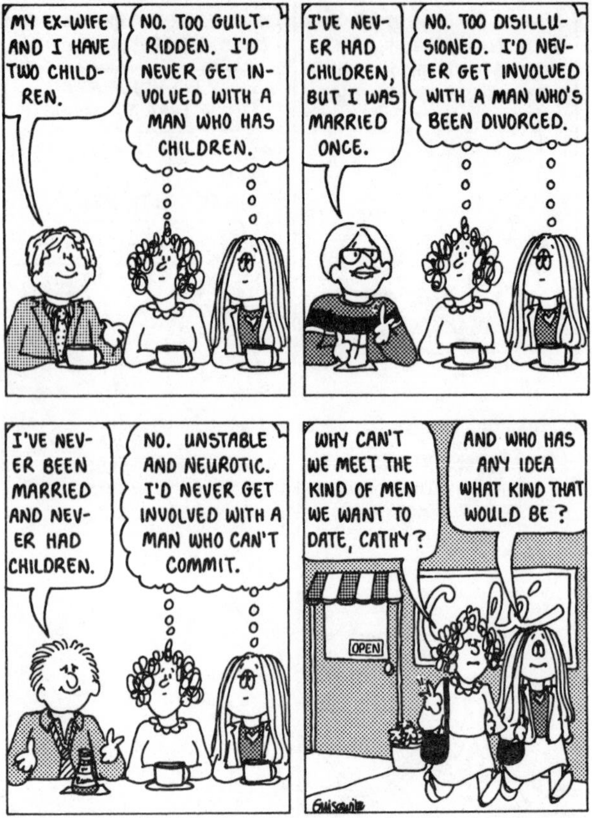
MY EX-WIFE AND I HAVE TWO CHILDREN.
NO. TOO GUILT-RIDDEN. I'D NEVER GET INVOLVED WITH A MAN WHO HAS CHILDREN.
I'VE NEVER HAD CHILDREN, BUT I WAS MARRIED ONCE.
NO. TOO DISILLUSIONED. I'D NEVER GET INVOLVED WITH A MAN WHO'S BEEN DIVORCED.
I'VE NEVER BEEN MARRIED AND NEVER HAD CHILDREN.
NO. UNSTABLE AND NEUROTIC. I'D NEVER GET INVOLVED WITH A MAN WHO CAN'T COMMIT.
WHY CAN'T WE MEET THE KIND OF MEN WE WANT TO DATE, CATHY?
AND WHO HAS ANY IDEA WHAT KIND THAT WOULD BE?
OPEN
Guisewite

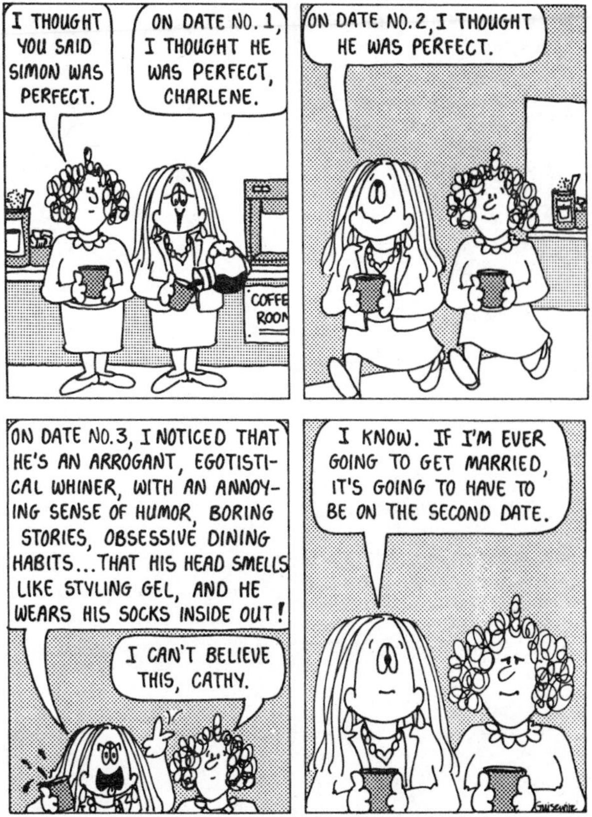
I THOUGHT YOU SAID SIMON WAS PERFECT.
ON DATE NO. 1, I THOUGHT HE WAS PERFECT, CHARLENE.
COFFE ROOM
ON DATE NO. 2, I THOUGHT HE WAS PERFECT.
ON DATE NO. 3, I NOTICED THAT HE'S AN ARROGANT, EGOTISTICAL WHINER, WITH AN ANNOYING SENSE OF HUMOR, BORING STORIES, OBSESSIVE DINING HABITS... THAT HIS HEAD SMELLS LIKE STYLING GEL, AND HE WEARS HIS SOCKS INSIDE OUT!
I CAN'T BELIEVE THIS, CATHY.
I KNOW. IF I'M EVER GOING TO GET MARRIED, IT'S GOING TO HAVE TO BE ON THE SECOND DATE.

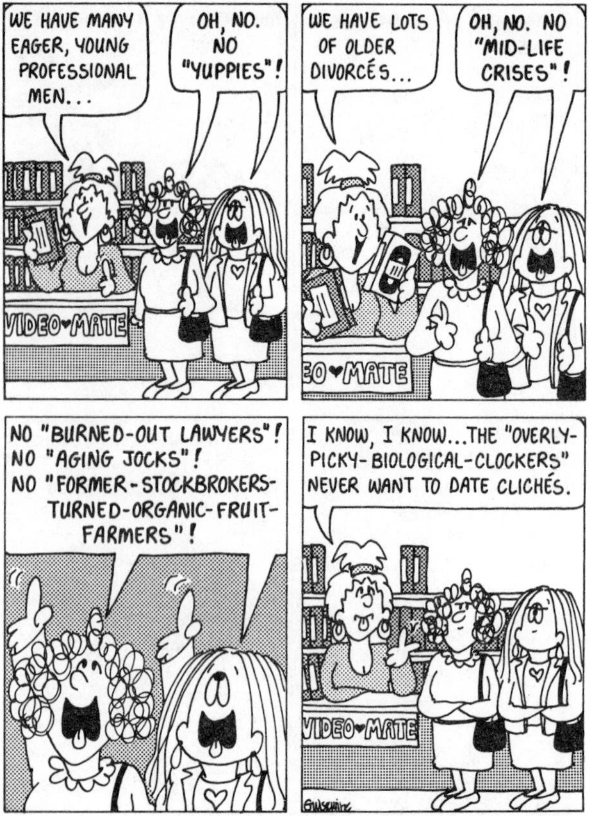
WE HAVE MANY EAGER, YOUNG PROFESSIONAL MEN...
OH, NO. NO "YUPPIES"!
VIDEO♥MATE
WE HAVE LOTS OF OLDER DIVORCÉS...
OH, NO. NO "MID-LIFE CRISES"!
EO♥MATE
NO "BURNED-OUT LAWYERS"! NO "AGING JOCKS"! NO "FORMER-STOCKBROKERS-TURNED-ORGANIC-FRUIT-FARMERS"!
I KNOW, I KNOW...THE "OVERLY-PICKY-BIOLOGICAL-CLOCKERS" NEVER WANT TO DATE CLICHÉS.
VIDEO♥MATE

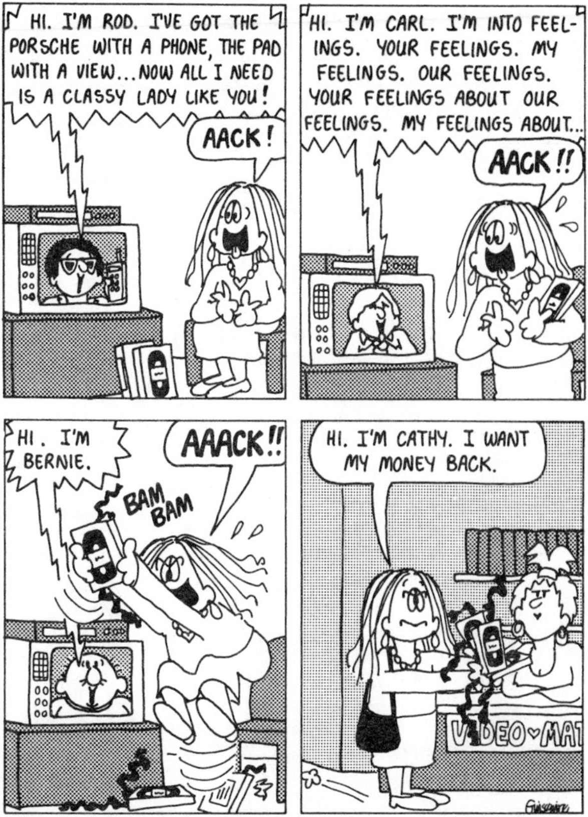
HI. I'M ROD. I'VE GOT THE PORSCHE WITH A PHONE, THE PAD WITH A VIEW... NOW ALL I NEED IS A CLASSY LADY LIKE YOU!
AACK!
HI. I'M CARL. I'M INTO FEELINGS. YOUR FEELINGS. MY FEELINGS. OUR FEELINGS. YOUR FEELINGS ABOUT OUR FEELINGS. MY FEELINGS ABOUT...
AACK!!
HI. I'M BERNIE.
AAACK!!
BAM BAM
HI. I'M CATHY. I WANT MY MONEY BACK.
VIDEO♥MAT

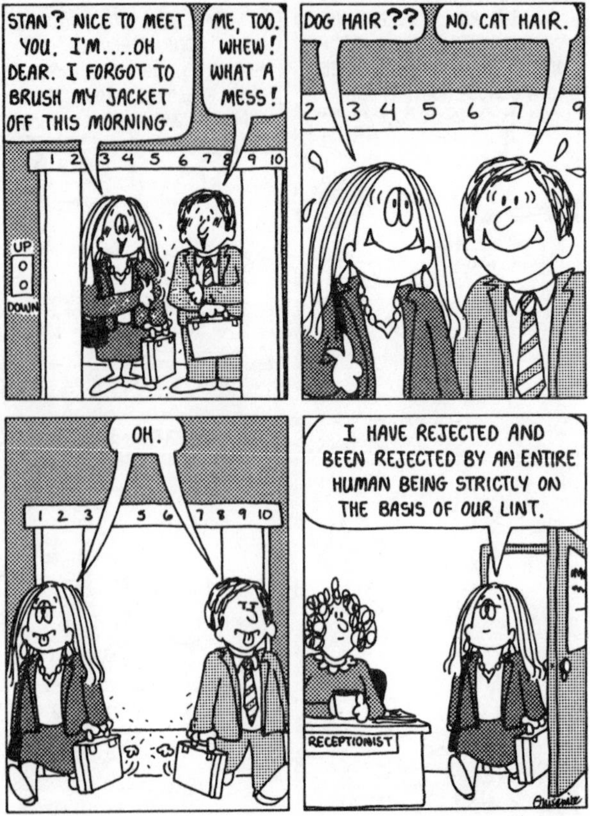
STAN? NICE TO MEET YOU. I'M....OH, DEAR. I FORGOT TO BRUSH MY JACKET OFF THIS MORNING.
ME, TOO. WHEW! WHAT A MESS!
UP
DOWN
DOG HAIR??
NO. CAT HAIR.
OH.
I HAVE REJECTED AND BEEN REJECTED BY AN ENTIRE HUMAN BEING STRICTLY ON THE BASIS OF OUR LINT.
RECEPTIONIST

1980: INCOMPATIBLE MILEAGE PROGRAMS.

I'M DELTA. I'M UNITED.

TOO BAD. IT WILL NEVER WORK.

Vino

1990: INCOMPATIBLE OPERATING SYSTEMS.

I'M MAC. I'M PC.

TOO BAD. IT WILL NEVER WORK.

ague

AFTER DECADES OF SUPERFICIAL JUDGMENTS, PEOPLE ARE FINALLY FOCUSING ON SOMETHING A LITTLE CLOSER TO HOME:

2000: INCOMPATIBLE HOME FURNISHINGS.

I'M PINE. I'M DECO.

TOO BAD. IT WILL NEVER WORK.

Latte

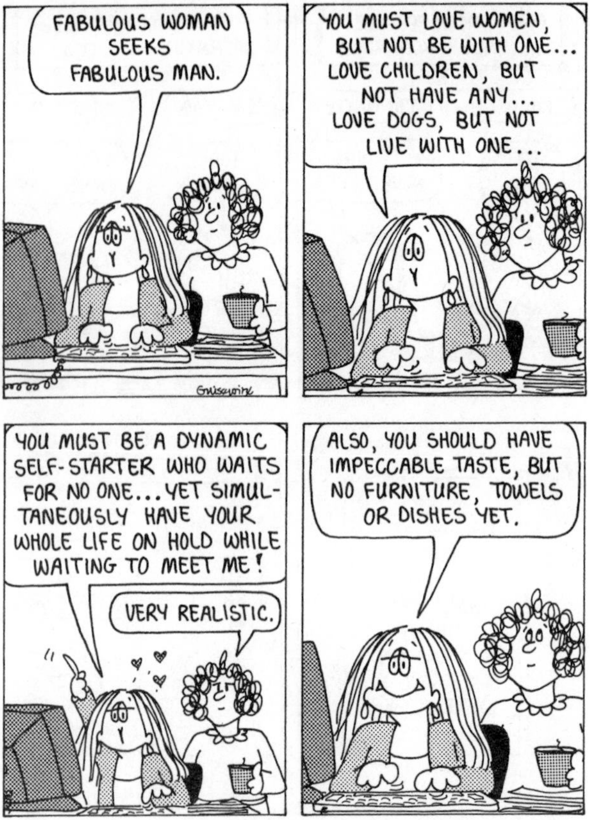
FABULOUS WOMAN SEEKS FABULOUS MAN.
YOU MUST LOVE WOMEN, BUT NOT BE WITH ONE... LOVE CHILDREN, BUT NOT HAVE ANY... LOVE DOGS, BUT NOT LIVE WITH ONE...
YOU MUST BE A DYNAMIC SELF-STARTER WHO WAITS FOR NO ONE... YET SIMULTANEOUSLY HAVE YOUR WHOLE LIFE ON HOLD WHILE WAITING TO MEET ME!
VERY REALISTIC.
ALSO, YOU SHOULD HAVE IMPECCABLE TASTE, BUT NO FURNITURE, TOWELS OR DISHES YET.

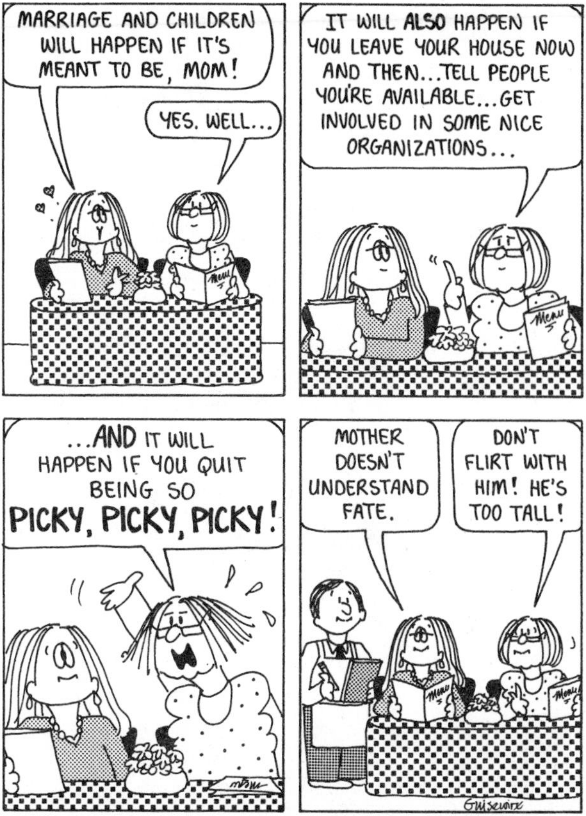
MARRIAGE AND CHILDREN WILL HAPPEN IF IT'S MEANT TO BE, MOM!
YES. WELL...
IT WILL ALSO HAPPEN IF YOU LEAVE YOUR HOUSE NOW AND THEN...TELL PEOPLE YOU'RE AVAILABLE...GET INVOLVED IN SOME NICE ORGANIZATIONS...
...AND IT WILL HAPPEN IF YOU QUIT BEING SO PICKY, PICKY, PICKY!
MOTHER DOESN'T UNDERSTAND FATE.
DON'T FLIRT WITH HIM! HE'S TOO TALL!
Guisewite

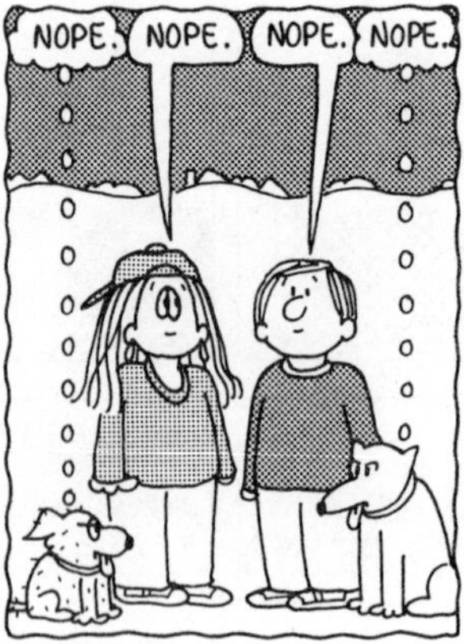
NOPE.
NOPE.
NOPE.
NOPE.

Mr. Wrongs

When I was young, I believed what people said:
There is one special man out there for all of us.

As I got older, I realized what people meant: There is ONE special man out there for ALL of us.

Ninety-five zillion eligible women.

One eligible guy.

One available, acceptable man.

One Mr. Right.

So many, many, many Mr. Wrongs.

Mr. Liberation, 1977:

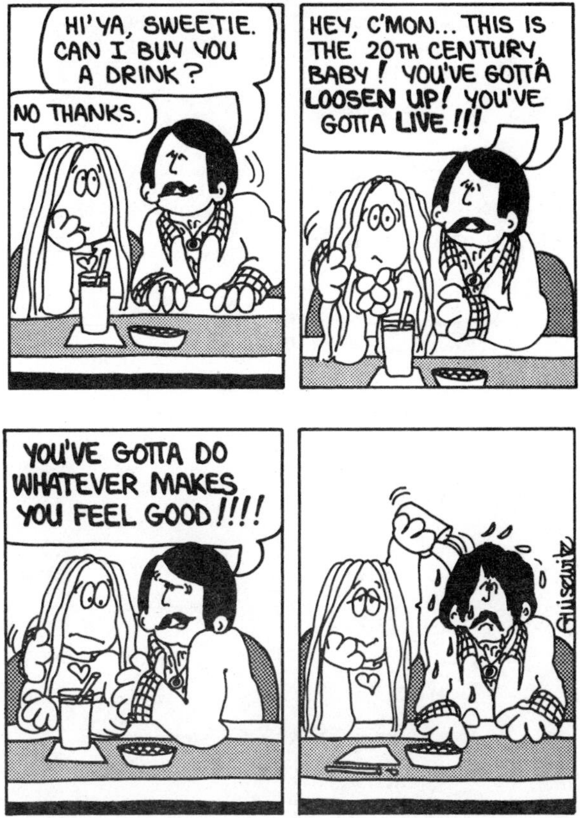
HI'YA, SWEETIE. CAN I BUY YOU A DRINK?
NO THANKS.
HEY, C'MON... THIS IS THE 20TH CENTURY, BABY! YOU'VE GOTTA LOOSEN UP! YOU'VE GOTTA LIVE!!!
YOU'VE GOTTA DO WHATEVER MAKES YOU FEEL GOOD!!!!
Guisewite

Mr. Unlucky, 1981:

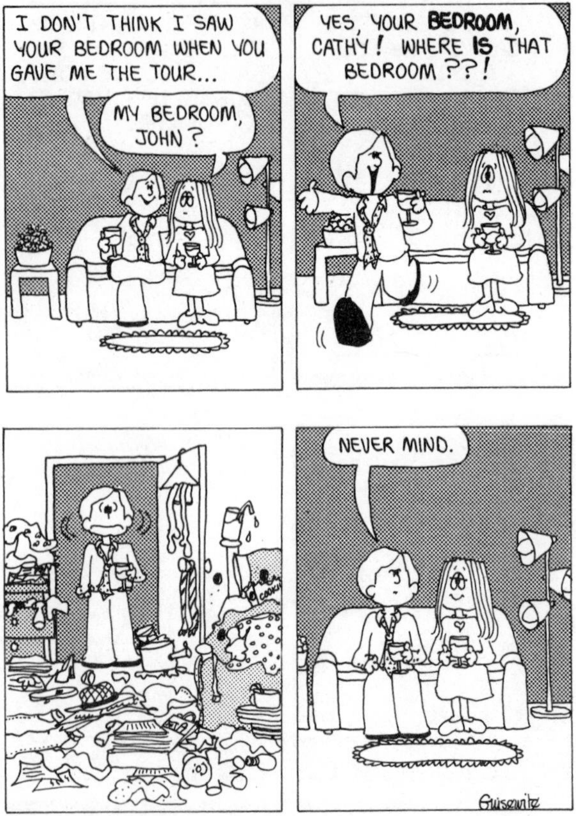
I DON'T THINK I SAW YOUR BEDROOM WHEN YOU GAVE ME THE TOUR...
MY BEDROOM, JOHN?
YES, YOUR **BEDROOM**, CATHY! WHERE **IS** THAT BEDROOM??!
NEVER MIND.
Guisewite

Mr. Enlightenment Seminar Graduate, 1982:

Mr. Oblivious, 1982:

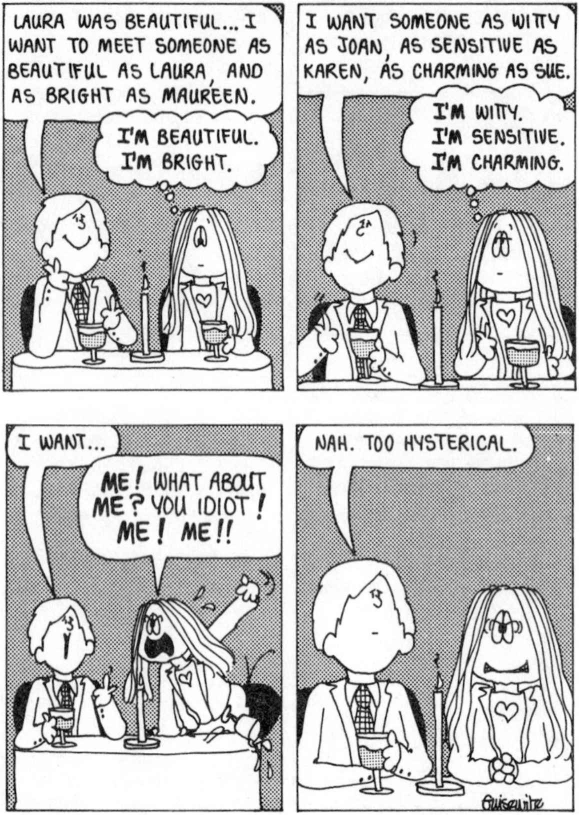

LAURA WAS BEAUTIFUL... I WANT TO MEET SOMEONE AS BEAUTIFUL AS LAURA, AND AS BRIGHT AS MAUREEN.
I'M BEAUTIFUL. I'M BRIGHT.
I WANT SOMEONE AS WITTY AS JOAN, AS SENSITIVE AS KAREN, AS CHARMING AS SUE.
I'M WITTY. I'M SENSITIVE. I'M CHARMING.
I WANT...
ME! WHAT ABOUT ME? YOU IDIOT! ME! ME!!
NAH. TOO HYSTERICAL.
Guisewite

Mr. Blank, 1985:

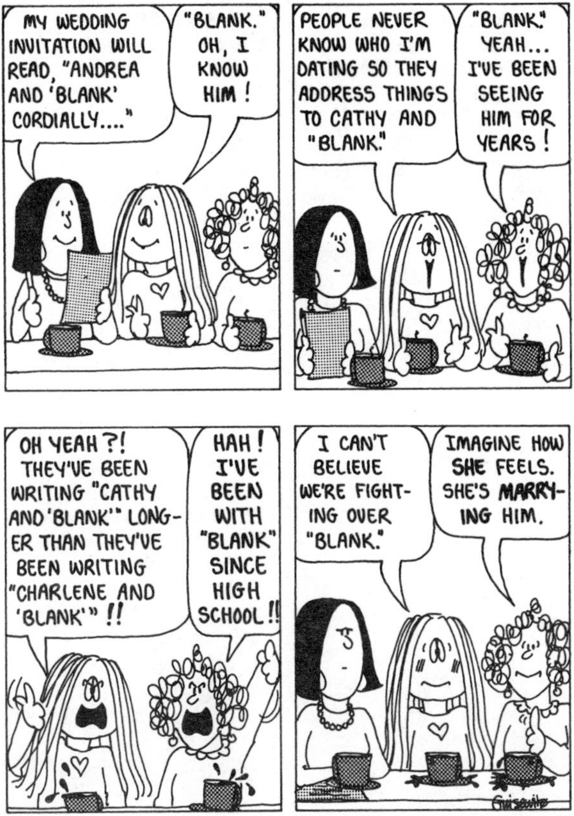
MY WEDDING INVITATION WILL READ, "ANDREA AND 'BLANK' CORDIALLY...."
"BLANK." OH, I KNOW HIM!
PEOPLE NEVER KNOW WHO I'M DATING SO THEY ADDRESS THINGS TO CATHY AND "BLANK."
"BLANK." YEAH... I'VE BEEN SEEING HIM FOR YEARS!
OH YEAH?! THEY'VE BEEN WRITING "CATHY AND 'BLANK'" LONGER THAN THEY'VE BEEN WRITING "CHARLENE AND 'BLANK'"!!
HAH! I'VE BEEN WITH "BLANK" SINCE HIGH SCHOOL!!
I CAN'T BELIEVE WE'RE FIGHTING OVER "BLANK."
IMAGINE HOW SHE FEELS. SHE'S MARRYING HIM.
Guisewite

Mr. Innocence, 1986:

I WAS GOING TO CALL!
I TRIED TO CALL!
I LOST YOUR NUMBER!
I FORGOT YOUR LAST NAME!
YOUR LINE WAS BUSY!
MY PHONE IS BROKEN!
YOUR PHONE IS BROKEN!
YOUR ANSWERING MACHINE
   IS BROKEN!

I'VE BEEN SICK!
I HAD A WORK CRISIS!
A FAMILY CRISIS!
A NATURAL DISASTER!
I'VE BEEN OUT OF TOWN!
I WAS INTIMIDATED!
I WAS CONFUSED!
AN OLD GIRLFRIEND RE-
   SURFACED!

...(pant, pant)
ANYTHING??
ANYTHING AT ALL?
(pant, pant)....

NOT
EVEN
CLOSE.

MY MOTHER IS VISITING!
MY GRANDMOTHER IS VISITING!
I WAS BEING COY!
MY APARTMENT FLOODED!
I HAD DENTAL SURGERY!
I WAS ROBBED!
I HAD FOOD POISONING!
I'M BEING TRANSFERRED!
I'VE HAD AMNESIA!
I LOST MY HOUSE KEYS!
I LOST MY CONTACTS!
I LOS   ADDR   OOK!
I'VE   DEPR   !
I WA   KEN   !
I   EP!

Mr. Adventure, 1987:

IRVING, WHAT'S HAPPENED TO YOU??

MEN HAVE HAD IT WITH WIMP CLOTHES, CATHY.

LOOK AT THIS STUFF... EXPEDITION CANVAS PANTS TOUGH ENOUGH TO SURVIVE A ROCK SLIDE... VESTS THAT CAN LUG 100 POUNDS OF GEAR WHILE BLOCKING GALE-FORCE WINDS... FATIGUE SOCKS... STORM FLAPS... GROMMET VENTS... TRAMPING BOOTS...

THIS HAT ALONE CAN WITHSTAND EVERYTHING FROM THE SCORCHING HEAT OF THE AMAZON TO THE FRIGID BLASTS OF THE ANTARCTIC.

OH, FORGET IT. LET'S JUST GO GET SOMETHING TO EAT.

IT'S DRIZZLING OUT.

Mr. Quick Thinker, 1987:

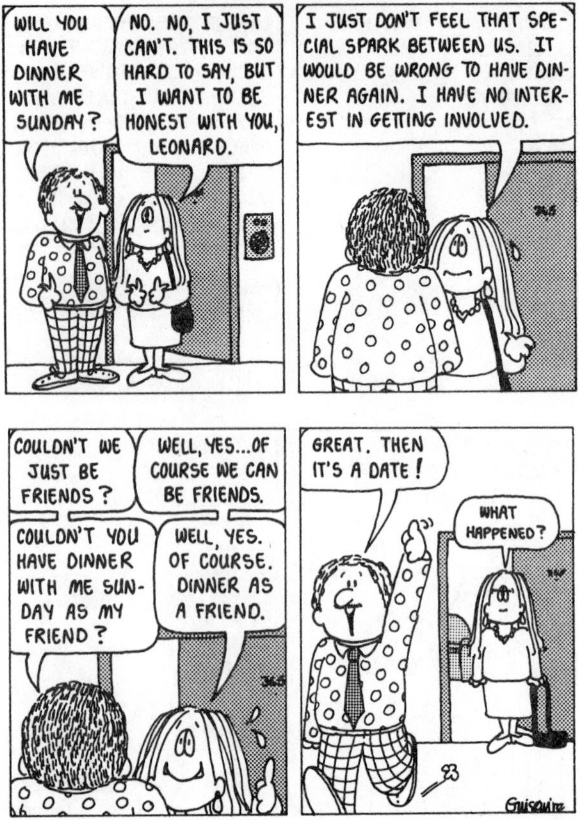
WILL YOU HAVE DINNER WITH ME SUNDAY?
NO. NO, I JUST CAN'T. THIS IS SO HARD TO SAY, BUT I WANT TO BE HONEST WITH YOU, LEONARD.
I JUST DON'T FEEL THAT SPECIAL SPARK BETWEEN US. IT WOULD BE WRONG TO HAVE DINNER AGAIN. I HAVE NO INTEREST IN GETTING INVOLVED.
COULDN'T WE JUST BE FRIENDS?
WELL, YES...OF COURSE WE CAN BE FRIENDS.
COULDN'T YOU HAVE DINNER WITH ME SUNDAY AS MY FRIEND?
WELL, YES. OF COURSE. DINNER AS A FRIEND.
GREAT. THEN IT'S A DATE!
WHAT HAPPENED?
Guisewite

Mr. Logo, 1989:

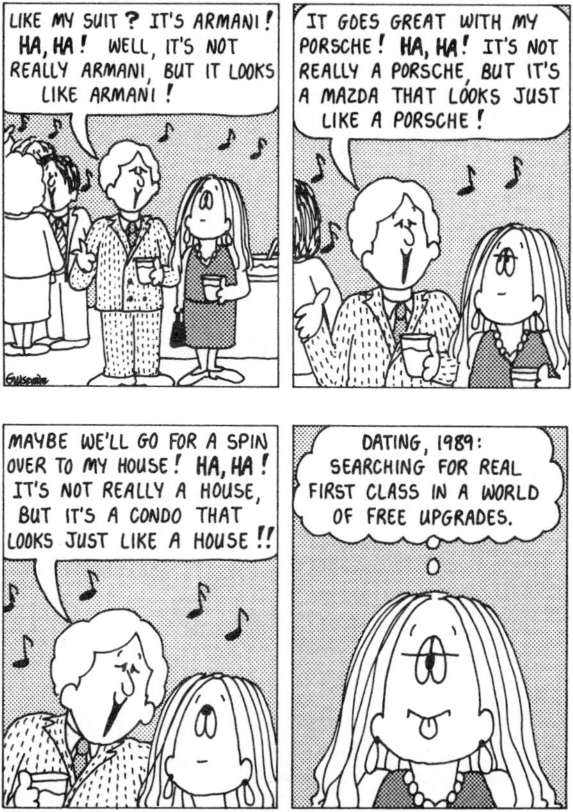
LIKE MY SUIT? IT'S ARMANI! HA, HA! WELL, IT'S NOT REALLY ARMANI, BUT IT LOOKS LIKE ARMANI!
IT GOES GREAT WITH MY PORSCHE! HA, HA! IT'S NOT REALLY A PORSCHE, BUT IT'S A MAZDA THAT LOOKS JUST LIKE A PORSCHE!
MAYBE WE'LL GO FOR A SPIN OVER TO MY HOUSE! HA, HA! IT'S NOT REALLY A HOUSE, BUT IT'S A CONDO THAT LOOKS JUST LIKE A HOUSE!!
DATING, 1989: SEARCHING FOR REAL FIRST CLASS IN A WORLD OF FREE UPGRADES.

Mr. Smooth, 1989:

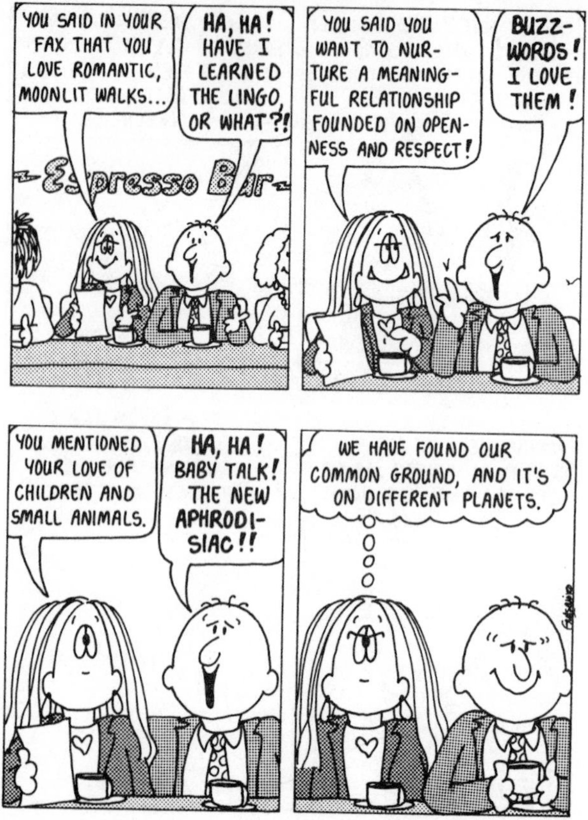
YOU SAID IN YOUR FAX THAT YOU LOVE ROMANTIC, MOONLIT WALKS...
HA, HA! HAVE I LEARNED THE LINGO, OR WHAT?!
Espresso Bar
YOU SAID YOU WANT TO NURTURE A MEANINGFUL RELATIONSHIP FOUNDED ON OPENNESS AND RESPECT!
BUZZWORDS! I LOVE THEM!
YOU MENTIONED YOUR LOVE OF CHILDREN AND SMALL ANIMALS.
HA, HA! BABY TALK! THE NEW APHRODISIAC!!
WE HAVE FOUND OUR COMMON GROUND, AND IT'S ON DIFFERENT PLANETS.

Mr. Too Good To Be True, 1990:

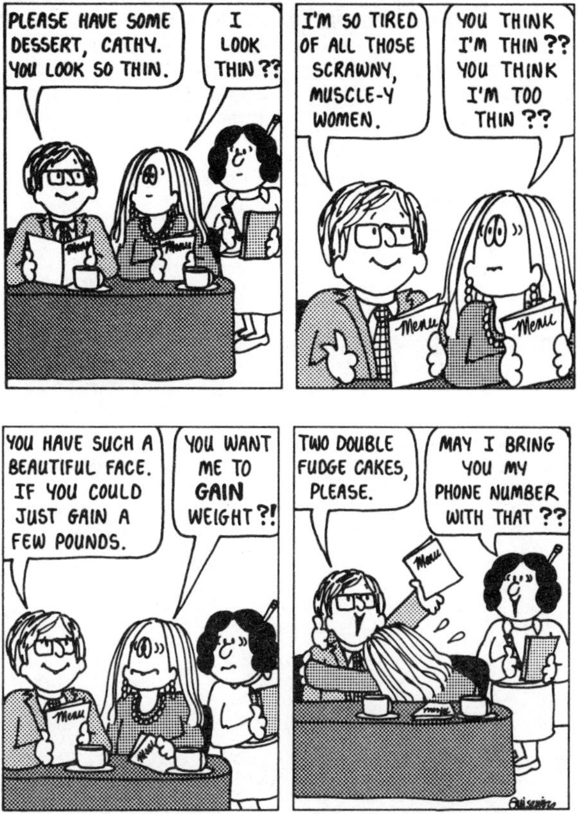
PLEASE HAVE SOME DESSERT, CATHY. YOU LOOK SO THIN.
I LOOK THIN??
I'M SO TIRED OF ALL THOSE SCRAWNY, MUSCLE-Y WOMEN.
YOU THINK I'M THIN?? YOU THINK I'M TOO THIN??
YOU HAVE SUCH A BEAUTIFUL FACE. IF YOU COULD JUST GAIN A FEW POUNDS.
YOU WANT ME TO GAIN WEIGHT?!
TWO DOUBLE FUDGE CAKES, PLEASE.
MAY I BRING YOU MY PHONE NUMBER WITH THAT??

Mr. Big Birthday, 1990:

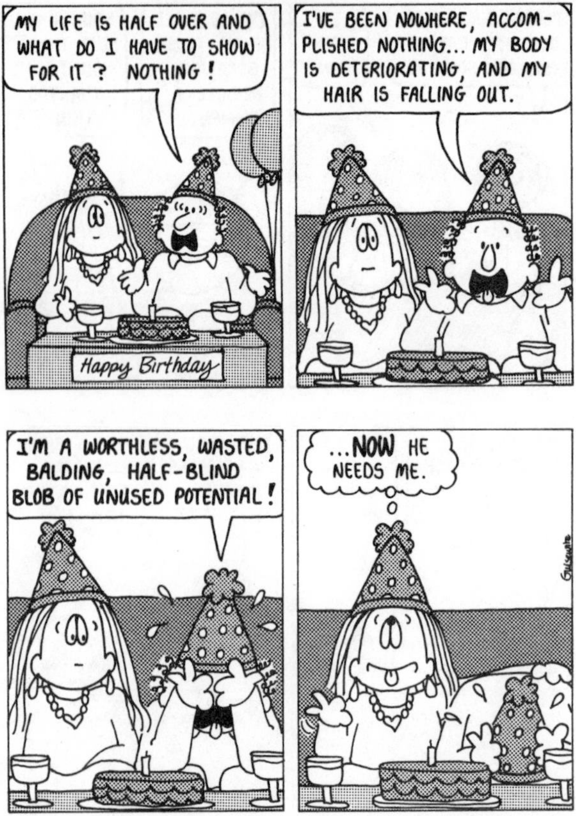
MY LIFE IS HALF OVER AND WHAT DO I HAVE TO SHOW FOR IT? NOTHING!
Happy Birthday
I'VE BEEN NOWHERE, ACCOMPLISHED NOTHING... MY BODY IS DETERIORATING, AND MY HAIR IS FALLING OUT.
I'M A WORTHLESS, WASTED, BALDING, HALF-BLIND BLOB OF UNUSED POTENTIAL!
...NOW HE NEEDS ME.

Mr. Outdoorsman, 1990:

DIGITAL HEARTRATE MONITOR...
CHECK.
BLOOD PRESSURE TRACKER...
CHECK.
ELECTRONIC SONIC DEEP-MUSCLE MASSAGER...
CHECK.
ALL-WEATHER KIDNEY-SUPPORT BELT WITH DETACHABLE KNEE, WRIST AND ANKLE BRACES.
CHECK.
PERIODONTIST-APPROVED, PLAQUE-FIGHTING, ELECTRIC TOOTHCARE SYSTEM...
CHECK.
INTERNATIONAL MINOXIDIL PRESCRIPTION...
CHECK.
THERE'S NOTHING LIKE VENTURING INTO THE GREAT OUTDOORS TO MAKE A MAN FEEL YOUNG AGAIN!

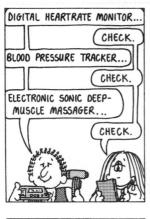

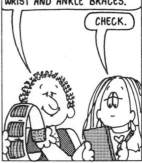

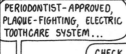

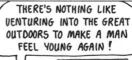

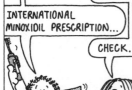

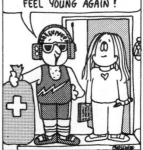

Mr. First and Last Date, 1991:

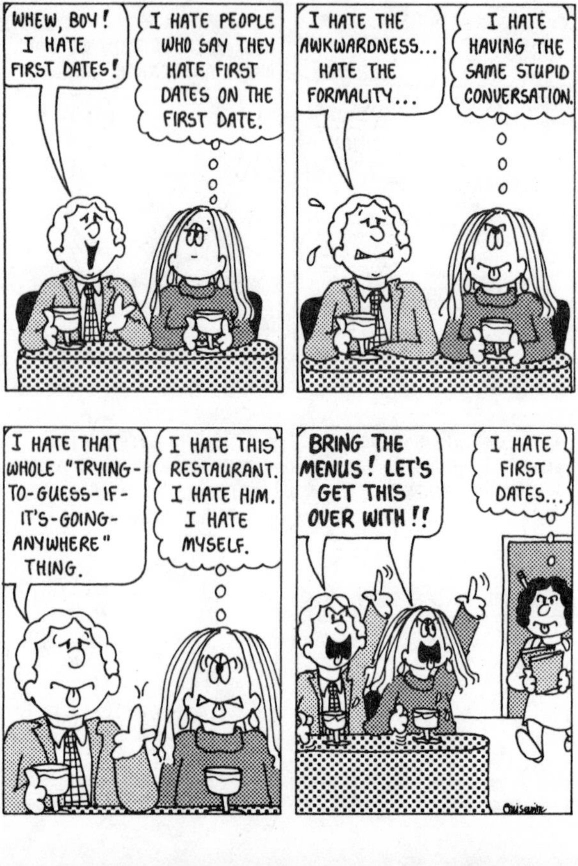
WHEW, BOY! I HATE FIRST DATES!
I HATE PEOPLE WHO SAY THEY HATE FIRST DATES ON THE FIRST DATE.
I HATE THE AWKWARDNESS... HATE THE FORMALITY...
I HATE HAVING THE SAME STUPID CONVERSATION.
I HATE THAT WHOLE "TRYING-TO-GUESS-IF-IT'S-GOING-ANYWHERE" THING.
I HATE THIS RESTAURANT. I HATE HIM. I HATE MYSELF.
BRING THE MENUS! LET'S GET THIS OVER WITH!!
I HATE FIRST DATES...
Guisewite

Mr. Golf, 1992:

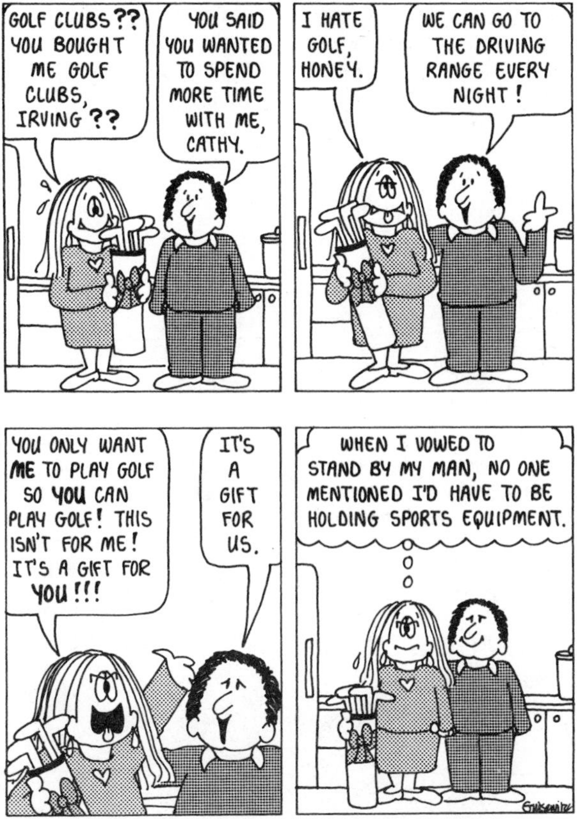
GOLF CLUBS?? YOU BOUGHT ME GOLF CLUBS, IRVING??
YOU SAID YOU WANTED TO SPEND MORE TIME WITH ME, CATHY.
I HATE GOLF, HONEY.
WE CAN GO TO THE DRIVING RANGE EVERY NIGHT!
YOU ONLY WANT ME TO PLAY GOLF SO YOU CAN PLAY GOLF! THIS ISN'T FOR ME! IT'S A GIFT FOR YOU!!!
IT'S A GIFT FOR US.
WHEN I VOWED TO STAND BY MY MAN, NO ONE MENTIONED I'D HAVE TO BE HOLDING SPORTS EQUIPMENT.
Guisewite

Mr. Unbelievable, 1993:

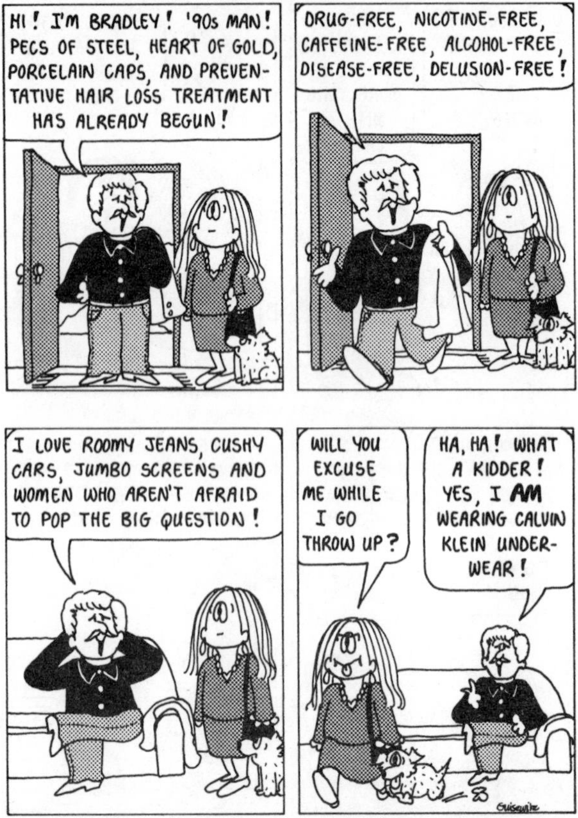

HI! I'M BRADLEY! '90s MAN! PECS OF STEEL, HEART OF GOLD, PORCELAIN CAPS, AND PREVENTATIVE HAIR LOSS TREATMENT HAS ALREADY BEGUN!
DRUG-FREE, NICOTINE-FREE, CAFFEINE-FREE, ALCOHOL-FREE, DISEASE-FREE, DELUSION-FREE!
I LOVE ROOMY JEANS, CUSHY CARS, JUMBO SCREENS AND WOMEN WHO AREN'T AFRAID TO POP THE BIG QUESTION!
WILL YOU EXCUSE ME WHILE I GO THROW UP?
HA, HA! WHAT A KIDDER! YES, I **AM** WEARING CALVIN KLEIN UNDERWEAR!

Mr. Really Unbelievable, 1993:

I WORK HARD, PLAY ROUGH, INVEST IN LONG-TERM GROWTH STOCKS AND PRE-RUMPLED KHAKI LEISURE WEAR.

I CAN QUOTE U2, SING SPRING-STEEN, DO THE ACHY-BREAKY, RUN WINDOWS, LIFT MY WEIGHT, PROGRAM MY VCR, AND WEEP IN PUBLIC!

I'VE BEATEN A SOUFFLÉ IN THE KITCHEN, A DRUM IN THE WOODS, MY HEAD AGAINST THE WALL... ...AND NOW I'M READY TO SNUGGLE UP WITH A SPECIAL LADY AND START CREATING LIT-TLE TINY VERSIONS OF MYSELF!

WHILE THE CITY SLEEPS, ANOTH-ER SINGLE WOMAN GATHERS MATERIAL FOR HER NOVEL.

YOU'RE TAKING NOTES! INCREDIBLE! AM I ON TONIGHT, OR WHAT?!

Guisewite

Mr. Really, Really Unbelievable, 1993:

Mr. Camper, 1994:

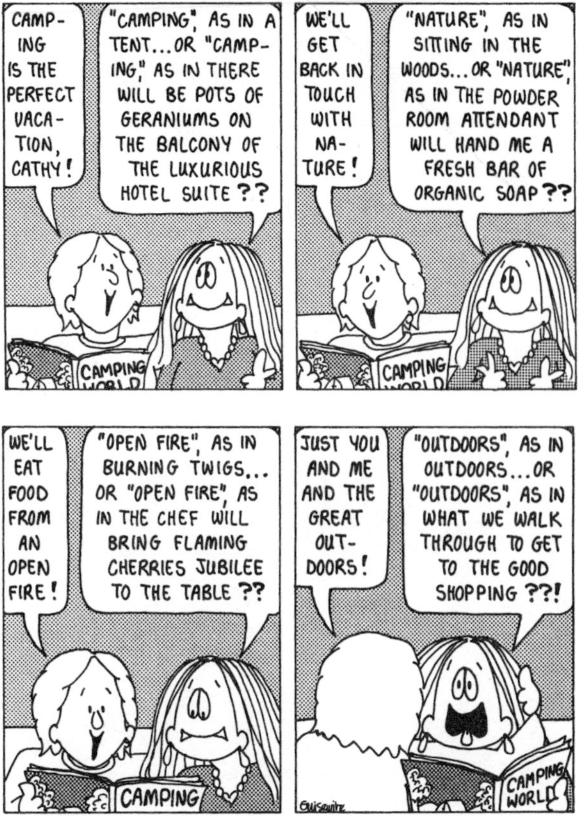
CAMPING IS THE PERFECT VACATION, CATHY!
"CAMPING", AS IN A TENT...OR "CAMPING," AS IN THERE WILL BE POTS OF GERANIUMS ON THE BALCONY OF THE LUXURIOUS HOTEL SUITE??
CAMPING WORLD
WE'LL GET BACK IN TOUCH WITH NATURE!
"NATURE", AS IN SITTING IN THE WOODS...OR "NATURE", AS IN THE POWDER ROOM ATTENDANT WILL HAND ME A FRESH BAR OF ORGANIC SOAP??
WE'LL EAT FOOD FROM AN OPEN FIRE!
"OPEN FIRE", AS IN BURNING TWIGS... OR "OPEN FIRE", AS IN THE CHEF WILL BRING FLAMING CHERRIES JUBILEE TO THE TABLE??
CAMPING
JUST YOU AND ME AND THE GREAT OUTDOORS!
"OUTDOORS", AS IN OUTDOORS...OR "OUTDOORS", AS IN WHAT WE WALK THROUGH TO GET TO THE GOOD SHOPPING??!
CAMPING WORLD
Guisewite

Dear Cathy,

I already feel closer to you than any woman I've ever known. I love how we can open up to each other online without the complications of physical involvement. May our love grow, and may we never be tempted to ruin it by actually meeting each other in person. Love, H.

Mr. Simple Life, 1996:

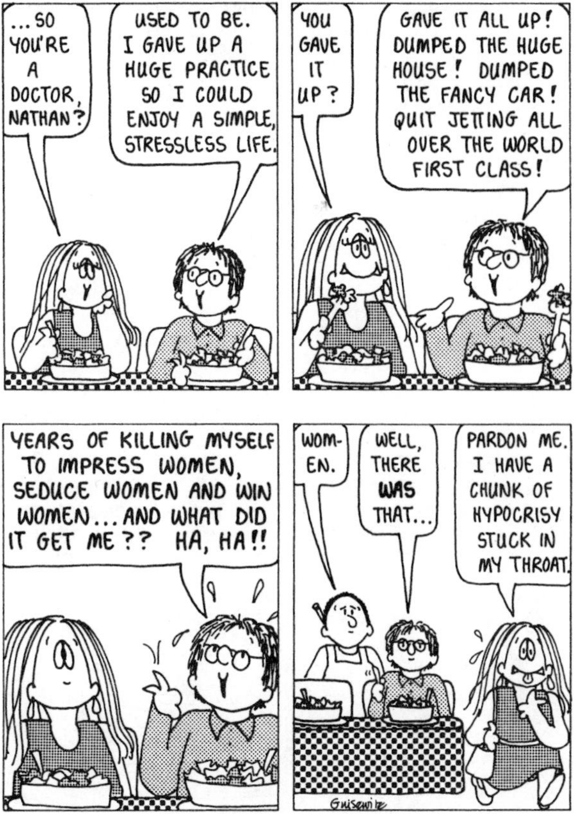

...SO YOU'RE A DOCTOR, NATHAN?
USED TO BE. I GAVE UP A HUGE PRACTICE SO I COULD ENJOY A SIMPLE, STRESSLESS LIFE.
YOU GAVE IT UP?
GAVE IT ALL UP! DUMPED THE HUGE HOUSE! DUMPED THE FANCY CAR! QUIT JETTING ALL OVER THE WORLD FIRST CLASS!
YEARS OF KILLING MYSELF TO IMPRESS WOMEN, SEDUCE WOMEN AND WIN WOMEN... AND WHAT DID IT GET ME?? HA, HA!!
WOM-EN.
WELL, THERE WAS THAT...
PARDON ME. I HAVE A CHUNK OF HYPOCRISY STUCK IN MY THROAT.
Guisewite

Mr. Communicator, 1997:

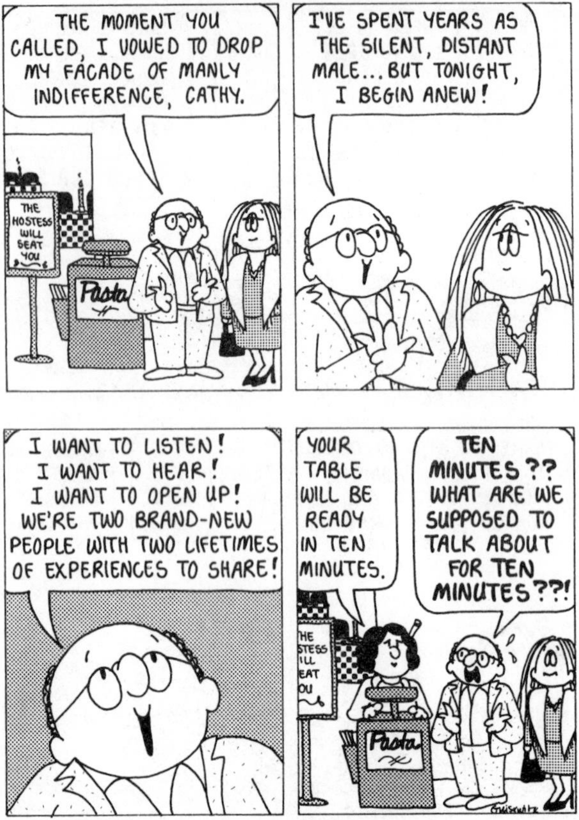
THE MOMENT YOU CALLED, I VOWED TO DROP MY FACADE OF MANLY INDIFFERENCE, CATHY.
THE HOSTESS WILL SEAT YOU
Pasta
I'VE SPENT YEARS AS THE SILENT, DISTANT MALE... BUT TONIGHT, I BEGIN ANEW!
I WANT TO LISTEN! I WANT TO HEAR! I WANT TO OPEN UP! WE'RE TWO BRAND-NEW PEOPLE WITH TWO LIFETIMES OF EXPERIENCES TO SHARE!
YOUR TABLE WILL BE READY IN TEN MINUTES.
TEN MINUTES?? WHAT ARE WE SUPPOSED TO TALK ABOUT FOR TEN MINUTES??!
Pasta

Mr. Inquisitive, 1997:

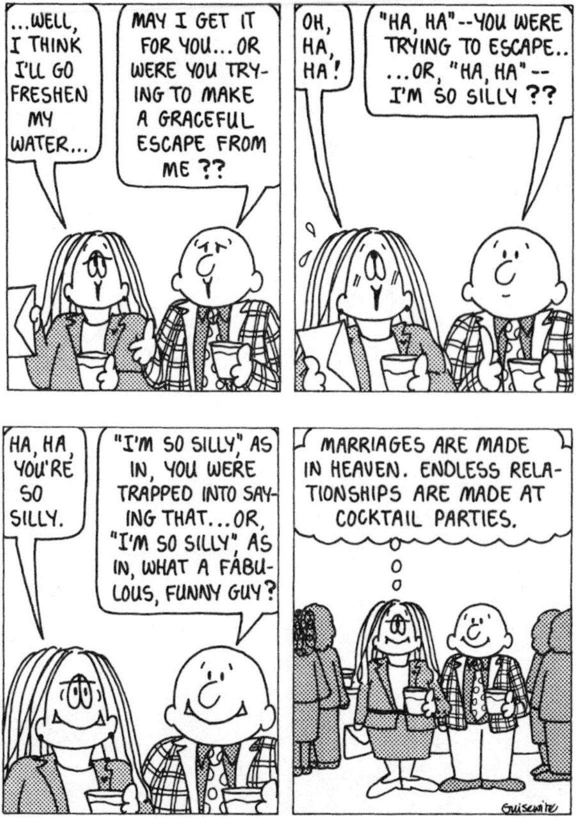
...WELL, I THINK I'LL GO FRESHEN MY WATER...
MAY I GET IT FOR YOU...OR WERE YOU TRYING TO MAKE A GRACEFUL ESCAPE FROM ME ??
OH, HA, HA!
"HA, HA"--YOU WERE TRYING TO ESCAPE.. ...OR, "HA, HA"-- I'M SO SILLY ??
HA, HA, YOU'RE SO SILLY.
"I'M SO SILLY," AS IN, YOU WERE TRAPPED INTO SAYING THAT...OR, "I'M SO SILLY," AS IN, WHAT A FABULOUS, FUNNY GUY?
MARRIAGES ARE MADE IN HEAVEN. ENDLESS RELATIONSHIPS ARE MADE AT COCKTAIL PARTIES.
Guisewite

Mr. Me, 1998:

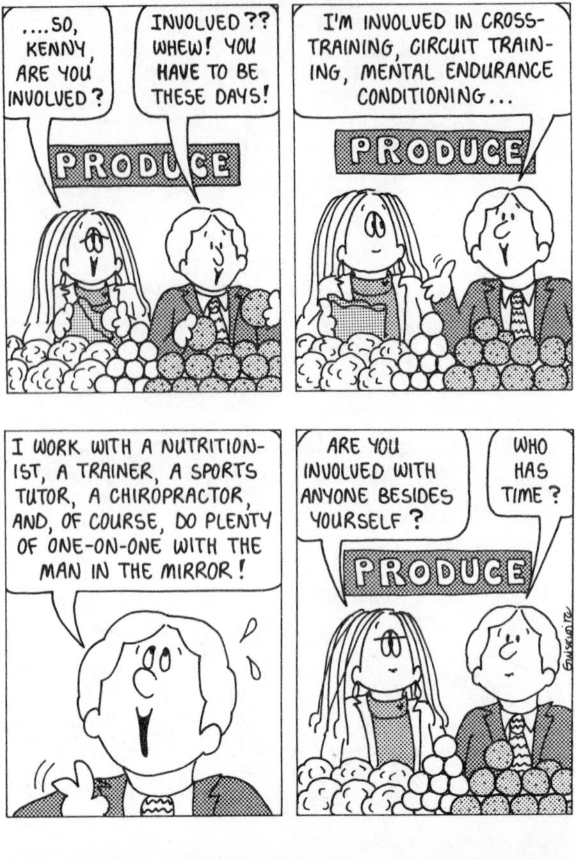

....SO, KENNY, ARE YOU INVOLVED?
INVOLVED?? WHEW! YOU HAVE TO BE THESE DAYS!
PRODUCE
I'M INVOLVED IN CROSS-TRAINING, CIRCUIT TRAINING, MENTAL ENDURANCE CONDITIONING...
PRODUCE
I WORK WITH A NUTRITIONIST, A TRAINER, A SPORTS TUTOR, A CHIROPRACTOR, AND, OF COURSE, DO PLENTY OF ONE-ON-ONE WITH THE MAN IN THE MIRROR!
ARE YOU INVOLVED WITH ANYONE BESIDES YOURSELF?
WHO HAS TIME?
PRODUCE

Mr. Fitness, 1998:

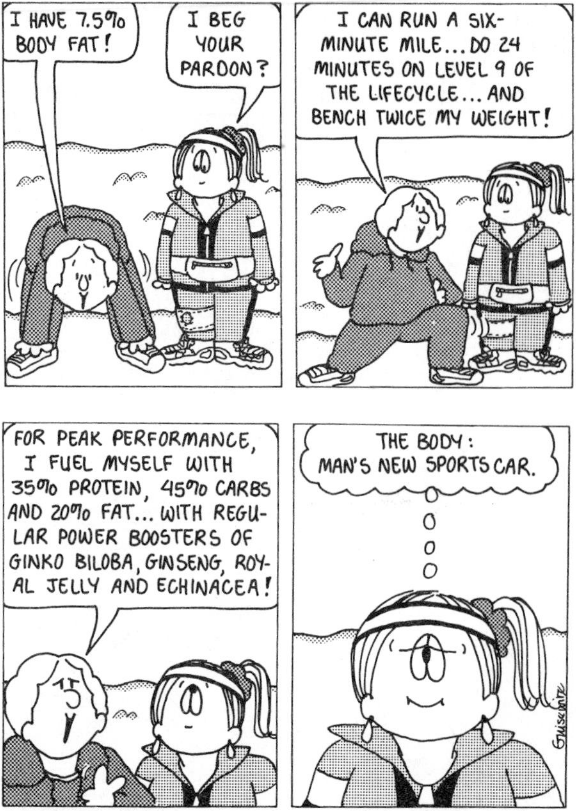
I HAVE 7.5% BODY FAT!
I BEG YOUR PARDON?
I CAN RUN A SIX-MINUTE MILE... DO 24 MINUTES ON LEVEL 9 OF THE LIFECYCLE... AND BENCH TWICE MY WEIGHT!
FOR PEAK PERFORMANCE, I FUEL MYSELF WITH 35% PROTEIN, 45% CARBS AND 20% FAT... WITH REGULAR POWER BOOSTERS OF GINKO BILOBA, GINSENG, ROYAL JELLY AND ECHINACEA!
THE BODY: MAN'S NEW SPORTS CAR.
GUISEWITE

Mr. Herb, 1998:

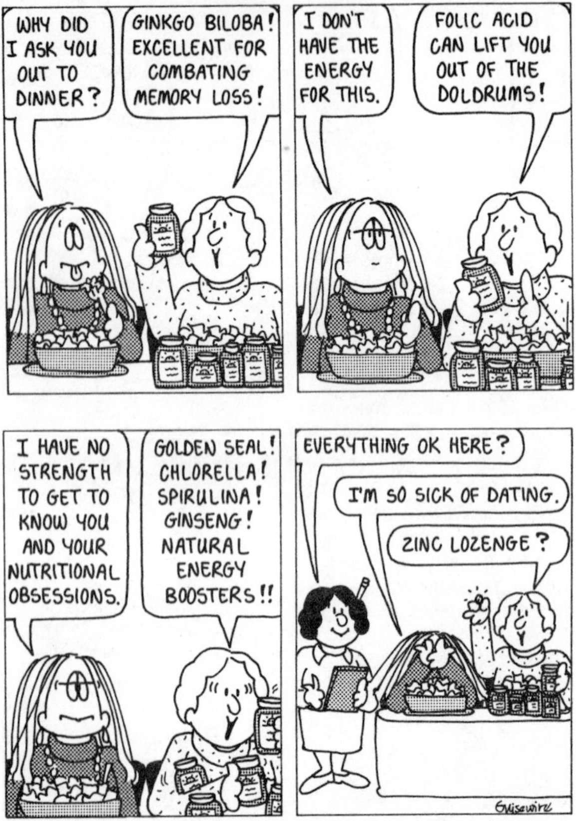
WHY DID I ASK YOU OUT TO DINNER?
GINKGO BILOBA! EXCELLENT FOR COMBATING MEMORY LOSS!
I DON'T HAVE THE ENERGY FOR THIS.
FOLIC ACID CAN LIFT YOU OUT OF THE DOLDRUMS!
I HAVE NO STRENGTH TO GET TO KNOW YOU AND YOUR NUTRITIONAL OBSESSIONS.
GOLDEN SEAL! CHLORELLA! SPIRULINA! GINSENG! NATURAL ENERGY BOOSTERS!!
EVERYTHING OK HERE?
I'M SO SICK OF DATING.
ZINC LOZENGE?
Guisewite

Mr. Dog Person, 1998:

WELL, **HI**, THERE...OH, AREN'T YOU SWEET?..AREN'T YOU GORGEOUS?...WHAT'S YOUR NAME?...YOU HAVE SUCH BEAUTIFUL EYES...SUCH WONDERFUL HAIR... **YES, YOU DO!**...YOU WANT TO KISS ME?...OH, YES.. ...I WANT TO KISS YOU, TOO...**KISS**...**KISS**....

HELLO.

HELLO.

WHY IS IT SO MUCH EASIER TO MAKE DOG CONTACT THAN EYE CONTACT?...

Guisewite

Mr. Never Mind, 1999

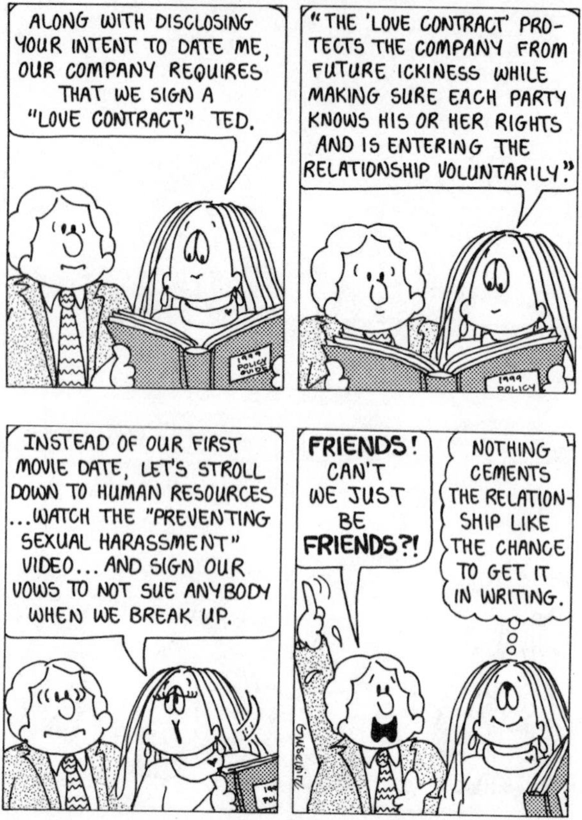
ALONG WITH DISCLOSING YOUR INTENT TO DATE ME, OUR COMPANY REQUIRES THAT WE SIGN A "LOVE CONTRACT," TED.
1999 POLICY GUIDE
"THE 'LOVE CONTRACT' PROTECTS THE COMPANY FROM FUTURE ICKINESS WHILE MAKING SURE EACH PARTY KNOWS HIS OR HER RIGHTS AND IS ENTERING THE RELATIONSHIP VOLUNTARILY."
1999 POLICY
INSTEAD OF OUR FIRST MOVIE DATE, LET'S STROLL DOWN TO HUMAN RESOURCES ...WATCH THE "PREVENTING SEXUAL HARASSMENT" VIDEO... AND SIGN OUR VOWS TO NOT SUE ANYBODY WHEN WE BREAK UP.
FRIENDS! CAN'T WE JUST BE FRIENDS?!
NOTHING CEMENTS THE RELATIONSHIP LIKE THE CHANCE TO GET IT IN WRITING.
GUISEWITE

Mr. Grandpa, 1999:

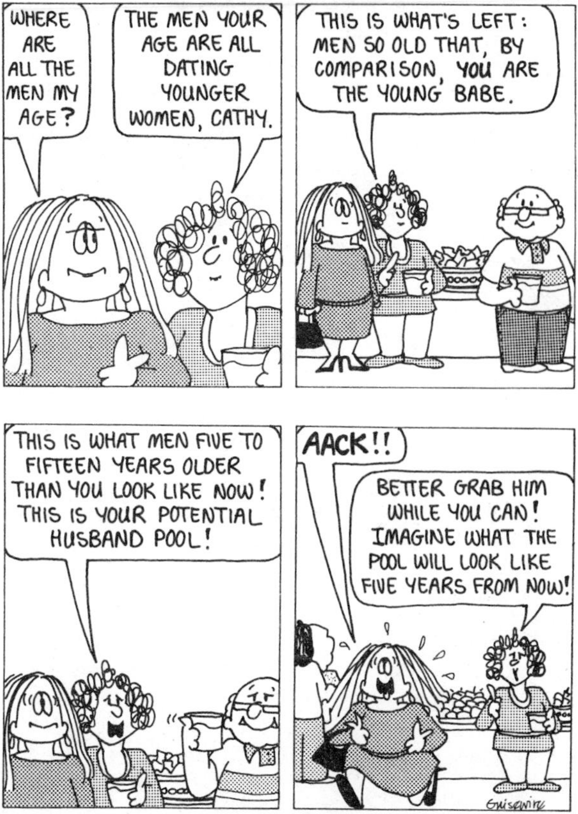
WHERE ARE ALL THE MEN MY AGE?
THE MEN YOUR AGE ARE ALL DATING YOUNGER WOMEN, CATHY.
THIS IS WHAT'S LEFT: MEN SO OLD THAT, BY COMPARISON, YOU ARE THE YOUNG BABE.
THIS IS WHAT MEN FIVE TO FIFTEEN YEARS OLDER THAN YOU LOOK LIKE NOW! THIS IS YOUR POTENTIAL HUSBAND POOL!
AACK!!
BETTER GRAB HIM WHILE YOU CAN! IMAGINE WHAT THE POOL WILL LOOK LIKE FIVE YEARS FROM NOW!
Guisewite

Mr. Millennium, 1999:

IT'S THE NEW ME, CATHY, **MILLENNIUM MAN!**

NET-SAVVY, HDTV-READY, 100% Y2K COMPLIANT!

I GOT MY LEASE AT 8%... MY MORTGAGE AT 6%... AND MY AMAZON.COM STOCK AT $20!

AND JUST IN CASE IT ALL GOES BELLY-UP, I KEEP A THREE-MONTH SUPPLY OF FAT-FREE SURVIVAL RATIONS STRAPPED TO ME AT ALL TIMES.

BEEF JERKY

I, FOR ONE, WILL BE RUNNING FULL SPEED ON JANUARY 1, 2000!

THIS CENTURY'S DOUBLE ESPRESSOS WON'T HAVE WORN OFF YET...

Mr. Sports Injury, 2000:

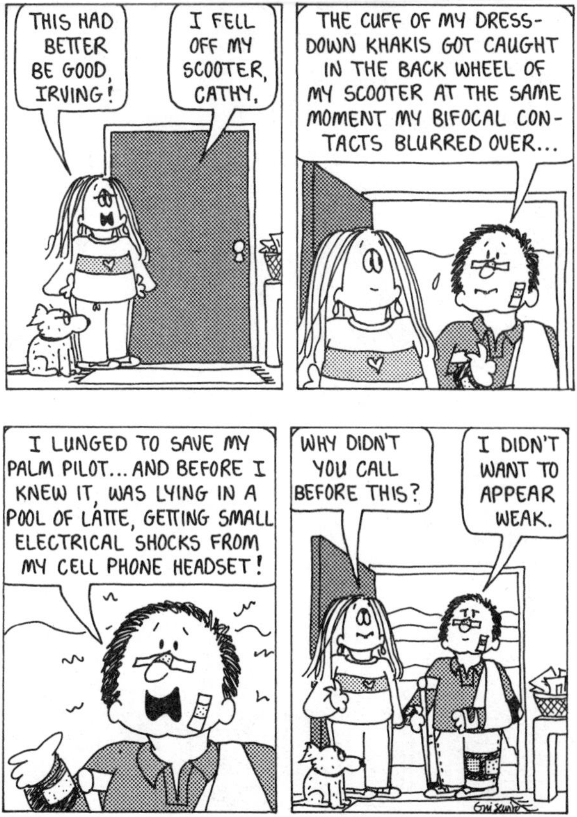
THIS HAD BETTER BE GOOD, IRVING!
I FELL OFF MY SCOOTER, CATHY.
THE CUFF OF MY DRESS-DOWN KHAKIS GOT CAUGHT IN THE BACK WHEEL OF MY SCOOTER AT THE SAME MOMENT MY BIFOCAL CONTACTS BLURRED OVER...
I LUNGED TO SAVE MY PALM PILOT... AND BEFORE I KNEW IT, WAS LYING IN A POOL OF LATTE, GETTING SMALL ELECTRICAL SHOCKS FROM MY CELL PHONE HEADSET!
WHY DIDN'T YOU CALL BEFORE THIS?
I DIDN'T WANT TO APPEAR WEAK.

Mr. Introspection, 2001:

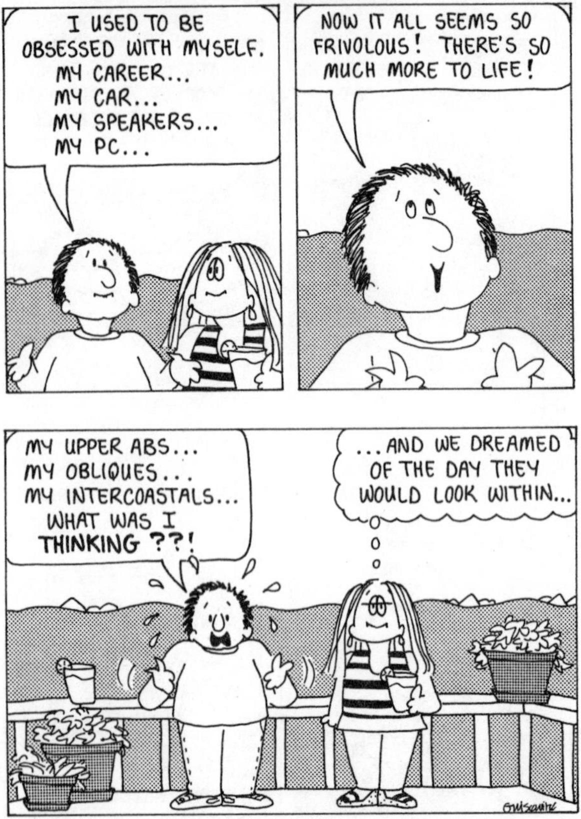
I USED TO BE OBSESSED WITH MYSELF. MY CAREER... MY CAR... MY SPEAKERS... MY PC...
NOW IT ALL SEEMS SO FRIVOLOUS! THERE'S SO MUCH MORE TO LIFE!
MY UPPER ABS... MY OBLIQUES... MY INTERCOASTALS... WHAT WAS I THINKING ??!
...AND WE DREAMED OF THE DAY THEY WOULD LOOK WITHIN...

Mr. Mid-Life Crisis, 2001:

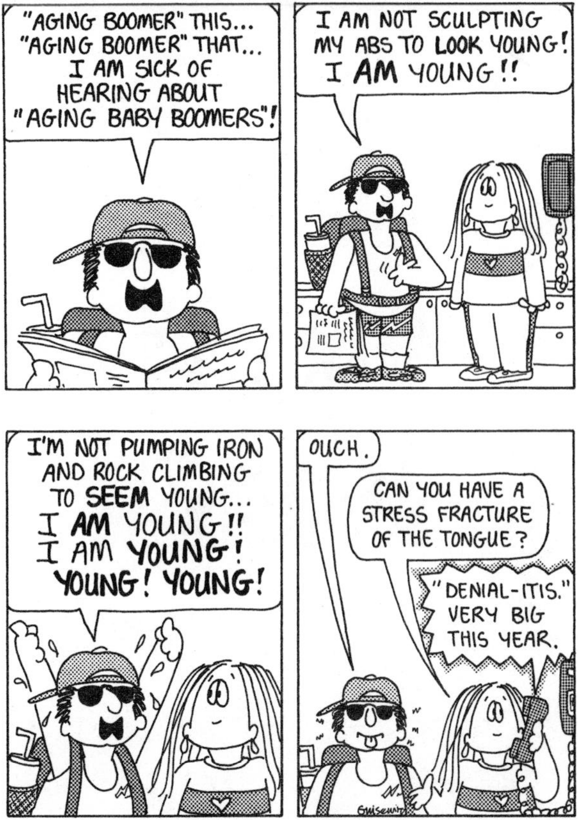

"AGING BOOMER" THIS... "AGING BOOMER" THAT... I AM SICK OF HEARING ABOUT "AGING BABY BOOMERS"!
I AM NOT SCULPTING MY ABS TO LOOK YOUNG! I AM YOUNG!!
I'M NOT PUMPING IRON AND ROCK CLIMBING TO SEEM YOUNG... I AM YOUNG!! I AM YOUNG! YOUNG! YOUNG!
OUCH.
CAN YOU HAVE A STRESS FRACTURE OF THE TONGUE?
"DENIAL-ITIS." VERY BIG THIS YEAR.

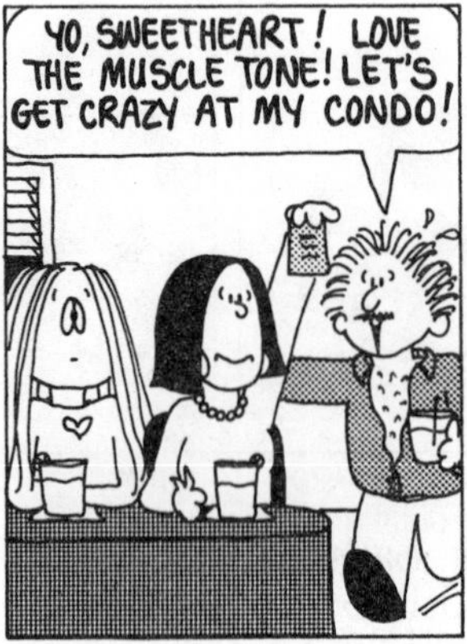
YO, SWEETHEART! LOVE THE MUSCLE TONE! LET'S GET CRAZY AT MY CONDO!

The Male Brain

Most of what we know about the male brain we've learned from women's magazines.

Some we've learned from girlfriends.

The rest we've made up on our own. Little 4,500 calorie insights, carbohydrate rush conclusions—the dangerous combination of horoscopes, classic romance movies, take-out menus, frozen chocolate, an empty voice mail box, some really, really long Saturday nights, and a house full of positive self-image affirmations.

In fairness, we've tried asking men:

We've tried asking men in general:

We've tried asking the universe:

For all the study, research, seminars, books, tapes, lectures, workshops, retreats, courses, magazines, thousands of hours with Mom on the phone, millions of hours with girlfriends, zillions of hours in private meditation...

For all the astrological charts, palm readings, tarot card readings, Chinese tea leaves, psychics, biorhythms, and meditations . . .

For all the private therapy, couple's therapy, group therapy, regression therapy, and rebirthing therapy...

For all the enlightenment, understanding, compassion, unburdening, sharing, and weeping . . .

For a full quarter-century quest to break down barriers, get past stereotypes, erase expectations, and really discover who men are, this is what we've come up with:

Men's hearing is different.

Men are really, really self-aware.

Men are vulnerable to all women except us.

Mars is an understatement.

Men have a limited use of the language.

Men's ears are different.

PERFECT SOUND. MEN LOVE IT! MEN LUST FOR IT! LOOK! THIS REMOTE CD PLAYER HAS A 95db SIGNAL-TO-NOISE RATIO, 95db DYNAMIC RANGE, 5hz TO 20,000hz FREQUENCY RESPONSE AND HARMONIC DISTORTION OF JUST 0.003%!!

THIS BABY TAKES BASS TO 26hz WITH A SUB-BASS ACOUSTIC SUSPENSION DRIVER!! FRONT-MOUNTED EXPONENTIAL TWEETERS BLAST TO 21,500hz! A 38mm VOICE COIL GOES TO 200°C!! AND SHE'S FUSE-PROTECTED TO 200 WATTS PEAK!

IT'S ENDLESS! SMASH THE CYMBALS AT 16,000hz! BLOW OUT THE SAX AT 19,500! 20 EQUALIZER CONTROLS! TEN VU METERS! AUDIO ECSTASY! REVERB ONE NOTE INTO A 3-D EXPLOSION OF PURE, PERFECT, DIGITAL SOUND!!

DO YOU HAVE ANYTHING THAT WILL MAKE MY BOYFRIEND LISTEN TO ME?

CAN YOU PLAY KEYBOARD?

Men have only one available brain cell.

Men only understand certain words.

Men are easy to excite.

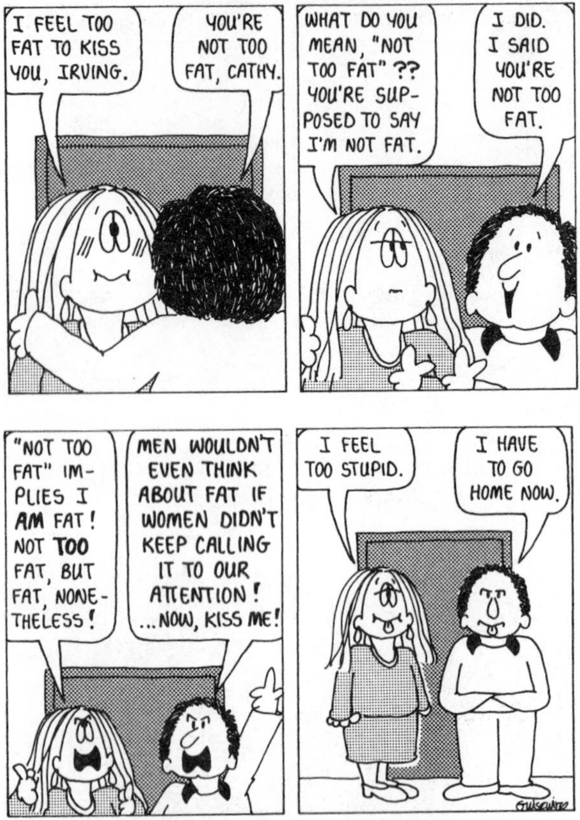
I FEEL TOO FAT TO KISS YOU, IRVING.
YOU'RE NOT TOO FAT, CATHY.
WHAT DO YOU MEAN, "NOT TOO FAT"?? YOU'RE SUPPOSED TO SAY I'M NOT FAT.
I DID. I SAID YOU'RE NOT TOO FAT.
"NOT TOO FAT" IMPLIES I AM FAT! NOT TOO FAT, BUT FAT, NONETHELESS!
MEN WOULDN'T EVEN THINK ABOUT FAT IF WOMEN DIDN'T KEEP CALLING IT TO OUR ATTENTION! ...NOW, KISS ME!
I FEEL TOO STUPID.
I HAVE TO GO HOME NOW.
GUISEWITE

Men are hard to excite.

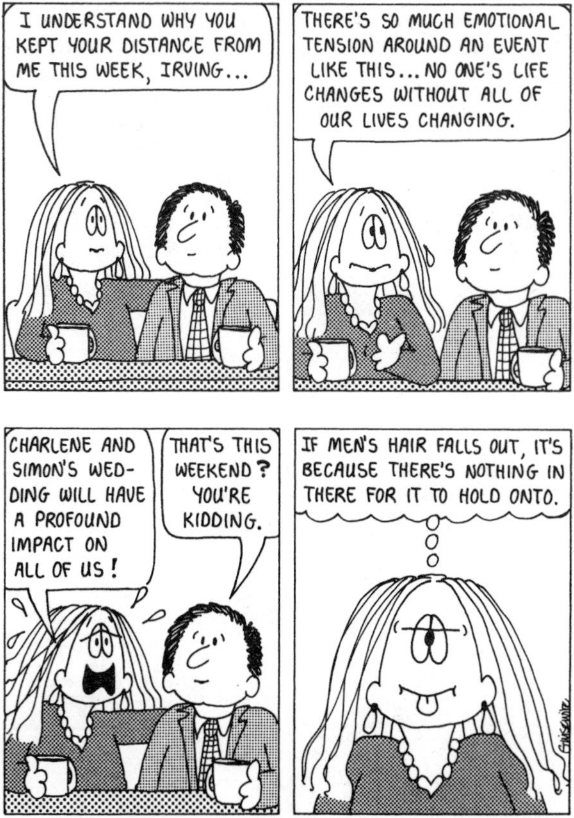
I UNDERSTAND WHY YOU KEPT YOUR DISTANCE FROM ME THIS WEEK, IRVING...
THERE'S SO MUCH EMOTIONAL TENSION AROUND AN EVENT LIKE THIS... NO ONE'S LIFE CHANGES WITHOUT ALL OF OUR LIVES CHANGING.
CHARLENE AND SIMON'S WEDDING WILL HAVE A PROFOUND IMPACT ON ALL OF US!
THAT'S THIS WEEKEND? YOU'RE KIDDING.
IF MEN'S HAIR FALLS OUT, IT'S BECAUSE THERE'S NOTHING IN THERE FOR IT TO HOLD ONTO.

Men don't like to watch sports with us.

WHAT HAPPENED WHILE I WAS IN THE KITCHEN?

THE MAN WITH THE MISTY HAZEL EYES PASSED TO THE GUY WITH THE GORGEOUS LIPS.

THE ONE WITH THE CUTE SEAT STOLE THE BALL AND SHOT IT OVER TO THE GUY WITH THE GLISTENING MUSCLE-Y SHOULDERS.

THEN THE GUY WITH THE FABULOUS JAW TOSSED BACK HIS AUBURN HAIR, AND PASSED TO THE GUY WITH THE GREAT LEGS WHO SMASHED THAT BABY IN FOR A SCORE!!

WHAT ARE YOU SO MAD FOR? I'M STARTING TO LIKE THIS SPORT.

Guisewite

Men are not like us.

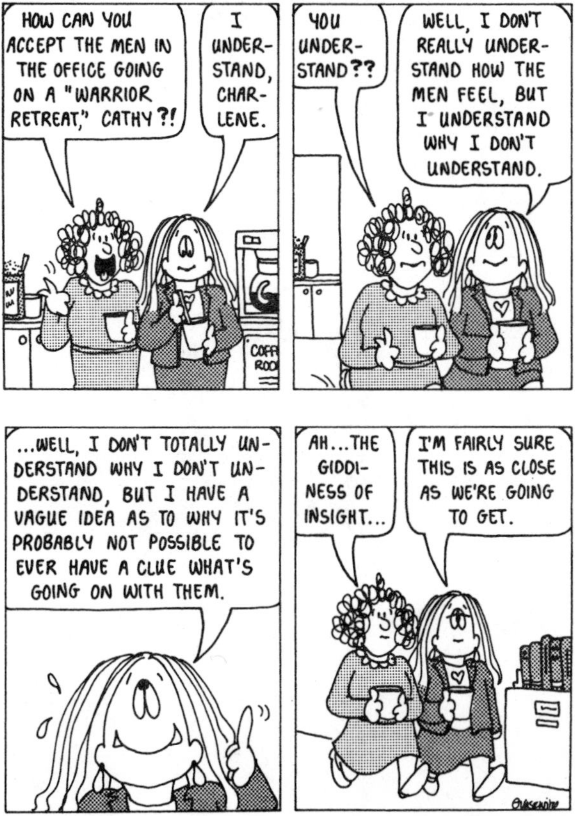
HOW CAN YOU ACCEPT THE MEN IN THE OFFICE GOING ON A "WARRIOR RETREAT," CATHY?!
I UNDERSTAND, CHARLENE.
YOU UNDERSTAND??
WELL, I DON'T REALLY UNDERSTAND HOW THE MEN FEEL, BUT I UNDERSTAND WHY I DON'T UNDERSTAND.
...WELL, I DON'T TOTALLY UNDERSTAND WHY I DON'T UNDERSTAND, BUT I HAVE A VAGUE IDEA AS TO WHY IT'S PROBABLY NOT POSSIBLE TO EVER HAVE A CLUE WHAT'S GOING ON WITH THEM.
AH...THE GIDDINESS OF INSIGHT...
I'M FAIRLY SURE THIS IS AS CLOSE AS WE'RE GOING TO GET.

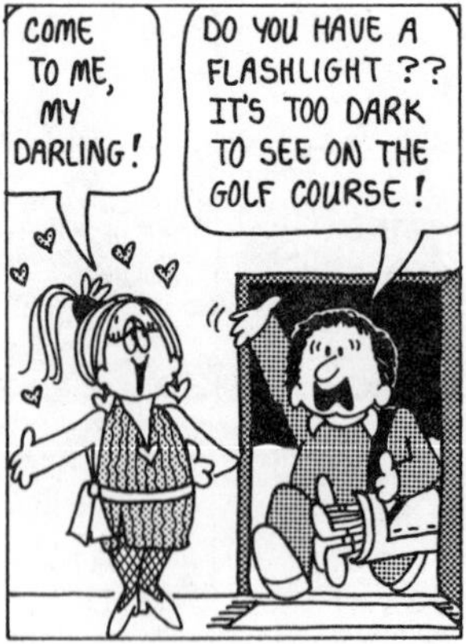
COME TO ME, MY DARLING!
DO YOU HAVE A FLASHLIGHT?? IT'S TOO DARK TO SEE ON THE GOLF COURSE!

The Ladies' Room

HIM: Watch ball game.

HER: Try on dress. Try on pants. Try on jeans. Try on long skirt. Try on short skirt. Try on medium skirt. Try on dressy medium skirt. Try on casual short skirt. Try on medium long skirt. Try on tops. Try on shoes.

HIM: Read paper.
HER: Call girlfriend. Call Mom. Call store. Drive to mall. Shop. Call. Shop. Call. Shop. Call. Shop.

HIM: Eat chips.
HER: Clean kitchen. Clean bathroom. Clean living room. Clean bedroom. Clean inside of car. Clean closet. Clean purse. Clean refrigerator.

HIM: Change channel.
HER: Change dress. Change shoes. Change underwear. Change jewelry. Change hair. Change mind. Change shoes. Change shoes. Change shoes. Change purse.

HIM: Jump in shower.
HER: Do hair. Do facial. Do makeup. Do fingernails. Do toenails. Iron top. Rehem bottom. Rearrange furniture. Rethink life.

HIM: Catch end of game in car.
HER: Read affirmations.
Recite affirmations
Study astrological chart.
Study world events.
Practice flirting.
Practice aloofness.
Practice disdain.
Practice vulnerability.
Fix contacts.
Fix hair.
De-lint sweater.
De-grease face.
Look in mirror.
Look out peephole.
Look in mirror.
Look out peephole.
Beg dog for forgiveness.
Change outfit.
Redo hair.

By the end of each year, men have at least two full months more time than women do.

Men's and women's dressing differences run exactly parallel to men's and women's language differences.

"I don't know," spoken by a man apparently actually means "I don't know."

"I don't know," spoken by a woman can mean 500 things, including "I don't know how I could have ever been attracted to someone who doesn't know I'm hoping he'll beg me to discuss all the other things I'm thinking when I say 'I don't know'!"

"Just wear jeans" to a man means "Just wear jeans."

"Just wear jeans" to a woman means 5,000 jeans options—dressy, casual, ripped, faded, medium-toned, dark-toned, low cut, high cut, boot cut, flared, straight leg, loose fit, tight fit, excruciating fit, studded, embroidered, wide enough for boots, long enough for tall heels, short enough for flats, 10,000 top choices, 10,000 footwear/sock options, belts, bags, jewelry—a full time job, if one surrendered to it, to create a unique, yet appropriate-for-the-occasion, "jeans" look.

If women are more concerned with where the relationship is going, maybe it's because we have a little more invested in each get-together.

Men, after all, are preparing to go to the movies. Women are preparing to create life.

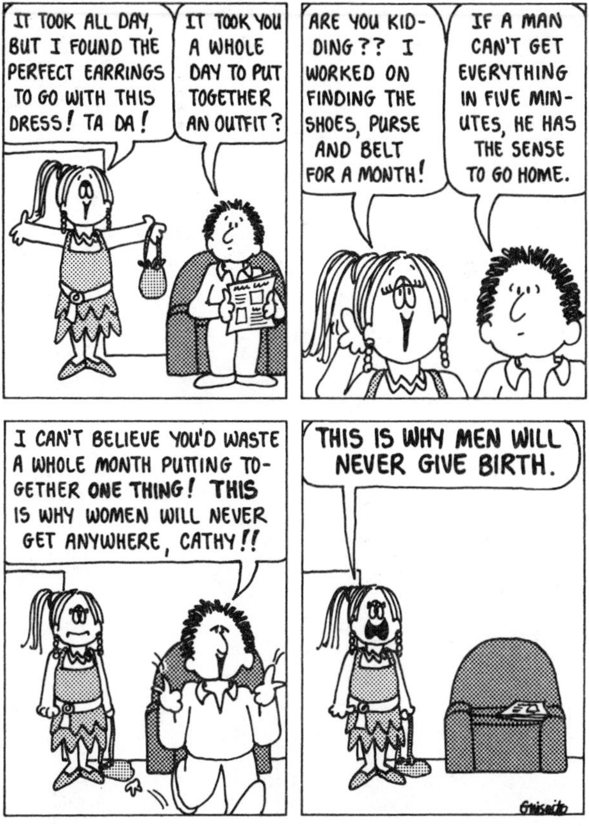
IT TOOK ALL DAY, BUT I FOUND THE PERFECT EARRINGS TO GO WITH THIS DRESS! TA DA!
IT TOOK YOU A WHOLE DAY TO PUT TOGETHER AN OUTFIT?
ARE YOU KIDDING?? I WORKED ON FINDING THE SHOES, PURSE AND BELT FOR A MONTH!
IF A MAN CAN'T GET EVERYTHING IN FIVE MINUTES, HE HAS THE SENSE TO GO HOME.
I CAN'T BELIEVE YOU'D WASTE A WHOLE MONTH PUTTING TOGETHER ONE THING! THIS IS WHY WOMEN WILL NEVER GET ANYWHERE, CATHY!!
THIS IS WHY MEN WILL NEVER GIVE BIRTH.
Guisewite

We reinvent our outsides.

We reinvent our insides.

We rethink our soles.

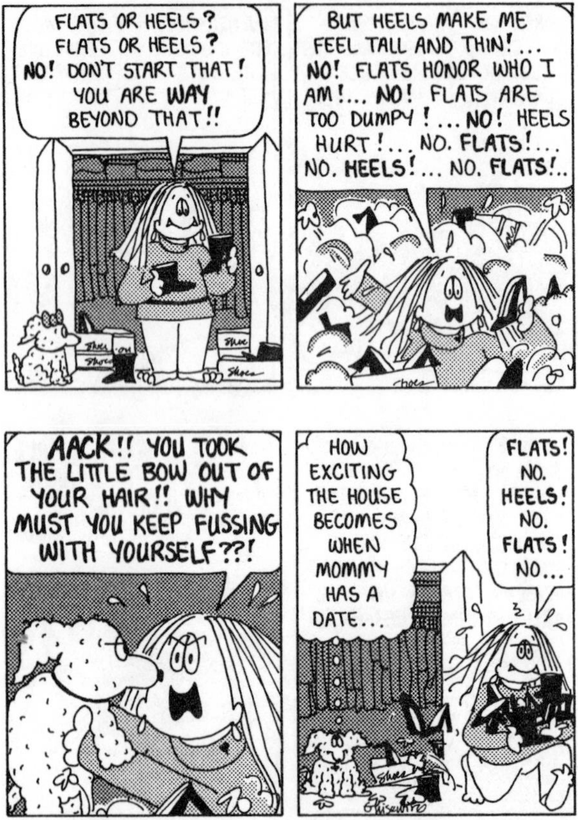
FLATS OR HEELS? FLATS OR HEELS? NO! DON'T START THAT! YOU ARE WAY BEYOND THAT!!
BUT HEELS MAKE ME FEEL TALL AND THIN!... NO! FLATS HONOR WHO I AM!... NO! FLATS ARE TOO DUMPY!... NO! HEELS HURT!... NO. FLATS!... NO. HEELS!... NO. FLATS!..
AACK!! YOU TOOK THE LITTLE BOW OUT OF YOUR HAIR!! WHY MUST YOU KEEP FUSSING WITH YOURSELF??!
HOW EXCITING THE HOUSE BECOMES WHEN MOMMY HAS A DATE...
FLATS! NO. HEELS! NO. FLATS! NO...

We dress the refrigerator.

AN OPENED BOTTLE OF WINE TO MAKE IT LOOK AS THOUGH I'VE HAD COMPANY RECENTLY...

A PLATE OF BARBEQUED RIBS... HALF A JAR OF MUSTARD... RYE BREAD... LEFTOVER POTATO SALAD... ..BREAKFAST SAUSAGES...

MEN'S FOOD! HA, HA! JUST ENOUGH OF IT SO THAT, IF HE OPENS THE DOOR, HE'LL SEE ME AS A BUSY, DESIRABLE AND POSSIBLY ALREADY-SPOKEN-FOR WOMAN!

ALL WOMEN DRESS THEMSELVES FOR A DATE. THE GREAT ONES ALSO DRESS THE INSIDES OF OUR REFRIGERATORS.

We dress the living room.

IF I'M GOING TO MEET SOMEONE NEW, I HAVE TO EXPAND MY UNIVERSE.

IF I'M GOING TO EXPAND MY UNIVERSE, I HAVE TO HAVE PEOPLE OVER.

IF I'M GOING TO HAVE PEOPLE OVER, I HAVE TO MAKE MY HOME LOOK FABULOUS.

WOMEN USED TO ATTRACT LOVE BY DABBING ON SOME COLOGNE.

NOW WE BUILD FURNITURE.

NOT NOW, MOTHER! I'M ASSEMBLING MY SEXY WALL UNIT!!

We try it all.

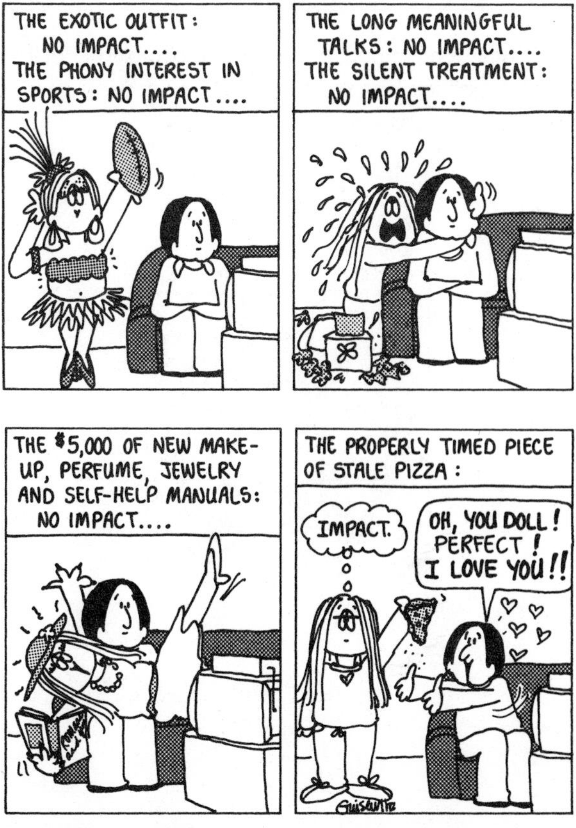
THE EXOTIC OUTFIT: NO IMPACT....
THE PHONY INTEREST IN SPORTS: NO IMPACT....
THE LONG MEANINGFUL TALKS: NO IMPACT....
THE SILENT TREATMENT: NO IMPACT....
THE $5,000 OF NEW MAKE-UP, PERFUME, JEWELRY AND SELF-HELP MANUALS: NO IMPACT....
THE PROPERLY TIMED PIECE OF STALE PIZZA:
IMPACT.
OH, YOU DOLL! PERFECT! I LOVE YOU!!
GUISEWITE

Finally, we gather in the ladies' room to check to see if the lipstick has worn off and/or if the brain has completely disappeared.

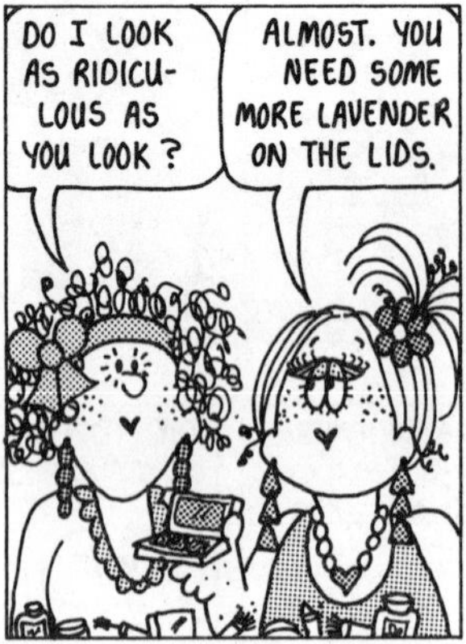
DO I LOOK AS RIDICU-LOUS AS YOU LOOK?
ALMOST. YOU NEED SOME MORE LAVENDER ON THE LIDS.

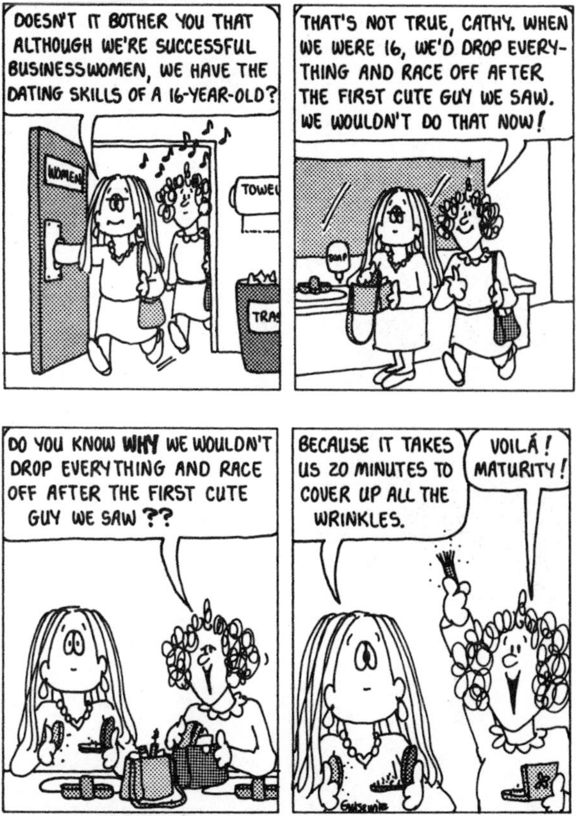
DOESN'T IT BOTHER YOU THAT ALTHOUGH WE'RE SUCCESSFUL BUSINESSWOMEN, WE HAVE THE DATING SKILLS OF A 16-YEAR-OLD?
WOMEN
TOWEL
TRA
THAT'S NOT TRUE, CATHY. WHEN WE WERE 16, WE'D DROP EVERYTHING AND RACE OFF AFTER THE FIRST CUTE GUY WE SAW. WE WOULDN'T DO THAT NOW!
SOAP
DO YOU KNOW WHY WE WOULDN'T DROP EVERYTHING AND RACE OFF AFTER THE FIRST CUTE GUY WE SAW??
BECAUSE IT TAKES US 20 MINUTES TO COVER UP ALL THE WRINKLES.
VOILÁ! MATURITY!

ANXIOUS TO LOOK ATTRACTIVE AND AVAILABLE, I PLASTER THE MAKEUP ON...

EMBARRASSED THAT I LOOK AS IF I'M **TRYING** TO LOOK AVAILABLE, I WIPE THE MAKEUP OFF.

ANNOYED THAT I SPENT $50 ON MAKEUP I'M EMBARRASSED TO WEAR, I PLASTER THE MAKEUP BACK ON...FURIOUS THAT I LET A SALESCLERK TALK ME INTO A LOOK I DON'T LIKE, I WIPE THE MAKEUP BACK OFF.....

THE QUESTION IS NOT WHY THERE'S ALWAYS A LINE TO GET INTO THE LADIES' ROOM... THE QUESTION IS HOW A WOMAN EVER GETS OUT OF ONE.

The ladies' room is our clubhouse. Our locker room. Our regrouping center. Our refuge. Our frame of reference. Our motivational speech auditorium.

When we're single, the ladies' room is our ego check. When we're older, it's our reality check. When we're married mothers of a couple of children, five minutes alone in the ladies' room is our summer vacation.

I love to stand in the ladies' room and see the dreams rush in and out. I love the drama: woman versus bad hair, woman versus contact lens, woman versus broken zipper, woman wishing she could crawl out the window and leave her blind date stranded at the table.

I love to see that I'm not the only woman on a two-hour date with a 45-pound evening bag.

I love to hear the conversations that start between complete strangers: diet failures, wrinkle remedies, shoe compliments, price comparisons, parenting tips, flirtation strategies . . .

Seventy-five women desperately competing for the same two stalls, sharing intimate details, grand triumphs, and little humiliations like lifelong best friends.

I love that women are so essentially connected that a broken strap can induce a 20-purse search for a safety pin; one tear shed in a ladies room can summon an instant 15-member support/therapy/advice group.

On some level, every relationship between a man and a woman is made possible by a friendship between a woman and a woman.

The ladies' room is a microcosm of the world at large—a universe of female spirits cheering, guiding, advising, consoling, and commiserating with each other.

To win one of our hearts, men usually have to win a whole bunch of our hearts.

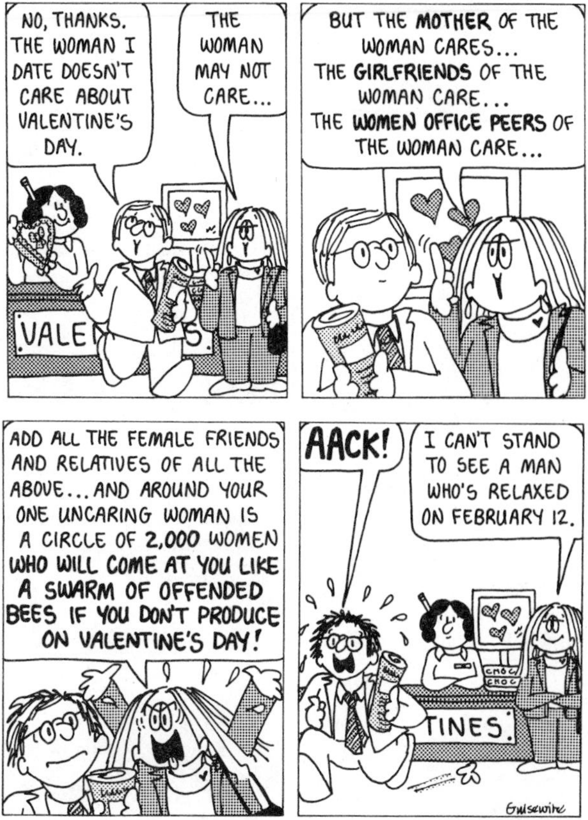
NO, THANKS. THE WOMAN I DATE DOESN'T CARE ABOUT VALENTINE'S DAY.
THE WOMAN MAY NOT CARE...
VALE
S
BUT THE MOTHER OF THE WOMAN CARES... THE GIRLFRIENDS OF THE WOMAN CARE... THE WOMEN OFFICE PEERS OF THE WOMAN CARE...
ADD ALL THE FEMALE FRIENDS AND RELATIVES OF ALL THE ABOVE... AND AROUND YOUR ONE UNCARING WOMAN IS A CIRCLE OF 2,000 WOMEN WHO WILL COME AT YOU LIKE A SWARM OF OFFENDED BEES IF YOU DON'T PRODUCE ON VALENTINE'S DAY!
AACK!
I CAN'T STAND TO SEE A MAN WHO'S RELAXED ON FEBRUARY 12.
CHOC
CHOC
TINES
Guisewite

Break up with one of us, and lose us all.

NO WONDER LYDIA BROKE UP WITH YOU! YOU DON'T EVEN HAVE A PICTURE OF HER??

I SAW HER ALL THE TIME. WHY DID I NEED A PICTURE?

BECAUSE SHE WAS YOUR GIRLFRIEND! SHE PROBABLY HAD **YOUR** PICTURE ALL OVER HER HOME AND OFFICE!... YOU COULDN'T EVEN TUCK ONE OF **HER** INTO A HIDDEN COMPARTMENT IN YOUR WALLET??

FOR WHAT?

THAT'S DESPICABLE! **JUST** DESPICABLE!

WHEN ONE DUMPS YOU, THEY ALL DUMP YOU.

From the time we're little, girlfriends are our anchors. Our rocks. Our personal team of soul-sisters filling a hundred different roles.

Girlfriend as Cheerleader:

I'M GOING TO PROPOSE TO IRVING, CHARLENE.

YES! BRAVO! GO FOR IT, CATHY!!

I'LL HELP YOU PLAN WHAT TO SAY! I'LL HELP YOU DECIDE WHAT TO WEAR! I'LL BE THERE FOR YOU 24 HOURS A DAY!! I'M SO PROUD OF YOU! I'M SO HAPPY FOR YOU!!

BUT IF YOU GET MARRIED, I'LL KILL YOU! I'LL NEVER FORGIVE YOU! IF YOU DESERT ME FOR A HUSBAND, I'LL NEVER SPEAK TO YOU AGAIN!!!!

I LOVE THE CLEAR MESSAGES I GET FROM MY WOMEN FRIENDS.

Girlfriend as Interpreter:

Girlfriend as Magnified Makeup Mirror:

Girlfriend as Support Group:

Girlfriend as Advisor:

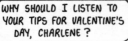

WHY SHOULD I LISTEN TO YOUR TIPS FOR VALENTINE'S DAY, CHARLENE?

YOUR LOVE LIFE IS PATHETIC. YOU DATE LOSERS. YOU DON'T HAVE THE SLIGHTEST CONCEPT OF HOW TO KEEP A DECENT RELATIONSHIP GOING FOR MORE THAN FIVE MINUTES!

FINE. WHY NOT ASK YOUR **MOTHER** FOR TIPS? SHE'S BEEN HAPPILY MARRIED TO A WONDERFUL MAN FOR 40 YEARS.

SORRY. WHAT WAS I THINKING?

NOW, FOR THE VALENTINE'S DAY WARDROBE, I RECOMMEND....

Girlfriend as Reality Check:

Girlfriend as Role Model:

Girlfriend as Lawmaker:

THERE ARE TWO LAWS OF LIFE, CHARLENE. **NEVER STRETCH OUT ANOTHER WOMAN'S SHOES,** AND **NEVER LUST AFTER AN-OTHER WOMAN'S EX-BOYFRIEND!**

...NO. THERE ARE **THREE** LAWS. THE SHOE ONE, THE BOY-FRIEND ONE, AND **NEVER CHANGE THE SETTING ON ANOTHER WOMAN'S SCALE!**

...NO. THERE ARE **FOUR** LAWS. THE SHOES, THE BOYFRIEND, THE SCALE, AND **NEVER LOOK IN ANOTHER WOMAN'S PURSE!**

...NO. WAIT. THERE ARE FIVE...

CAN WE PUT A MUZZLE ON HER?

NO. THAT'S NUMBER FIFTEEN. NEVER SMEAR ANOTHER WOMAN'S LIP GLOSS.

Girlfriend as Compatibility Quiz:

Girlfriend as Bodyguard:

Girlfriend as Ex-therapist:

Girlfriend as Team Player:

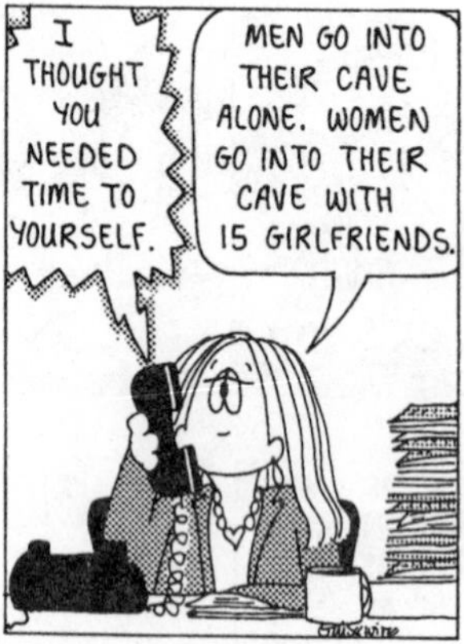
I THOUGHT YOU NEEDED TIME TO YOURSELF.
MEN GO INTO THEIR CAVE ALONE. WOMEN GO INTO THEIR CAVE WITH 15 GIRLFRIENDS.

The Phone

In no area of life has so much progress been made with so little actual improvement.

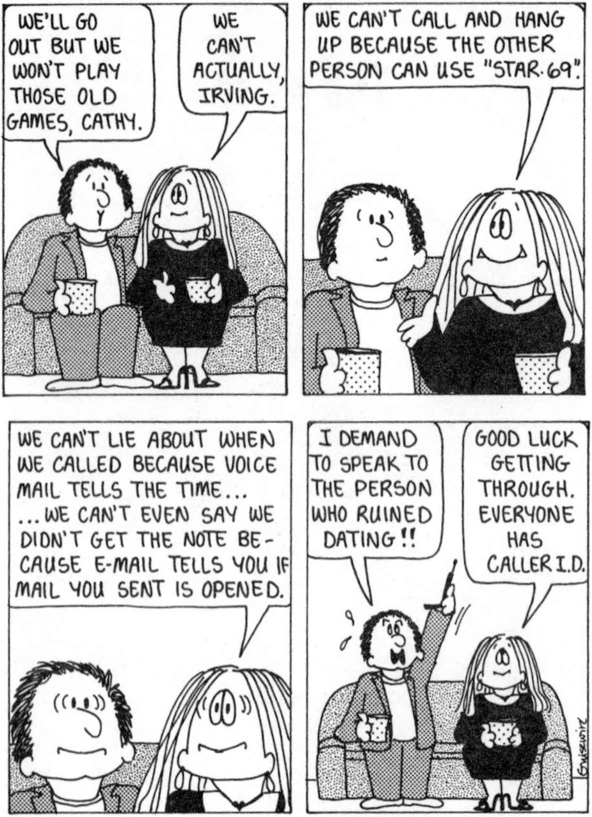
WE'LL GO OUT BUT WE WON'T PLAY THOSE OLD GAMES, CATHY.
WE CAN'T ACTUALLY, IRVING.
WE CAN'T CALL AND HANG UP BECAUSE THE OTHER PERSON CAN USE "STAR-69".
WE CAN'T LIE ABOUT WHEN WE CALLED BECAUSE VOICE MAIL TELLS THE TIME... ...WE CAN'T EVEN SAY WE DIDN'T GET THE NOTE BE-CAUSE E-MAIL TELLS YOU IF MAIL YOU SENT IS OPENED.
I DEMAND TO SPEAK TO THE PERSON WHO RUINED DATING!!
GOOD LUCK GETTING THROUGH. EVERYONE HAS CALLER I.D.
Guisewite

In spite of a universe of advanced communication devices, we have hung on to our inability to communicate with amazing fortitude.

In spite of the fact that we're all reachable 24/7, it's just as hard to make actual contact.

In spite of all the teensy little cells, the beepers, the voice mails, the call forwarding, and the caller ID, the conversation quality remains pretty much unchanged.

In spite of call waiting, the "waiting-and-waiting-and-waiting-for-a-call" function is still going strong.

In telephones, the human element appears to be the one unchangeable, irreplaceable, unrepairable, unupgradable component.

Waiting for a Call, 1982:

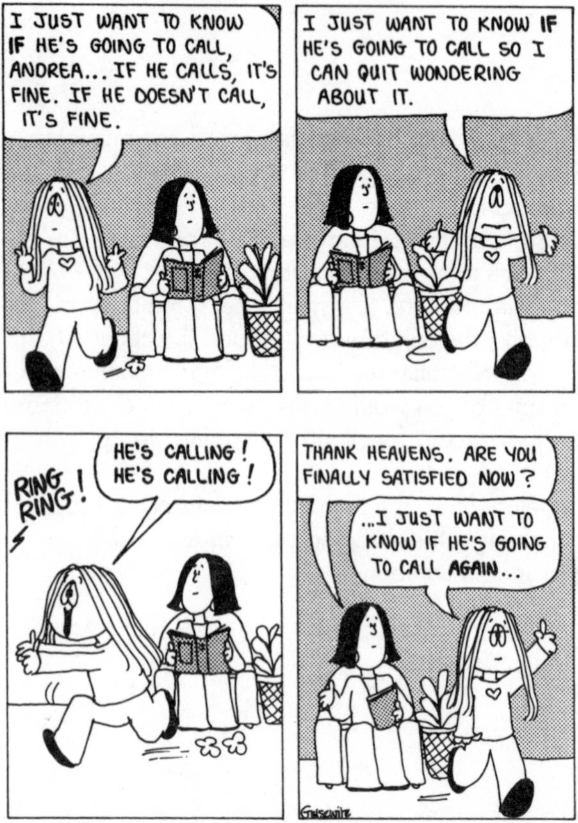
I JUST WANT TO KNOW IF HE'S GOING TO CALL, ANDREA... IF HE CALLS, IT'S FINE. IF HE DOESN'T CALL, IT'S FINE.
I JUST WANT TO KNOW IF HE'S GOING TO CALL SO I CAN QUIT WONDERING ABOUT IT.
RING RING!
HE'S CALLING! HE'S CALLING!
THANK HEAVENS. ARE YOU FINALLY SATISFIED NOW?
...I JUST WANT TO KNOW IF HE'S GOING TO CALL AGAIN...
Guisewite

Waiting for a Call, 2000:

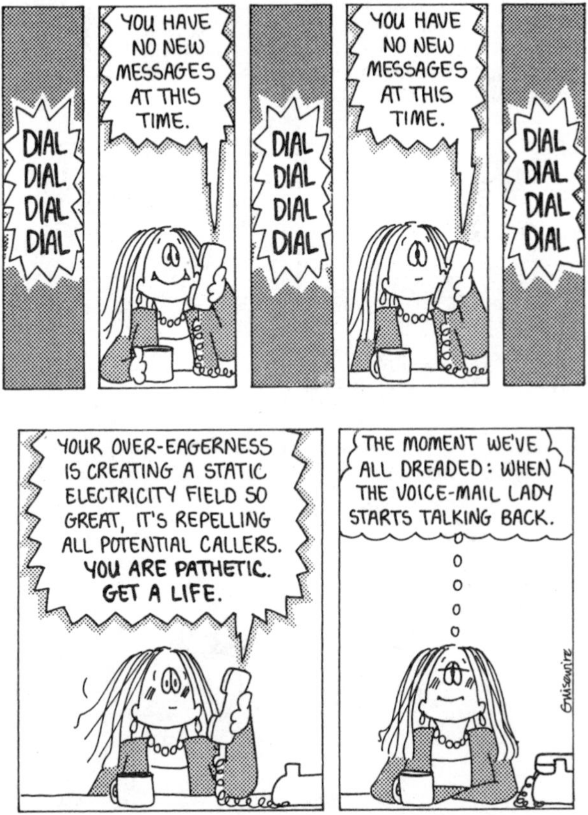
DIAL DIAL DIAL DIAL
YOU HAVE NO NEW MESSAGES AT THIS TIME.
DIAL DIAL DIAL DIAL
YOU HAVE NO NEW MESSAGES AT THIS TIME.
DIAL DIAL DIAL DIAL
YOUR OVER-EAGERNESS IS CREATING A STATIC ELECTRICITY FIELD SO GREAT, IT'S REPELLING ALL POTENTIAL CALLERS. YOU ARE PATHETIC. GET A LIFE.
THE MOMENT WE'VE ALL DREADED: WHEN THE VOICE-MAIL LADY STARTS TALKING BACK.
GUISEWITE

Regretting the Conversation, 1980:

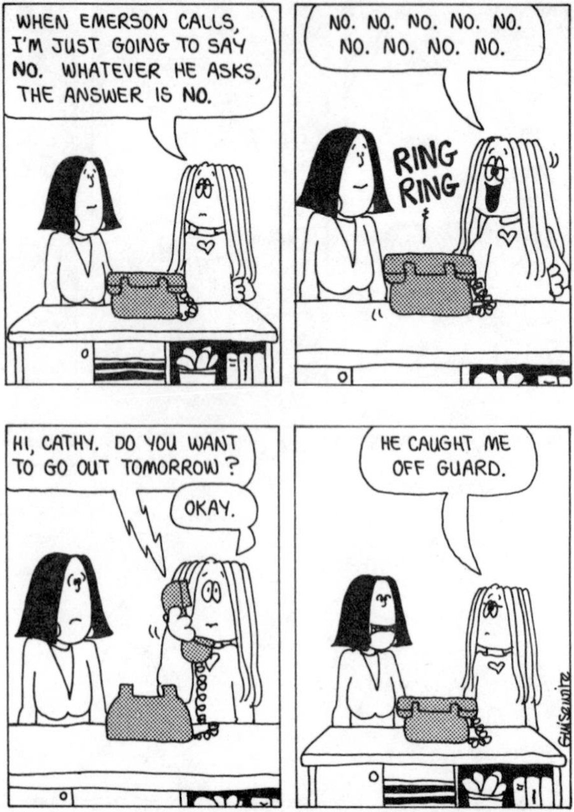
WHEN EMERSON CALLS, I'M JUST GOING TO SAY NO. WHATEVER HE ASKS, THE ANSWER IS NO.
NO. NO. NO. NO. NO. NO. NO. NO. NO.
RING RING
HI, CATHY. DO YOU WANT TO GO OUT TOMORROW?
OKAY.
HE CAUGHT ME OFF GUARD.
GUISEWITE

Regretting the Conversation, 1990:

Humiliating Oneself, 1982:

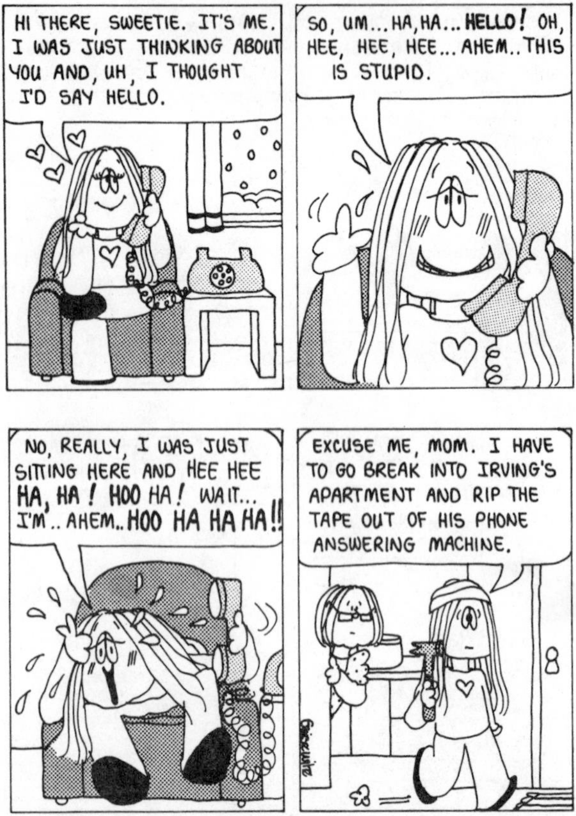

HI THERE, SWEETIE. IT'S ME. I WAS JUST THINKING ABOUT YOU AND, UH, I THOUGHT I'D SAY HELLO.
SO, UM... HA, HA... HELLO! OH, HEE, HEE, HEE... AHEM.. THIS IS STUPID.
NO, REALLY, I WAS JUST SITTING HERE AND HEE HEE HA, HA! HOO HA! WAIT... I'M.. AHEM.. HOO HA HA HA!!
EXCUSE ME, MOM. I HAVE TO GO BREAK INTO IRVING'S APARTMENT AND RIP THE TAPE OUT OF HIS PHONE ANSWERING MACHINE.

Humiliating Oneself, 1998:

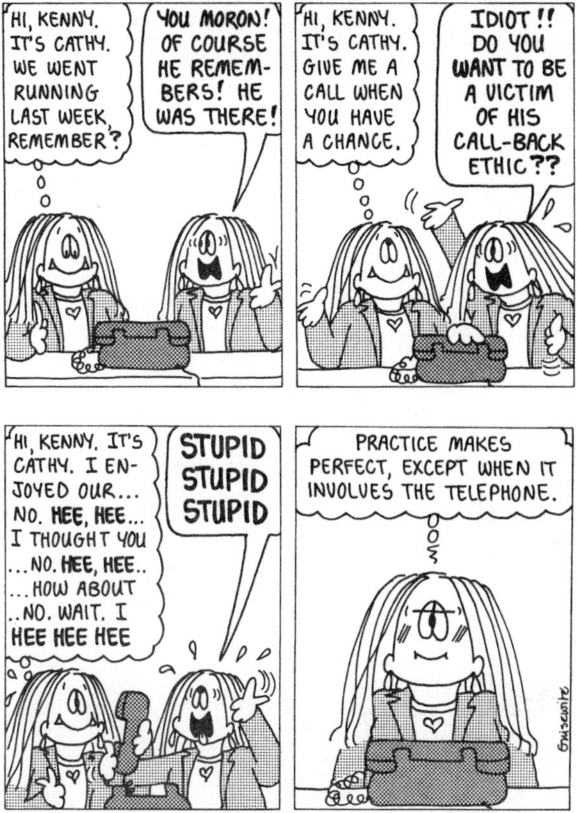
HI, KENNY. IT'S CATHY. WE WENT RUNNING LAST WEEK, REMEMBER?
YOU MORON! OF COURSE HE REMEMBERS! HE WAS THERE!
HI, KENNY. IT'S CATHY. GIVE ME A CALL WHEN YOU HAVE A CHANCE.
IDIOT!! DO YOU WANT TO BE A VICTIM OF HIS CALL-BACK ETHIC??
HI, KENNY. IT'S CATHY. I ENJOYED OUR... NO. HEE, HEE... I THOUGHT YOU ...NO. HEE, HEE.. ...HOW ABOUT ..NO. WAIT. I HEE HEE HEE
STUPID STUPID STUPID
PRACTICE MAKES PERFECT, EXCEPT WHEN IT INVOLVES THE TELEPHONE.
Guisewite

Defending Oneself, 1987:

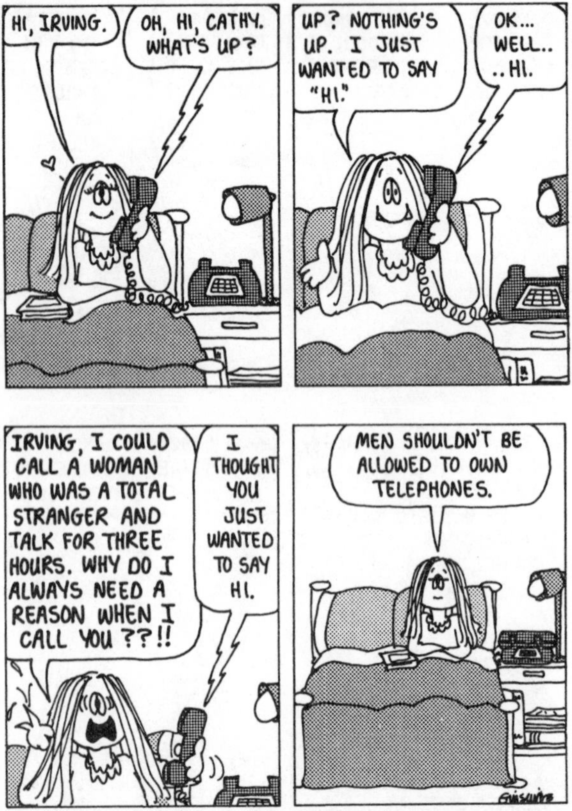
HI, IRVING.
OH, HI, CATHY. WHAT'S UP?
UP? NOTHING'S UP. I JUST WANTED TO SAY "HI."
OK... WELL.. ..HI.
IRVING, I COULD CALL A WOMAN WHO WAS A TOTAL STRANGER AND TALK FOR THREE HOURS. WHY DO I ALWAYS NEED A REASON WHEN I CALL YOU??!!
I THOUGHT YOU JUST WANTED TO SAY HI.
MEN SHOULDN'T BE ALLOWED TO OWN TELEPHONES.

Defending Oneself, 2000:

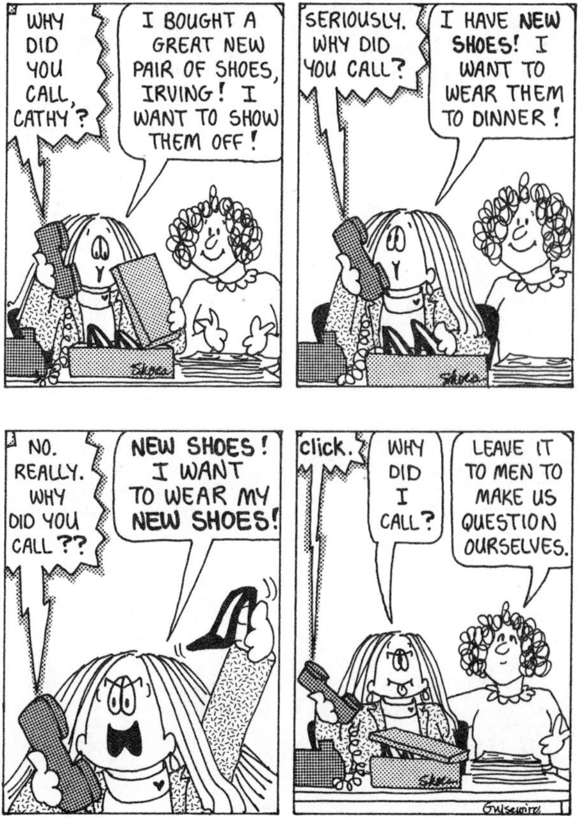
WHY DID YOU CALL, CATHY?
I BOUGHT A GREAT NEW PAIR OF SHOES, IRVING! I WANT TO SHOW THEM OFF!
SERIOUSLY. WHY DID YOU CALL?
I HAVE NEW SHOES! I WANT TO WEAR THEM TO DINNER!
NO. REALLY. WHY DID YOU CALL??
NEW SHOES! I WANT TO WEAR MY NEW SHOES!
click.
WHY DID I CALL?
LEAVE IT TO MEN TO MAKE US QUESTION OURSELVES.

Failed Connection, 1990:

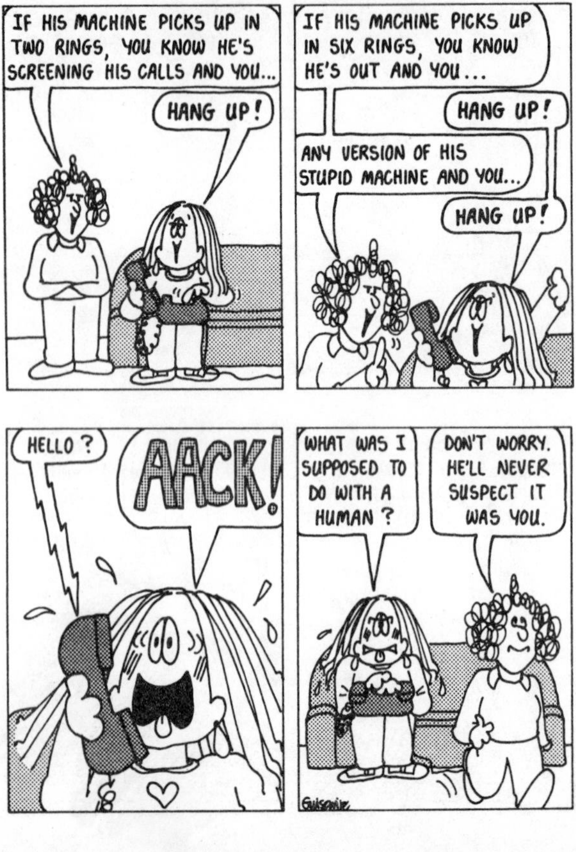
IF HIS MACHINE PICKS UP IN TWO RINGS, YOU KNOW HE'S SCREENING HIS CALLS AND YOU...
HANG UP!
IF HIS MACHINE PICKS UP IN SIX RINGS, YOU KNOW HE'S OUT AND YOU...
HANG UP!
ANY VERSION OF HIS STUPID MACHINE AND YOU...
HANG UP!
HELLO?
AACK!
WHAT WAS I SUPPOSED TO DO WITH A HUMAN?
DON'T WORRY. HE'LL NEVER SUSPECT IT WAS YOU.
GUISEWITE

Failed Connection, 1995:

HI, CATHY. IT'S ALEX. WHY DID YOU JUST CALL AND HANG UP?

ME?? CALL?? I DIDN'T CALL.

YES YOU DID. I HAVE THAT SERVICE THAT AUTOMATICALLY DIALS THE LAST PERSON WHO CALLED. YOU JUST CALLED.

WHY WOULD I CALL?? ME?? CALL?? HA, HA! NO!

WHY DID YOU CALL, AND WHY ARE YOU LYING ABOUT IT?

WHAT? I CAN'T HEAR YOU! THE PHONE IS ALL CRACKLY! **CRACKLE, CRACKLE**! HEAR THAT? OOPS! HAVE TO HANG UP!

CURSES ON MEN, AND NOW, CURSES ON THEIR ELECTRONIC GIZMOS.

Failed Connection, 1999:

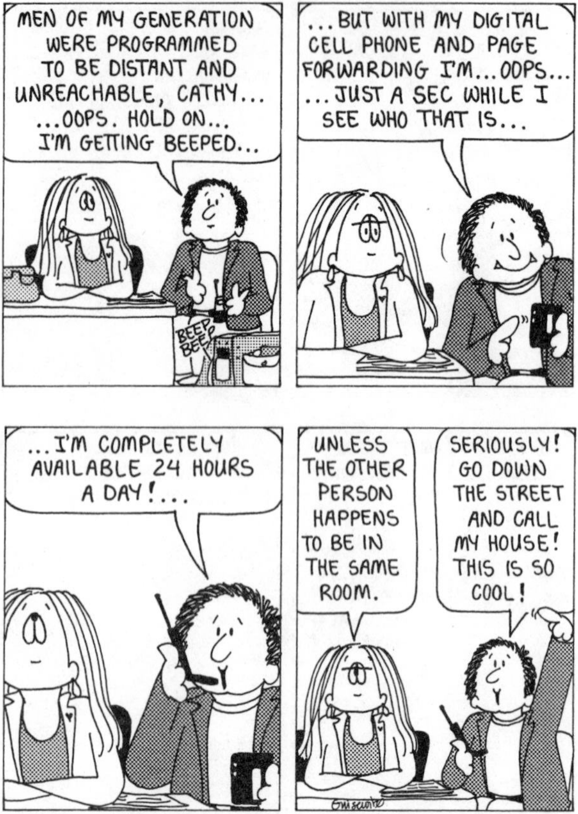
MEN OF MY GENERATION WERE PROGRAMMED TO BE DISTANT AND UNREACHABLE, CATHY... ...OOPS. HOLD ON... I'M GETTING BEEPED...
BEEP BEEP
...BUT WITH MY DIGITAL CELL PHONE AND PAGE FORWARDING I'M...OOPS... ...JUST A SEC WHILE I SEE WHO THAT IS...
...I'M COMPLETELY AVAILABLE 24 HOURS A DAY!...
UNLESS THE OTHER PERSON HAPPENS TO BE IN THE SAME ROOM.
SERIOUSLY! GO DOWN THE STREET AND CALL MY HOUSE! THIS IS SO COOL!

Failed Connection, 2001:

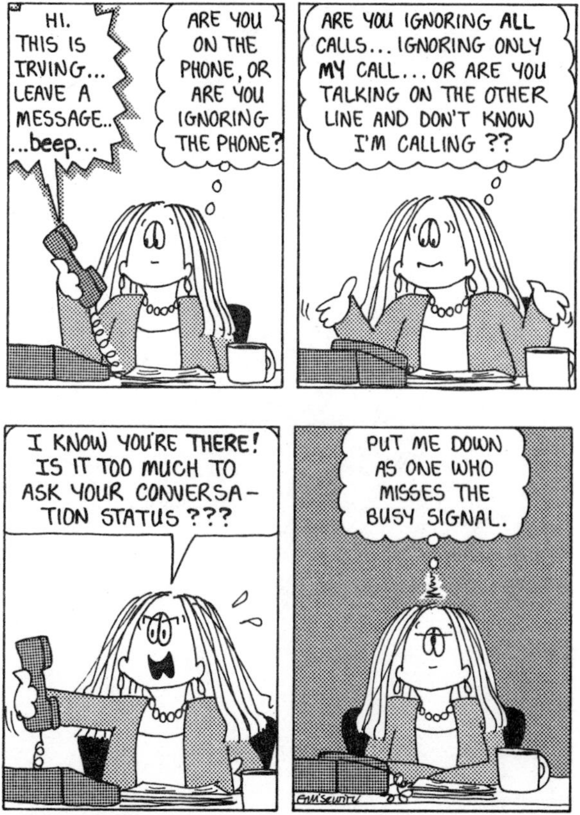
HI. THIS IS IRVING... LEAVE A MESSAGE.. ...beep...
ARE YOU ON THE PHONE, OR ARE YOU IGNORING THE PHONE?
ARE YOU IGNORING ALL CALLS... IGNORING ONLY MY CALL... OR ARE YOU TALKING ON THE OTHER LINE AND DON'T KNOW I'M CALLING ??
I KNOW YOU'RE THERE! IS IT TOO MUCH TO ASK YOUR CONVERSA-TION STATUS ???
PUT ME DOWN AS ONE WHO MISSES THE BUSY SIGNAL.
GUISEWITE

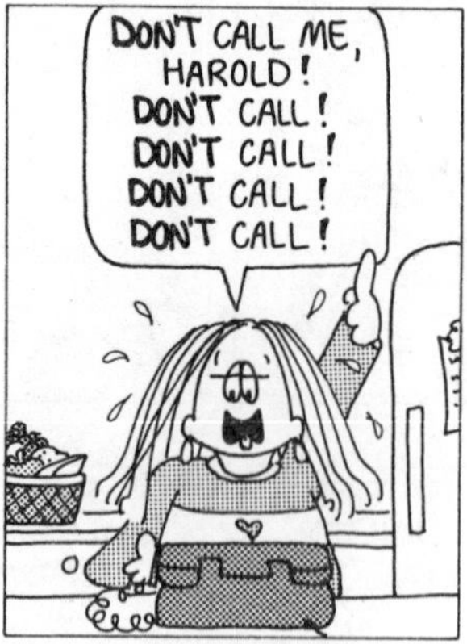
DON'T CALL ME, HAROLD! DON'T CALL! DON'T CALL! DON'T CALL! DON'T CALL!

The Commitment Problem

A man will joyfully discuss the standing of every player in every team in every division of every sport in history, but will choke if his girlfriend asks where she stands in their relationship.

A man will watch the recaps, the highlights, the roundups, the reviews, the replays—a thousand different versions of the exact same sports moment—from every angle and from every point of view, but if his loved one brings up the relationship conversation more than once every six months, he will accuse her of needing to "rehash" everything.

A man can remember the second shot of the third hole of a golf game that was played 11 years ago, but can't remember a promise to "talk about us" made six minutes ago.

Clearly, it isn't that men can't commit. They just have their commitment brain cells already used up on the wrong things.

After 25 years of research into human emotions . . .
25 years of open, caring dialogue between the sexes . . .
25 years of reaching out, healing, and learning to trust
and respect and strive for more meaningful levels of
connectedness . . . we have not only landed right back on
square one, but have built "His" and "Hers" mini-malls
there.

Commitment, Then:

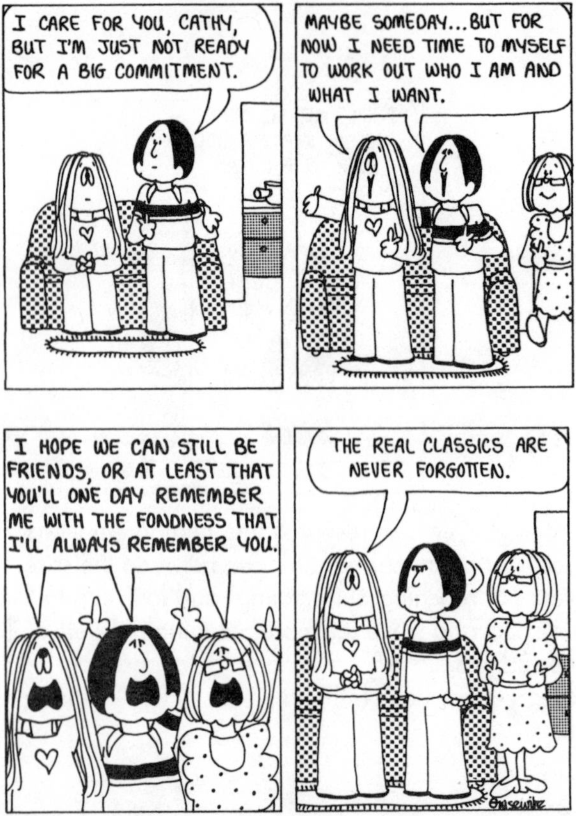
I CARE FOR YOU, CATHY, BUT I'M JUST NOT READY FOR A BIG COMMITMENT.
MAYBE SOMEDAY... BUT FOR NOW I NEED TIME TO MYSELF TO WORK OUT WHO I AM AND WHAT I WANT.
I HOPE WE CAN STILL BE FRIENDS, OR AT LEAST THAT YOU'LL ONE DAY REMEMBER ME WITH THE FONDNESS THAT I'LL ALWAYS REMEMBER YOU.
THE REAL CLASSICS ARE NEVER FORGOTTEN.
Guisewite

Commitment, Now:

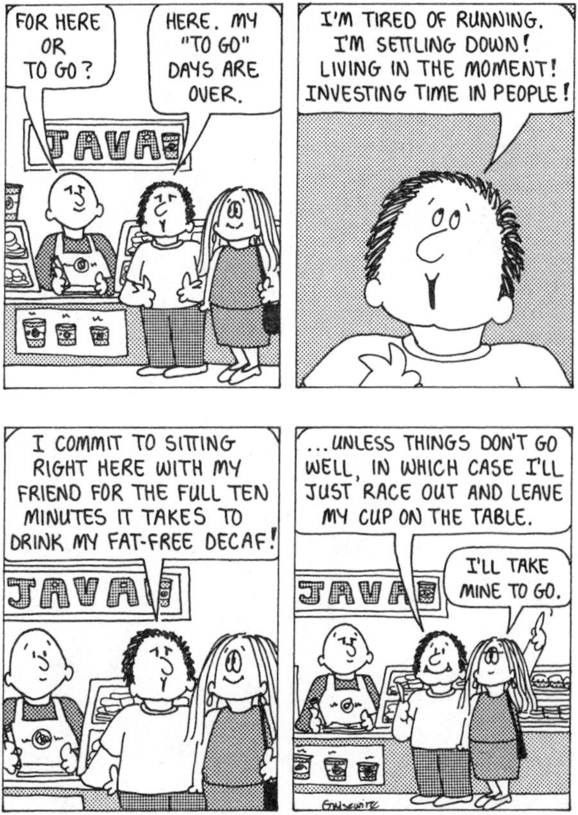
FOR HERE OR TO GO?
HERE. MY "TO GO" DAYS ARE OVER.
I'M TIRED OF RUNNING. I'M SETTLING DOWN! LIVING IN THE MOMENT! INVESTING TIME IN PEOPLE!
I COMMIT TO SITTING RIGHT HERE WITH MY FRIEND FOR THE FULL TEN MINUTES IT TAKES TO DRINK MY FAT-FREE DECAF!
...UNLESS THINGS DON'T GO WELL, IN WHICH CASE I'LL JUST RACE OUT AND LEAVE MY CUP ON THE TABLE.
I'LL TAKE MINE TO GO.
JAVA

Commitment, Then:

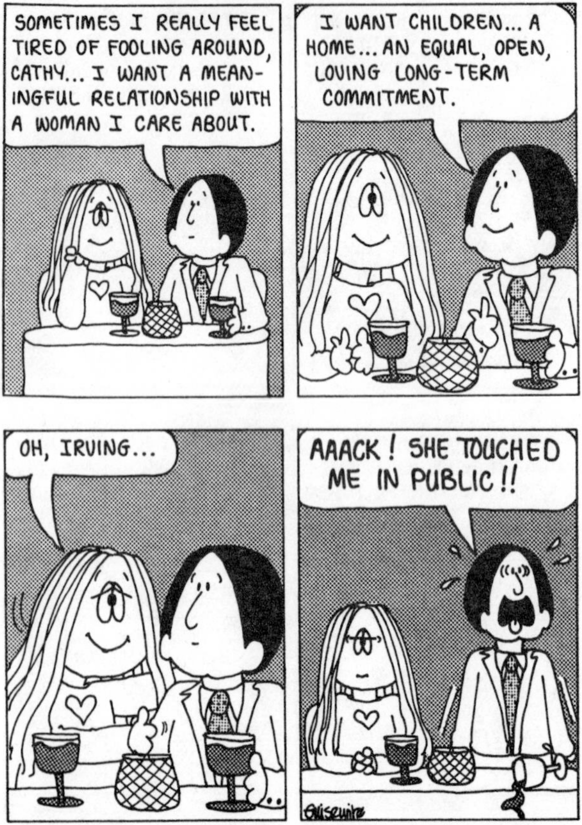
SOMETIMES I REALLY FEEL TIRED OF FOOLING AROUND, CATHY... I WANT A MEANINGFUL RELATIONSHIP WITH A WOMAN I CARE ABOUT.
I WANT CHILDREN... A HOME... AN EQUAL, OPEN, LOVING LONG-TERM COMMITMENT.
OH, IRVING...
AAACK! SHE TOUCHED ME IN PUBLIC!!
Guisewite

Commitment, Now:

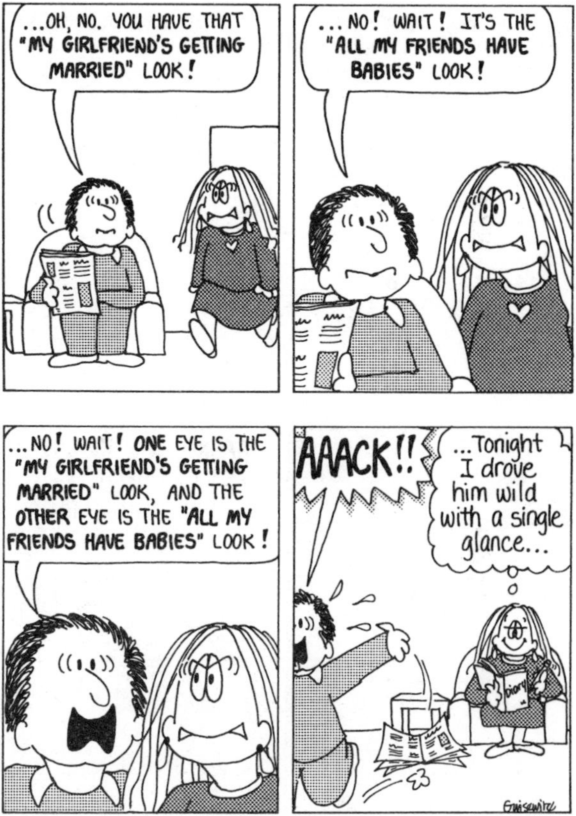

...OH, NO. YOU HAVE THAT "MY GIRLFRIEND'S GETTING MARRIED" LOOK!
...NO! WAIT! IT'S THE "ALL MY FRIENDS HAVE BABIES" LOOK!
...NO! WAIT! ONE EYE IS THE "MY GIRLFRIEND'S GETTING MARRIED" LOOK, AND THE OTHER EYE IS THE "ALL MY FRIENDS HAVE BABIES" LOOK!
AAACK!!
...Tonight I drove him wild with a single glance...
diary
Guisewite

Commitment, Then:

THIS IS WHAT MEN HATE, CATHY. I WENT WITH YOU A COUPLE OF TIMES, AND SUDDENLY YOU'RE MAKING ME FEEL THE PRESSURE OF A WHOLE RELATIONSHIP.

WE DON'T HAVE A RELATIONSHIP. WE HAD TWO GREAT DATES. WHO KNOWS? MAYBE WE'LL GO OUT AGAIN.

BUT UNTIL WE DO, I AM NOT GOING TO KISS THE GROUND YOU WALK ON, OR FEEL SOME HUGE GUILT BECAUSE I'M NOT DANCING THROUGH EVERY MOMENT OF MY LIFE WITH YOU!

WHAT DID GRANT SAY?

"GREAT DATES. GO OUT AGAIN. KISS AND DANCE."

Commitment, Now:

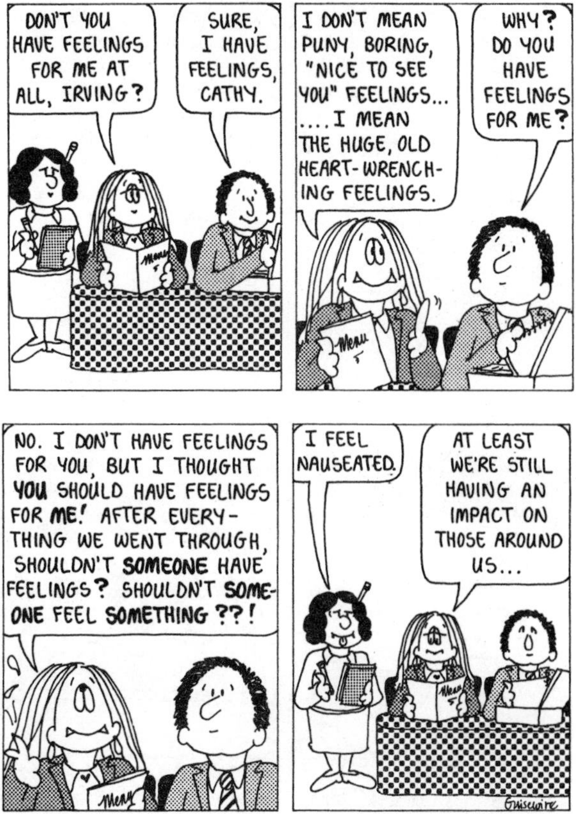
DON'T YOU HAVE FEELINGS FOR ME AT ALL, IRVING?
SURE, I HAVE FEELINGS, CATHY.
I DON'T MEAN PUNY, BORING, "NICE TO SEE YOU" FEELINGS... ....I MEAN THE HUGE, OLD HEART-WRENCHING FEELINGS.
WHY? DO YOU HAVE FEELINGS FOR ME?
NO. I DON'T HAVE FEELINGS FOR YOU, BUT I THOUGHT YOU SHOULD HAVE FEELINGS FOR ME! AFTER EVERYTHING WE WENT THROUGH, SHOULDN'T SOMEONE HAVE FEELINGS? SHOULDN'T SOMEONE FEEL SOMETHING??!
I FEEL NAUSEATED.
AT LEAST WE'RE STILL HAVING AN IMPACT ON THOSE AROUND US...
Guisewite

Commitment, Then:

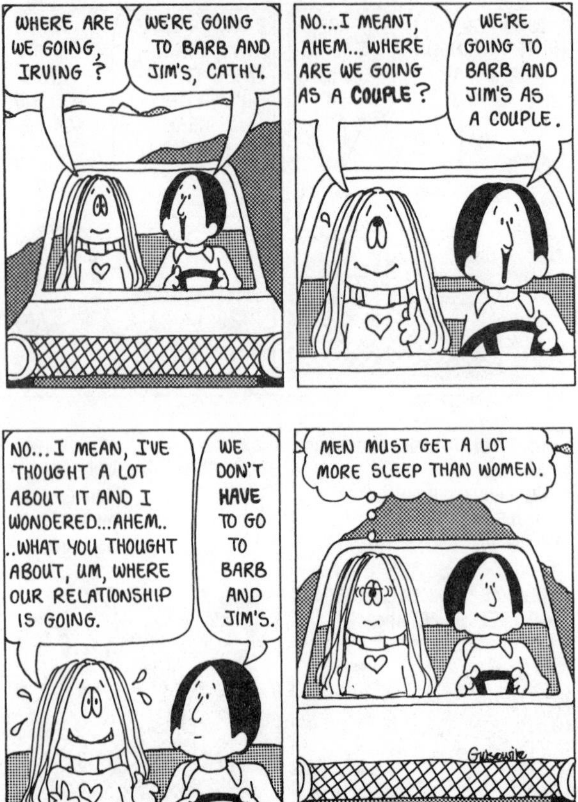
WHERE ARE WE GOING, IRVING?
WE'RE GOING TO BARB AND JIM'S, CATHY.
NO...I MEANT, AHEM... WHERE ARE WE GOING AS A **COUPLE**?
WE'RE GOING TO BARB AND JIM'S AS A COUPLE.
NO... I MEAN, I'VE THOUGHT A LOT ABOUT IT AND I WONDERED...AHEM.. ..WHAT YOU THOUGHT ABOUT, UM, WHERE OUR RELATIONSHIP IS GOING.
WE DON'T **HAVE** TO GO TO BARB AND JIM'S.
MEN MUST GET A LOT MORE SLEEP THAN WOMEN.
Guisewite

Commitment, Now:

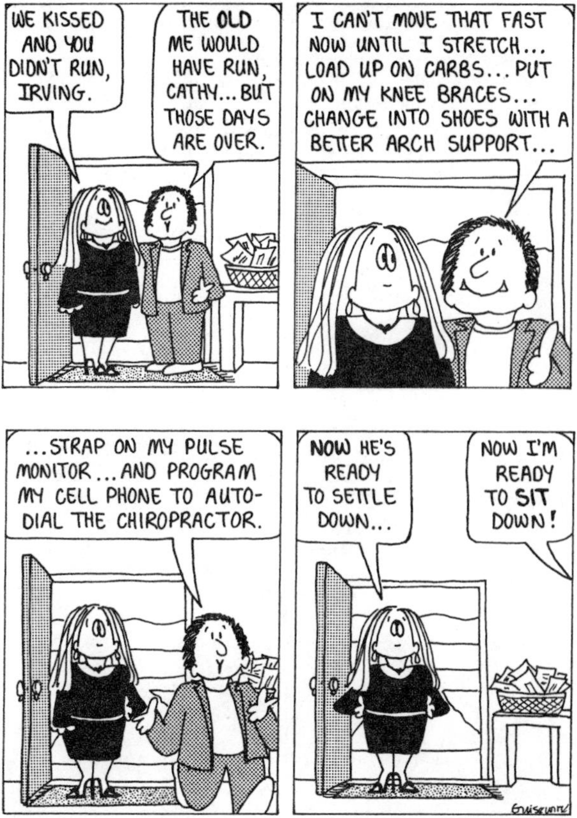
WE KISSED AND YOU DIDN'T RUN, IRVING.
THE OLD ME WOULD HAVE RUN, CATHY... BUT THOSE DAYS ARE OVER.
I CAN'T MOVE THAT FAST NOW UNTIL I STRETCH... LOAD UP ON CARBS... PUT ON MY KNEE BRACES... CHANGE INTO SHOES WITH A BETTER ARCH SUPPORT...
...STRAP ON MY PULSE MONITOR... AND PROGRAM MY CELL PHONE TO AUTO-DIAL THE CHIROPRACTOR.
NOW HE'S READY TO SETTLE DOWN...
NOW I'M READY TO SIT DOWN!

Commitment Then and Now:

And the ultimate commitment problem: fear of discussing commitment after proposing a lifetime of commitment.

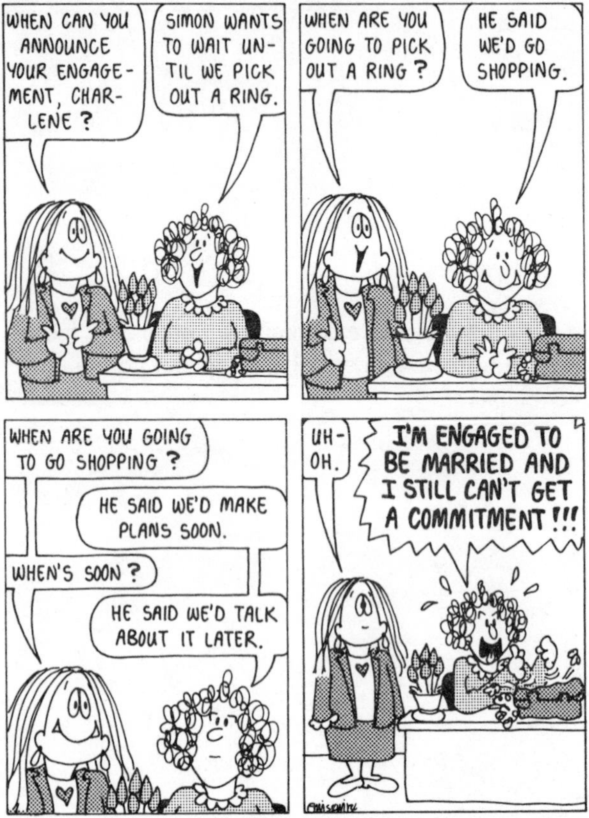

WHEN CAN YOU ANNOUNCE YOUR ENGAGE-MENT, CHAR-LENE?
SIMON WANTS TO WAIT UN-TIL WE PICK OUT A RING.
WHEN ARE YOU GOING TO PICK OUT A RING?
HE SAID WE'D GO SHOPPING.
WHEN ARE YOU GOING TO GO SHOPPING?
HE SAID WE'D MAKE PLANS SOON.
WHEN'S SOON?
HE SAID WE'D TALK ABOUT IT LATER.
UH-OH.
I'M ENGAGED TO BE MARRIED AND I STILL CAN'T GET A COMMITMENT!!!

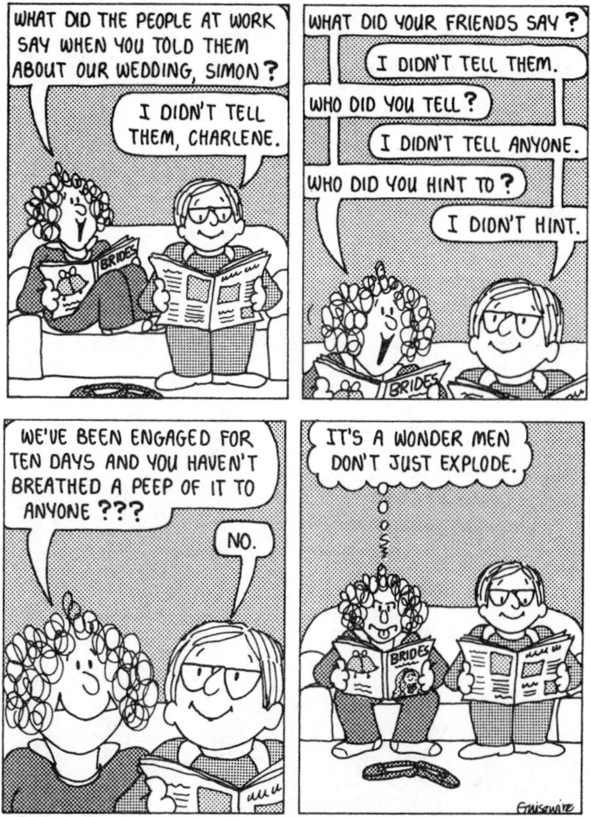
WHAT DID THE PEOPLE AT WORK SAY WHEN YOU TOLD THEM ABOUT OUR WEDDING, SIMON?
I DIDN'T TELL THEM, CHARLENE.
BRIDES
WHAT DID YOUR FRIENDS SAY?
I DIDN'T TELL THEM.
WHO DID YOU TELL?
I DIDN'T TELL ANYONE.
WHO DID YOU HINT TO?
I DIDN'T HINT.
BRIDES
WE'VE BEEN ENGAGED FOR TEN DAYS AND YOU HAVEN'T BREATHED A PEEP OF IT TO ANYONE???
NO.
IT'S A WONDER MEN DON'T JUST EXPLODE.
BRIDES
Guisewite

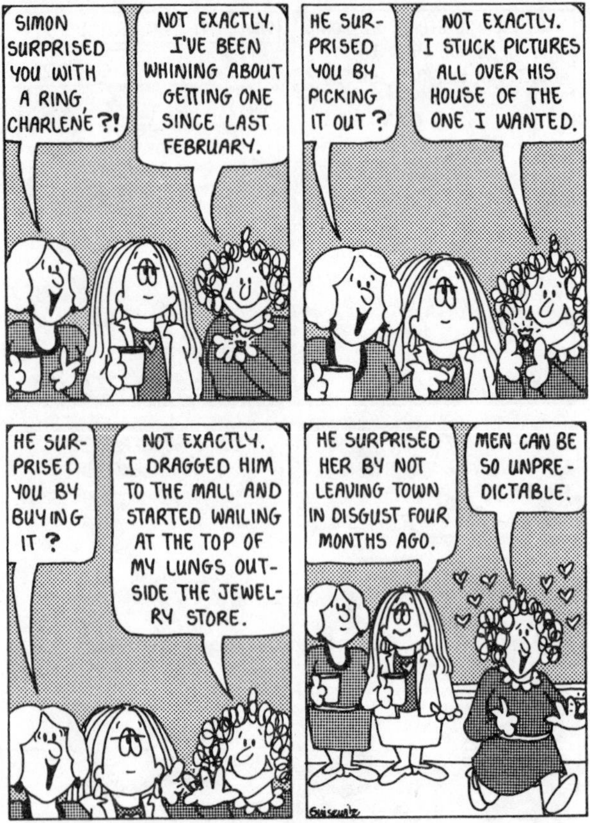
SIMON SURPRISED YOU WITH A RING, CHARLENE?!
NOT EXACTLY. I'VE BEEN WHINING ABOUT GETTING ONE SINCE LAST FEBRUARY.
HE SURPRISED YOU BY PICKING IT OUT?
NOT EXACTLY. I STUCK PICTURES ALL OVER HIS HOUSE OF THE ONE I WANTED.
HE SURPRISED YOU BY BUYING IT?
NOT EXACTLY. I DRAGGED HIM TO THE MALL AND STARTED WAILING AT THE TOP OF MY LUNGS OUTSIDE THE JEWELRY STORE.
HE SURPRISED HER BY NOT LEAVING TOWN IN DISGUST FOUR MONTHS AGO.
MEN CAN BE SO UNPREDICTABLE.
Guisewite

Commitment is scary, but definition is comforting.

While the marriage rates have gone up and down in the last two decades, there's been a steady rise in our desire to label whatever it is that we may or may not have with each other.

The Not a Couple, but Not a Noncouple:

The Couple, but Not a Golf Couple:

The Noncouple:

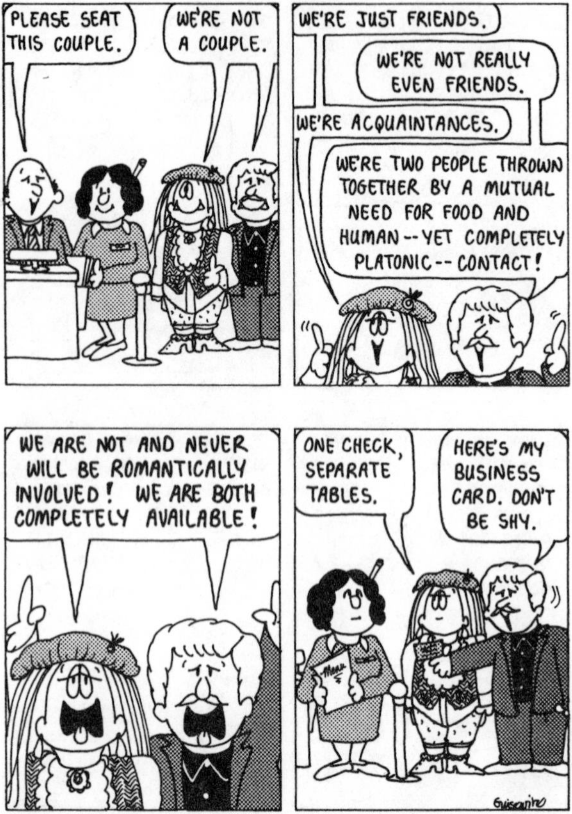
PLEASE SEAT THIS COUPLE.
WE'RE NOT A COUPLE.
WE'RE JUST FRIENDS.
WE'RE NOT REALLY EVEN FRIENDS.
WE'RE ACQUAINTANCES.
WE'RE TWO PEOPLE THROWN TOGETHER BY A MUTUAL NEED FOR FOOD AND HUMAN--YET COMPLETELY PLATONIC--CONTACT!
WE ARE NOT AND NEVER WILL BE ROMANTICALLY INVOLVED! WE ARE BOTH COMPLETELY AVAILABLE!
ONE CHECK, SEPARATE TABLES.
HERE'S MY BUSINESS CARD. DON'T BE SHY.
Guisewite

The Completely Uninvolved Couple:

The Paper Couple:

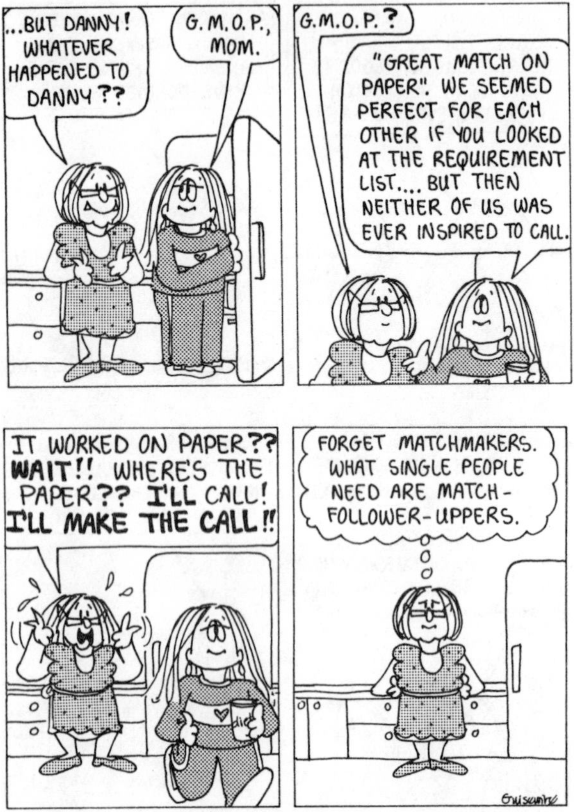
...BUT DANNY! WHATEVER HAPPENED TO DANNY??
G.M.O.P., MOM.
G.M.O.P.?
"GREAT MATCH ON PAPER". WE SEEMED PERFECT FOR EACH OTHER IF YOU LOOKED AT THE REQUIREMENT LIST.... BUT THEN NEITHER OF US WAS EVER INSPIRED TO CALL.
IT WORKED ON PAPER?? WAIT!! WHERE'S THE PAPER?? I'LL CALL! I'LL MAKE THE CALL!!
FORGET MATCHMAKERS. WHAT SINGLE PEOPLE NEED ARE MATCH-FOLLOWER-UPPERS.
GUISEWITE

The Pre-Ex-Couple:

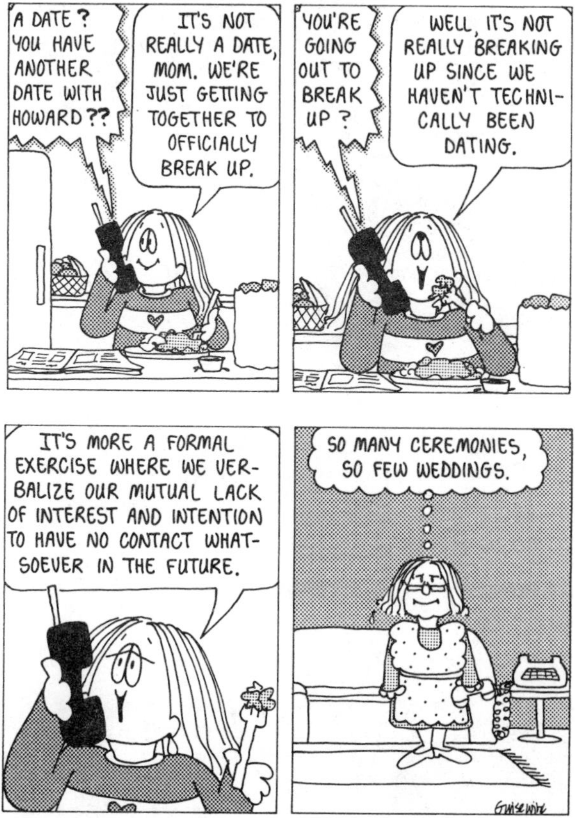
A DATE? YOU HAVE ANOTHER DATE WITH HOWARD??
IT'S NOT REALLY A DATE, MOM. WE'RE JUST GETTING TOGETHER TO OFFICIALLY BREAK UP.
YOU'RE GOING OUT TO BREAK UP?
WELL, IT'S NOT REALLY BREAKING UP SINCE WE HAVEN'T TECHNICALLY BEEN DATING.
IT'S MORE A FORMAL EXERCISE WHERE WE VERBALIZE OUR MUTUAL LACK OF INTEREST AND INTENTION TO HAVE NO CONTACT WHATSOEVER IN THE FUTURE.
SO MANY CEREMONIES, SO FEW WEDDINGS.
Guisewite

The Media-Generated Couple:

Friends:

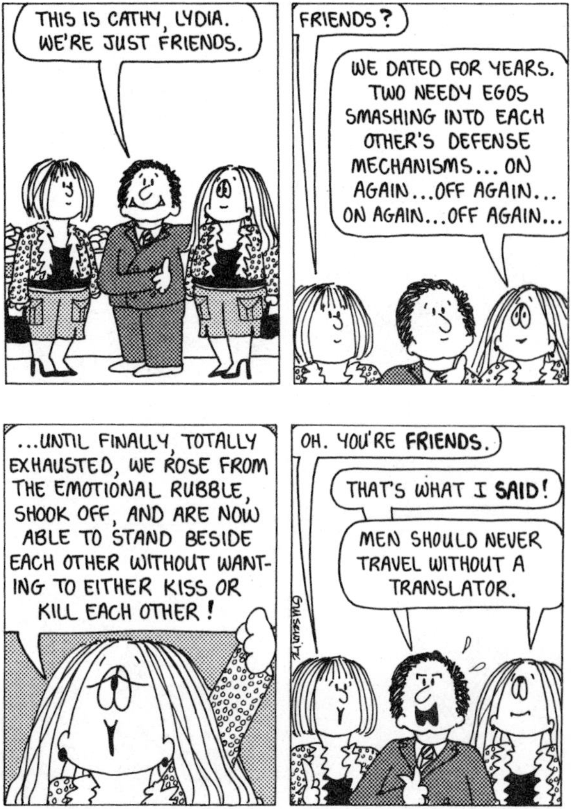
THIS IS CATHY, LYDIA. WE'RE JUST FRIENDS.
FRIENDS?
WE DATED FOR YEARS. TWO NEEDY EGOS SMASHING INTO EACH OTHER'S DEFENSE MECHANISMS... ON AGAIN...OFF AGAIN... ON AGAIN...OFF AGAIN...
...UNTIL FINALLY, TOTALLY EXHAUSTED, WE ROSE FROM THE EMOTIONAL RUBBLE, SHOOK OFF, AND ARE NOW ABLE TO STAND BESIDE EACH OTHER WITHOUT WANTING TO EITHER KISS OR KILL EACH OTHER!
OH. YOU'RE **FRIENDS**.
THAT'S WHAT I **SAID**!
MEN SHOULD NEVER TRAVEL WITHOUT A TRANSLATOR.
GUISEWITE

The Dinner Party:

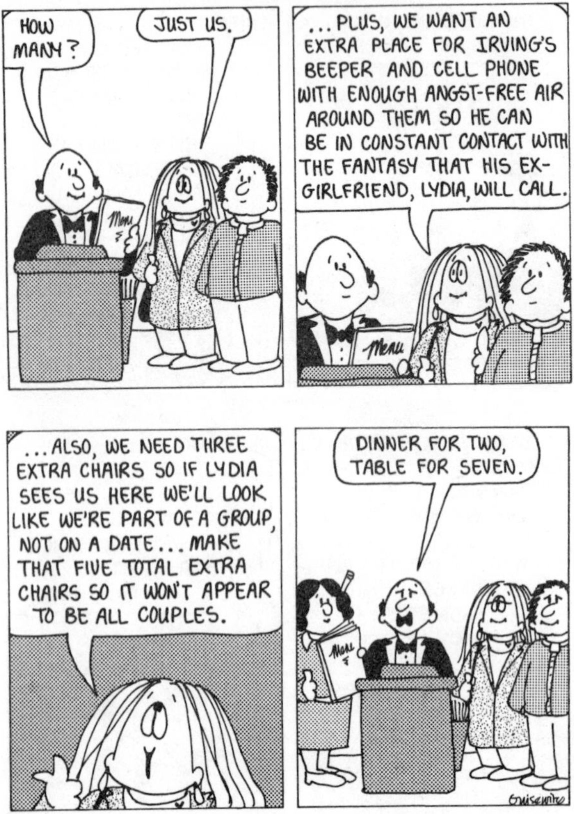
HOW MANY?
JUST US.
...PLUS, WE WANT AN EXTRA PLACE FOR IRVING'S BEEPER AND CELL PHONE WITH ENOUGH ANGST-FREE AIR AROUND THEM SO HE CAN BE IN CONSTANT CONTACT WITH THE FANTASY THAT HIS EX-GIRLFRIEND, LYDIA, WILL CALL.
...ALSO, WE NEED THREE EXTRA CHAIRS SO IF LYDIA SEES US HERE WE'LL LOOK LIKE WE'RE PART OF A GROUP, NOT ON A DATE... MAKE THAT FIVE TOTAL EXTRA CHAIRS SO IT WON'T APPEAR TO BE ALL COUPLES.
DINNER FOR TWO, TABLE FOR SEVEN.
Guisewite

The Mini-Marriage:

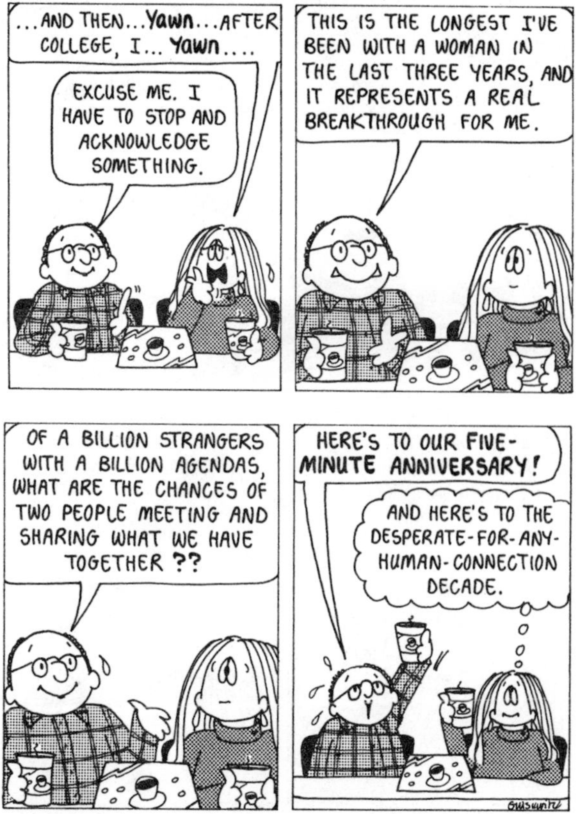
...AND THEN...Yawn...AFTER COLLEGE, I... Yawn....
EXCUSE ME. I HAVE TO STOP AND ACKNOWLEDGE SOMETHING.
THIS IS THE LONGEST I'VE BEEN WITH A WOMAN IN THE LAST THREE YEARS, AND IT REPRESENTS A REAL BREAKTHROUGH FOR ME.
OF A BILLION STRANGERS WITH A BILLION AGENDAS, WHAT ARE THE CHANCES OF TWO PEOPLE MEETING AND SHARING WHAT WE HAVE TOGETHER??
HERE'S TO OUR FIVE-MINUTE ANNIVERSARY!
AND HERE'S TO THE DESPERATE-FOR-ANY-HUMAN-CONNECTION DECADE.
GUISEWITE

The Transition People:

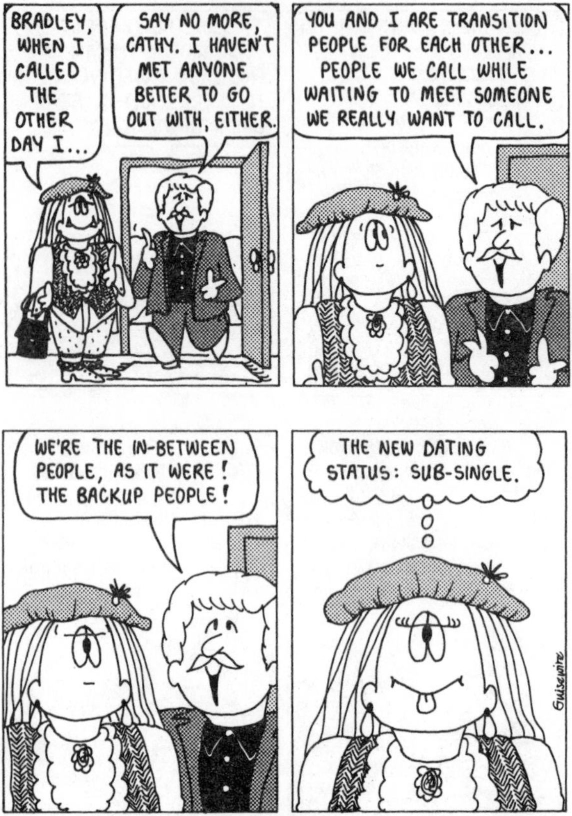
BRADLEY, WHEN I CALLED THE OTHER DAY I...
SAY NO MORE, CATHY. I HAVEN'T MET ANYONE BETTER TO GO OUT WITH, EITHER.
YOU AND I ARE TRANSITION PEOPLE FOR EACH OTHER... PEOPLE WE CALL WHILE WAITING TO MEET SOMEONE WE REALLY WANT TO CALL.
WE'RE THE IN-BETWEEN PEOPLE, AS IT WERE! THE BACKUP PEOPLE!
THE NEW DATING STATUS: SUB-SINGLE.
Guisewite

Apathy Mates:

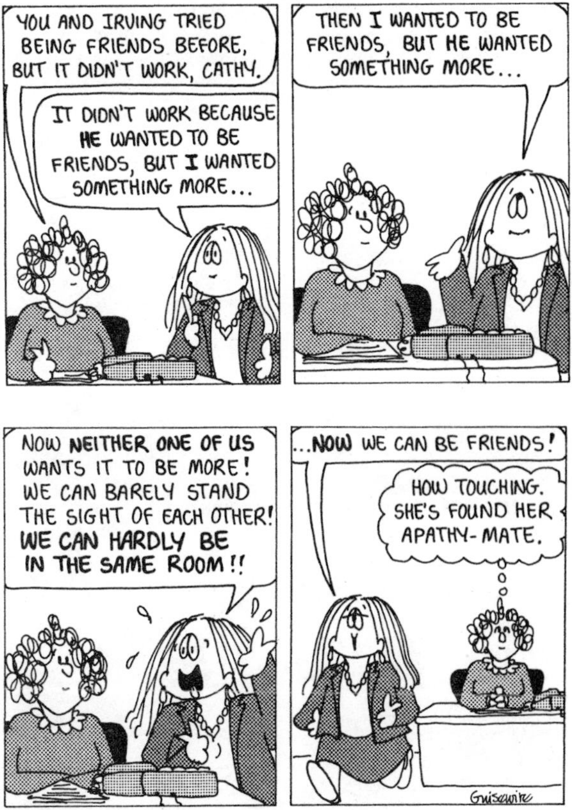
YOU AND IRVING TRIED BEING FRIENDS BEFORE, BUT IT DIDN'T WORK, CATHY.
IT DIDN'T WORK BECAUSE HE WANTED TO BE FRIENDS, BUT I WANTED SOMETHING MORE...
THEN I WANTED TO BE FRIENDS, BUT HE WANTED SOMETHING MORE...
NOW NEITHER ONE OF US WANTS IT TO BE MORE! WE CAN BARELY STAND THE SIGHT OF EACH OTHER! WE CAN HARDLY BE IN THE SAME ROOM!!
...NOW WE CAN BE FRIENDS!
HOW TOUCHING. SHE'S FOUND HER APATHY-MATE.
Guisewite

Standing Mates:

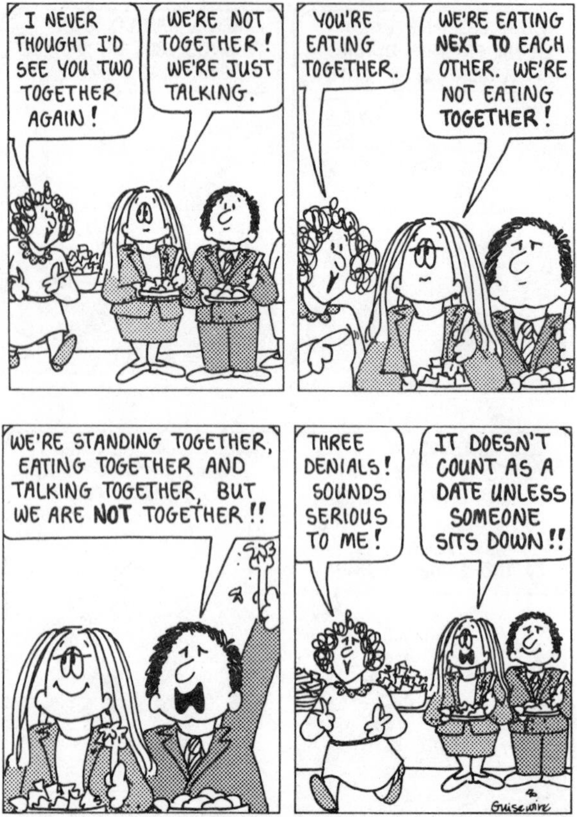
I NEVER THOUGHT I'D SEE YOU TWO TOGETHER AGAIN!
WE'RE NOT TOGETHER! WE'RE JUST TALKING.
YOU'RE EATING TOGETHER.
WE'RE EATING NEXT TO EACH OTHER. WE'RE NOT EATING TOGETHER!
WE'RE STANDING TOGETHER, EATING TOGETHER AND TALKING TOGETHER, BUT WE ARE NOT TOGETHER!!
THREE DENIALS! SOUNDS SERIOUS TO ME!
IT DOESN'T COUNT AS A DATE UNLESS SOMEONE SITS DOWN!!
Guisewite

The Non-relationship Relationship:

IF YOU CAN'T DEAL WITH THE "M" WORD, I'LL HAVE NO CHOICE BUT TO BRING UP THE "R" WORD, THE "T" WORD AND THE "E" WORD, WHICH WILL ONLY LEAD TO THE "Q" WORD... ...AND I DON'T THINK I HAVE TO MENTION WHAT WILL HAPPEN IF THE CONVERSATION DETERIORATES INTO THE "J" WORD!

The Dump

The only thing worse than trying to start a relationship, of course, is trying to end one.

Dating, at least, has some basic structure. Even though we did away with all the old rules, we created a bunch of new ones.

In dumping, there's always been only one rule, and it isn't even about how, when, or why it's done. It's only about taking turns.

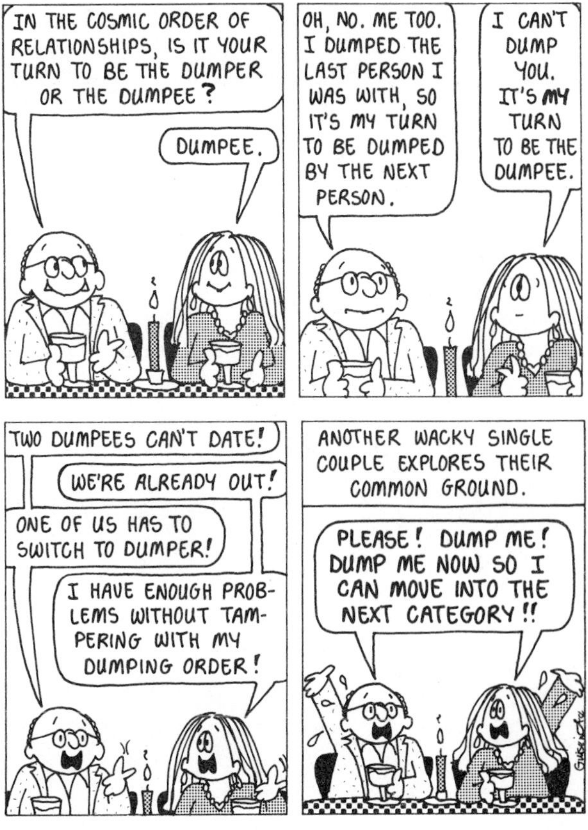
IN THE COSMIC ORDER OF RELATIONSHIPS, IS IT YOUR TURN TO BE THE DUMPER OR THE DUMPEE?
DUMPEE.
OH, NO. ME TOO. I DUMPED THE LAST PERSON I WAS WITH, SO IT'S MY TURN TO BE DUMPED BY THE NEXT PERSON.
I CAN'T DUMP YOU. IT'S MY TURN TO BE THE DUMPEE.
TWO DUMPEES CAN'T DATE!
WE'RE ALREADY OUT!
ONE OF US HAS TO SWITCH TO DUMPER!
I HAVE ENOUGH PROBLEMS WITHOUT TAMPERING WITH MY DUMPING ORDER!
ANOTHER WACKY SINGLE COUPLE EXPLORES THEIR COMMON GROUND.
PLEASE! DUMP ME! DUMP ME NOW SO I CAN MOVE INTO THE NEXT CATEGORY!!

Breaking up is a free-for-all. The only comfort comes from knowing that no matter how it's happened to you or how you've made it happen to someone else, it probably wasn't the first time.

Here, in alphabetical order, are some of the classics.

The Assisted Dump:

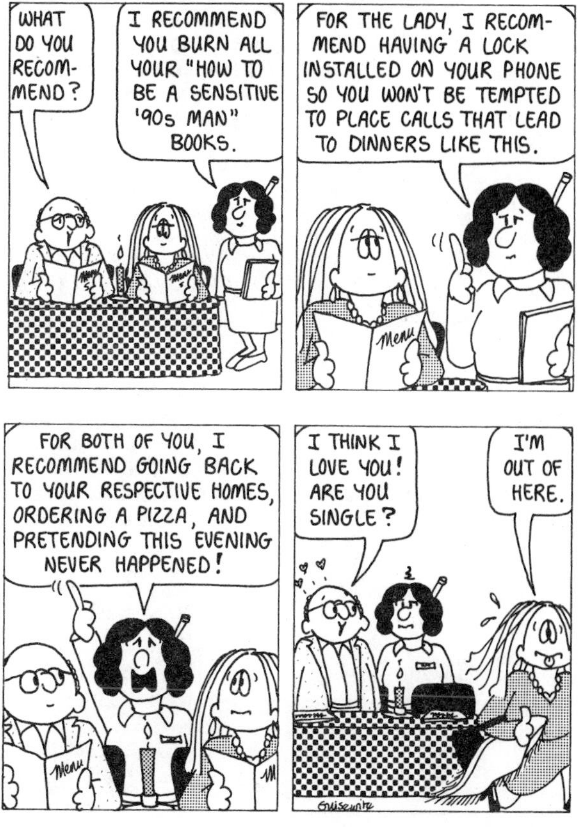
WHAT DO YOU RECOMMEND?
I RECOMMEND YOU BURN ALL YOUR "HOW TO BE A SENSITIVE '90s MAN" BOOKS.
FOR THE LADY, I RECOMMEND HAVING A LOCK INSTALLED ON YOUR PHONE SO YOU WON'T BE TEMPTED TO PLACE CALLS THAT LEAD TO DINNERS LIKE THIS.
Menu
FOR BOTH OF YOU, I RECOMMEND GOING BACK TO YOUR RESPECTIVE HOMES, ORDERING A PIZZA, AND PRETENDING THIS EVENING NEVER HAPPENED!
Menu
I THINK I LOVE YOU! ARE YOU SINGLE?
I'M OUT OF HERE.

The Auto Dump:

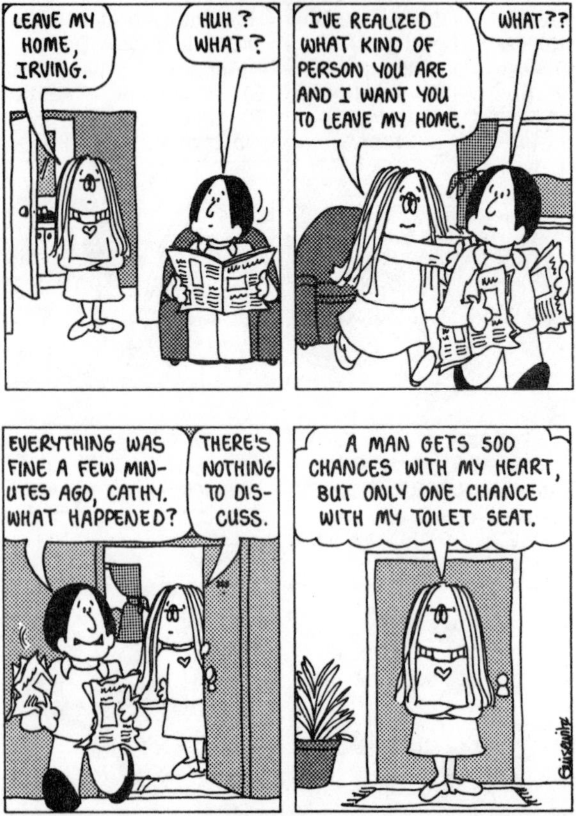

LEAVE MY HOME, IRVING.
HUH? WHAT?
I'VE REALIZED WHAT KIND OF PERSON YOU ARE AND I WANT YOU TO LEAVE MY HOME.
WHAT??
EVERYTHING WAS FINE A FEW MIN-UTES AGO, CATHY. WHAT HAPPENED?
THERE'S NOTHING TO DIS-CUSS.
A MAN GETS 500 CHANCES WITH MY HEART, BUT ONLY ONE CHANCE WITH MY TOILET SEAT.
Guisewite

The Competitive Dump:

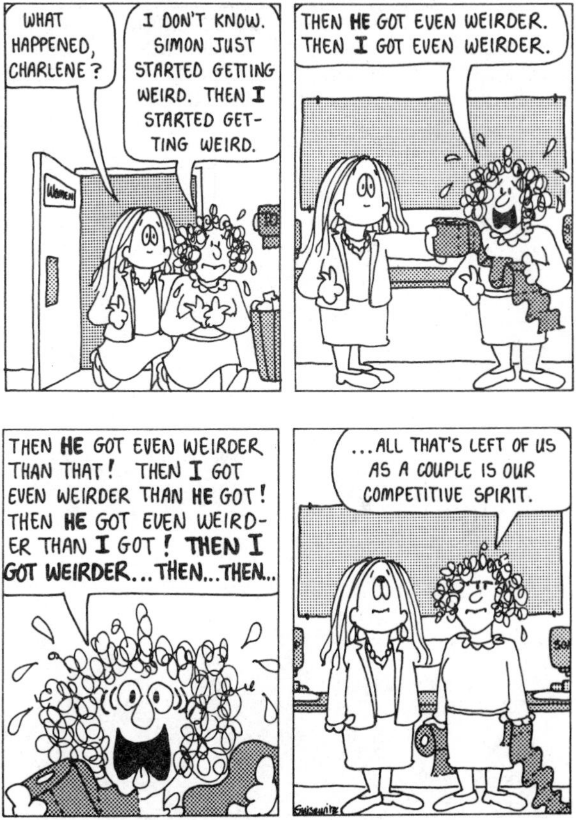
WHAT HAPPENED, CHARLENE?
I DON'T KNOW. SIMON JUST STARTED GETTING WEIRD. THEN I STARTED GET-TING WEIRD.
WOMEN
THEN HE GOT EVEN WEIRDER. THEN I GOT EVEN WEIRDER.
THEN HE GOT EVEN WEIRDER THAN THAT! THEN I GOT EVEN WEIRDER THAN HE GOT! THEN HE GOT EVEN WEIRD-ER THAN I GOT! THEN I GOT WEIRDER... THEN... THEN...
...ALL THAT'S LEFT OF US AS A COUPLE IS OUR COMPETITIVE SPIRIT.

The Cyber Dump:

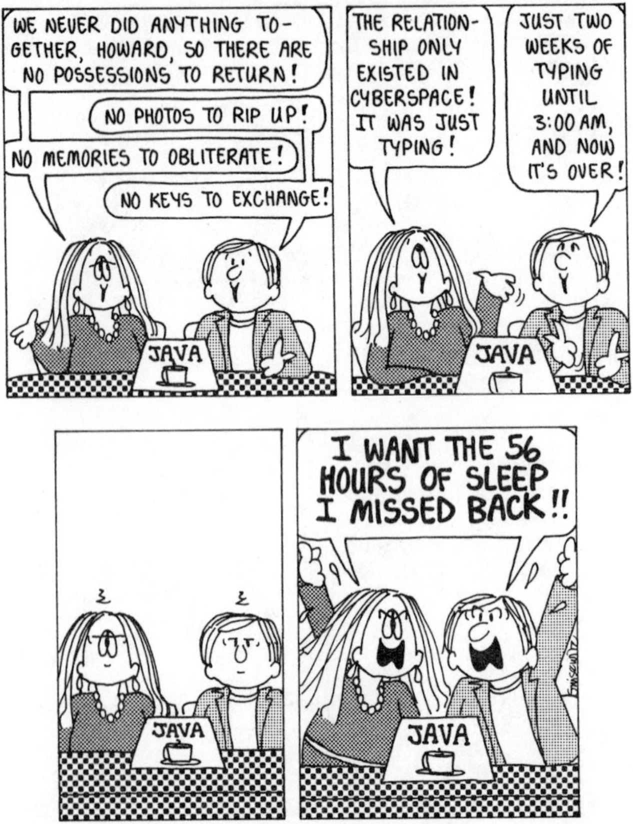

WE NEVER DID ANYTHING TOGETHER, HOWARD, SO THERE ARE NO POSSESSIONS TO RETURN!
NO PHOTOS TO RIP UP!
NO MEMORIES TO OBLITERATE!
NO KEYS TO EXCHANGE!
JAVA
THE RELATIONSHIP ONLY EXISTED IN CYBERSPACE! IT WAS JUST TYPING!
JUST TWO WEEKS OF TYPING UNTIL 3:00 AM, AND NOW IT'S OVER!
JAVA
JAVA
I WANT THE 56 HOURS OF SLEEP I MISSED BACK!!
JAVA

The Dumping Date:

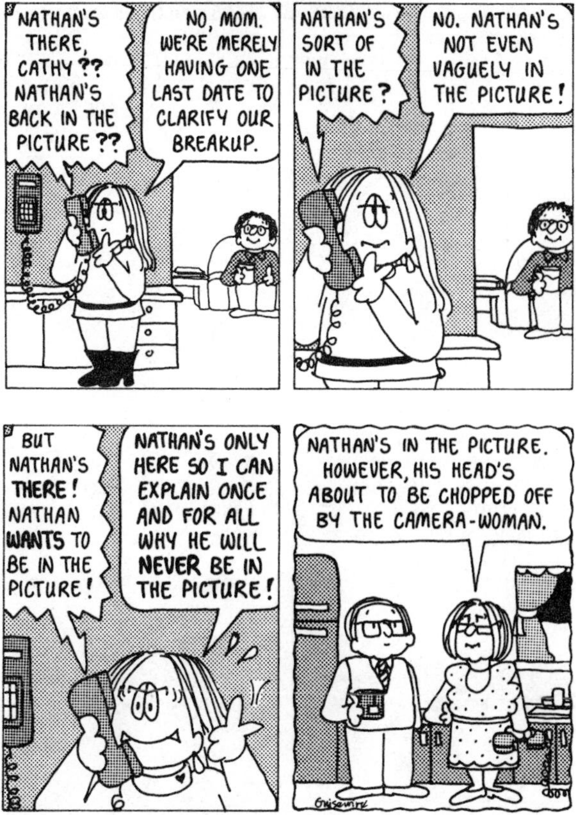
NATHAN'S THERE, CATHY?? NATHAN'S BACK IN THE PICTURE??
NO, MOM. WE'RE MERELY HAVING ONE LAST DATE TO CLARIFY OUR BREAKUP.
NATHAN'S SORT OF IN THE PICTURE?
NO. NATHAN'S NOT EVEN VAGUELY IN THE PICTURE!
BUT NATHAN'S THERE! NATHAN WANTS TO BE IN THE PICTURE!
NATHAN'S ONLY HERE SO I CAN EXPLAIN ONCE AND FOR ALL WHY HE WILL NEVER BE IN THE PICTURE!
NATHAN'S IN THE PICTURE. HOWEVER, HIS HEAD'S ABOUT TO BE CHOPPED OFF BY THE CAMERA-WOMAN.
Guisewite

The Dumping Wardrobe:

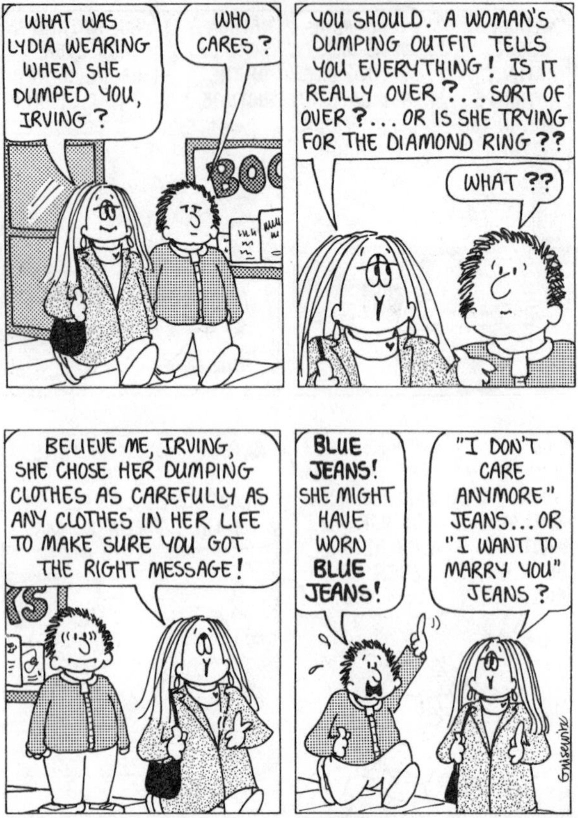
WHAT WAS LYDIA WEARING WHEN SHE DUMPED YOU, IRVING?
WHO CARES?
BOO
YOU SHOULD. A WOMAN'S DUMPING OUTFIT TELLS YOU EVERYTHING! IS IT REALLY OVER?... SORT OF OVER?... OR IS SHE TRYING FOR THE DIAMOND RING??
WHAT??
BELIEVE ME, IRVING, SHE CHOSE HER DUMPING CLOTHES AS CAREFULLY AS ANY CLOTHES IN HER LIFE TO MAKE SURE YOU GOT THE RIGHT MESSAGE!
KS
BLUE JEANS! SHE MIGHT HAVE WORN BLUE JEANS!
"I DON'T CARE ANYMORE" JEANS... OR "I WANT TO MARRY YOU" JEANS?
Guisewite

The Dump-o-rama:

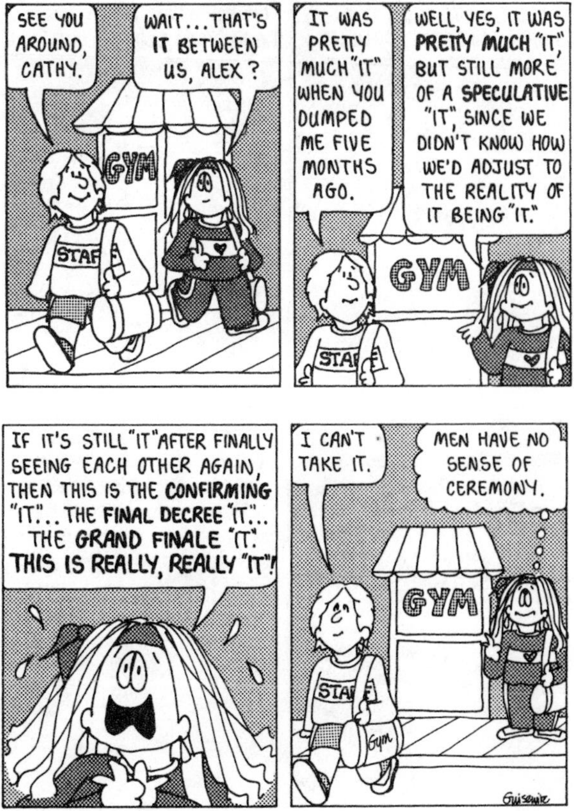
SEE YOU AROUND, CATHY.
WAIT... THAT'S IT BETWEEN US, ALEX?
GYM
STAFF
IT WAS PRETTY MUCH "IT" WHEN YOU DUMPED ME FIVE MONTHS AGO.
WELL, YES, IT WAS PRETTY MUCH "IT", BUT STILL MORE OF A SPECULATIVE "IT", SINCE WE DIDN'T KNOW HOW WE'D ADJUST TO THE REALITY OF IT BEING "IT."
IF IT'S STILL "IT" AFTER FINALLY SEEING EACH OTHER AGAIN, THEN THIS IS THE CONFIRMING "IT."... THE FINAL DECREE "IT."... THE GRAND FINALE "IT." THIS IS REALLY, REALLY "IT"!
I CAN'T TAKE IT.
MEN HAVE NO SENSE OF CEREMONY.
Gym
Guisewite

The Failed Dump:

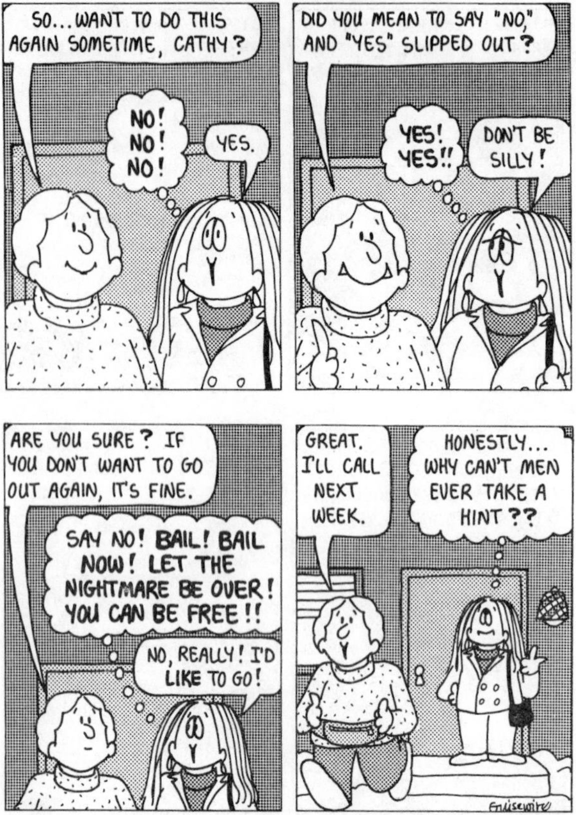
SO... WANT TO DO THIS AGAIN SOMETIME, CATHY?
NO! NO! NO!
YES.
DID YOU MEAN TO SAY "NO," AND "YES" SLIPPED OUT?
YES! YES!!
DON'T BE SILLY!
ARE YOU SURE? IF YOU DON'T WANT TO GO OUT AGAIN, IT'S FINE.
SAY NO! BAIL! BAIL NOW! LET THE NIGHTMARE BE OVER! YOU CAN BE FREE!!
NO, REALLY! I'D LIKE TO GO!
GREAT. I'LL CALL NEXT WEEK.
HONESTLY... WHY CAN'T MEN EVER TAKE A HINT??
Guisewite

The Going Steady Dump:

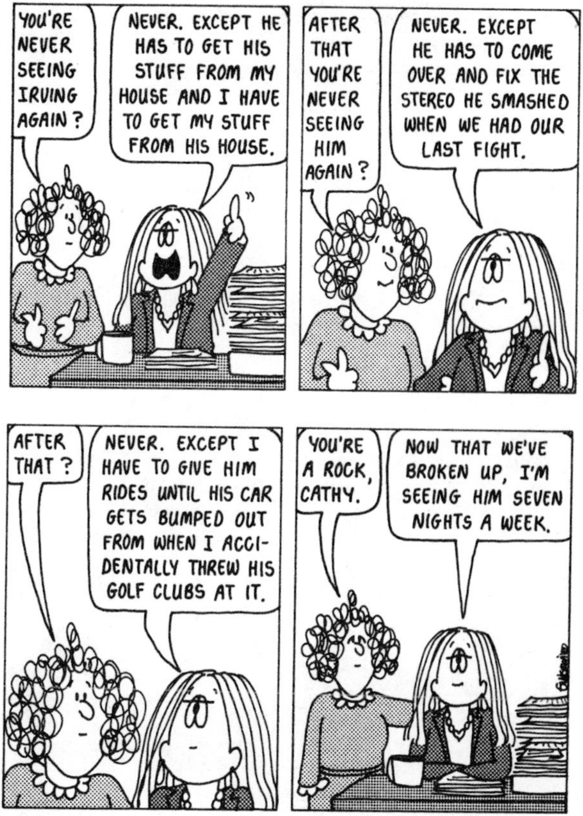
YOU'RE NEVER SEEING IRVING AGAIN?
NEVER. EXCEPT HE HAS TO GET HIS STUFF FROM MY HOUSE AND I HAVE TO GET MY STUFF FROM HIS HOUSE.
AFTER THAT YOU'RE NEVER SEEING HIM AGAIN?
NEVER. EXCEPT HE HAS TO COME OVER AND FIX THE STEREO HE SMASHED WHEN WE HAD OUR LAST FIGHT.
AFTER THAT?
NEVER. EXCEPT I HAVE TO GIVE HIM RIDES UNTIL HIS CAR GETS BUMPED OUT FROM WHEN I ACCI-DENTALLY THREW HIS GOLF CLUBS AT IT.
YOU'RE A ROCK, CATHY.
NOW THAT WE'VE BROKEN UP, I'M SEEING HIM SEVEN NIGHTS A WEEK.

The Grand Finale Dump:

I JUST NEED TO CALL IRVING ONCE TO MAKE SURE THERE'S NOTHING THERE ANYMORE, CHARLENE.

IF THERE'S NOTHING THERE ON THE PHONE, I'LL NEED TO SEE HIM ONCE AND MAKE SURE THERE'S NOTHING THERE IN PERSON.

IF THERE'S NOTHING THERE IN PERSON, I WILL HAVE TO KISS HIM ONCE TO MAKE REALLY, REALLY SURE THERE'S NOTHING THERE... AND IF THERE'S NOTHING THERE WHEN I KISS HIM, I'LL HAVE NO CHOICE BUT TO...

THE FLINGING YOURSELF INTO THE CHOCOLATE CAKE APPROACH TO BREAKING UP.

MARRIED PEOPLE KNOW NOTHING ABOUT CLOSURE.

The Guilt-Free Dump:

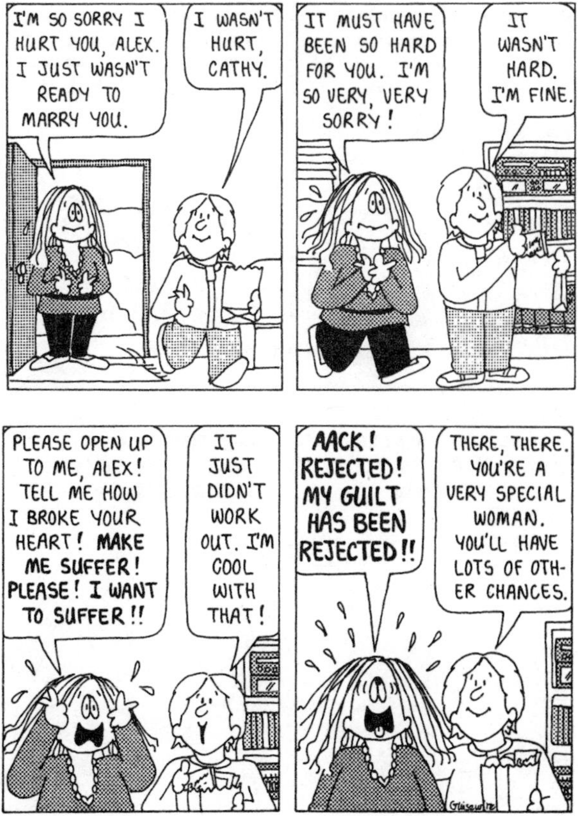
I'M SO SORRY I HURT YOU, ALEX. I JUST WASN'T READY TO MARRY YOU.
I WASN'T HURT, CATHY.
IT MUST HAVE BEEN SO HARD FOR YOU. I'M SO VERY, VERY SORRY!
IT WASN'T HARD. I'M FINE.
PLEASE OPEN UP TO ME, ALEX! TELL ME HOW I BROKE YOUR HEART! MAKE ME SUFFER! PLEASE! I WANT TO SUFFER!!
IT JUST DIDN'T WORK OUT. I'M COOL WITH THAT!
AACK! REJECTED! MY GUILT HAS BEEN REJECTED!!
THERE, THERE. YOU'RE A VERY SPECIAL WOMAN. YOU'LL HAVE LOTS OF OTHER CHANCES.
Guisewite

The Postponed Dump:

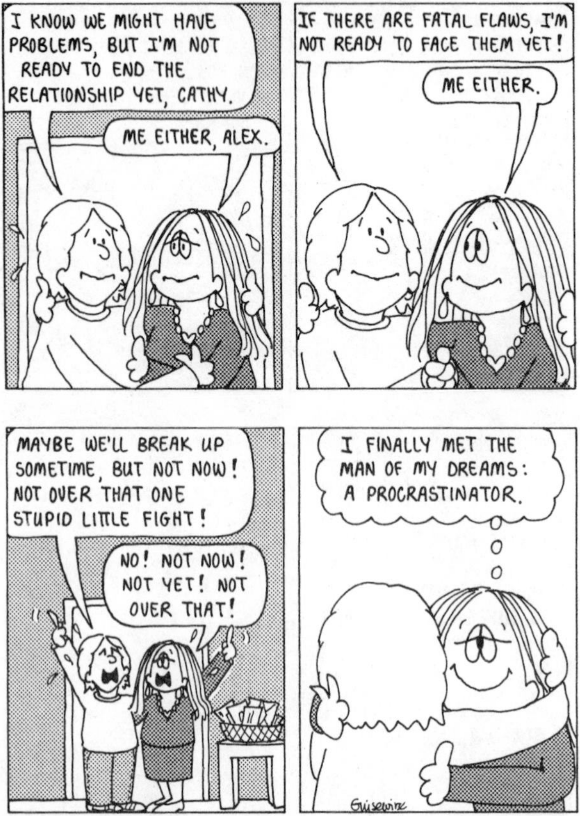
I KNOW WE MIGHT HAVE PROBLEMS, BUT I'M NOT READY TO END THE RELATIONSHIP YET, CATHY.
ME EITHER, ALEX.
IF THERE ARE FATAL FLAWS, I'M NOT READY TO FACE THEM YET!
ME EITHER.
MAYBE WE'LL BREAK UP SOMETIME, BUT NOT NOW! NOT OVER THAT ONE STUPID LITTLE FIGHT!
NO! NOT NOW! NOT YET! NOT OVER THAT!
I FINALLY MET THE MAN OF MY DREAMS: A PROCRASTINATOR.
Guisewite

The Pre-dating Dump:

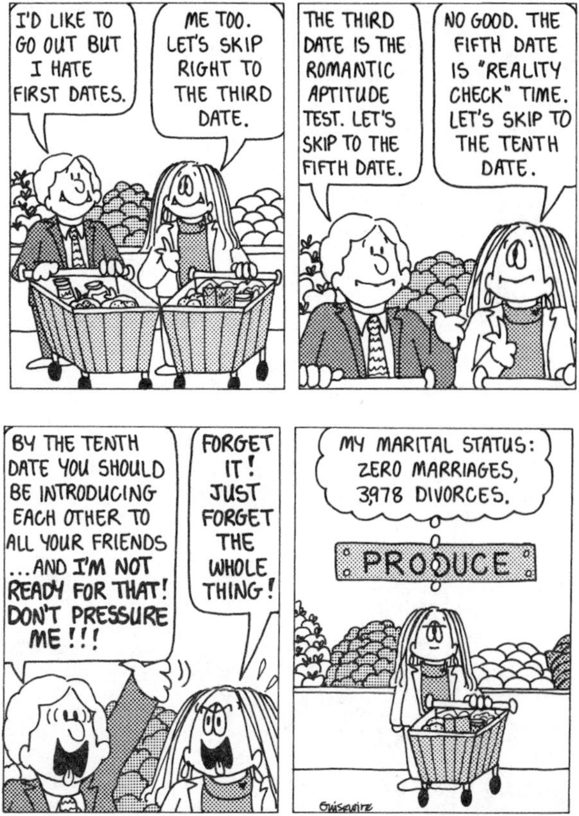
I'D LIKE TO GO OUT BUT I HATE FIRST DATES.
ME TOO. LET'S SKIP RIGHT TO THE THIRD DATE.
THE THIRD DATE IS THE ROMANTIC APTITUDE TEST. LET'S SKIP TO THE FIFTH DATE.
NO GOOD. THE FIFTH DATE IS "REALITY CHECK" TIME. LET'S SKIP TO THE TENTH DATE.
BY THE TENTH DATE YOU SHOULD BE INTRODUCING EACH OTHER TO ALL YOUR FRIENDS ...AND I'M NOT READY FOR THAT! DON'T PRESSURE ME!!!
FORGET IT! JUST FORGET THE WHOLE THING!
MY MARITAL STATUS: ZERO MARRIAGES, 3,978 DIVORCES.
PRODUCE

The Theoretical Dump:

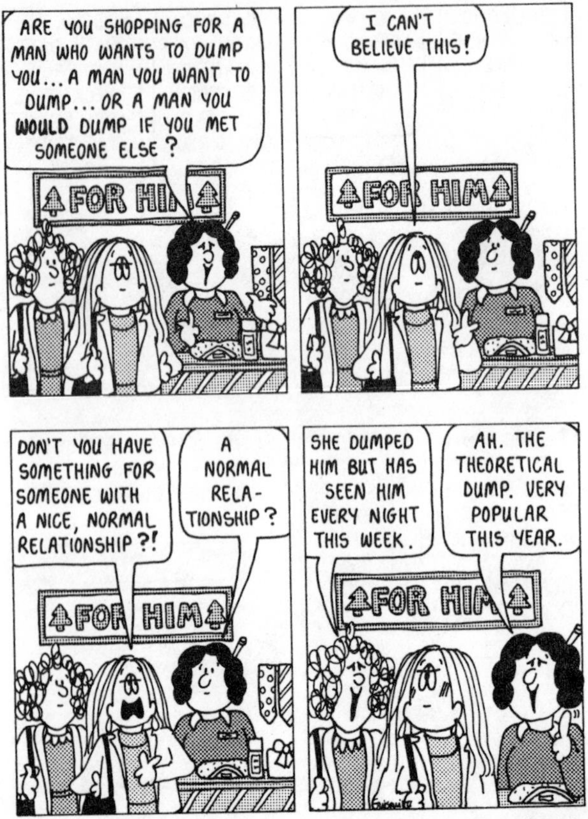
ARE YOU SHOPPING FOR A MAN WHO WANTS TO DUMP YOU... A MAN YOU WANT TO DUMP... OR A MAN YOU WOULD DUMP IF YOU MET SOMEONE ELSE?
FOR HIM
I CAN'T BELIEVE THIS!
FOR HIM
DON'T YOU HAVE SOMETHING FOR SOMEONE WITH A NICE, NORMAL RELATIONSHIP?!
A NORMAL RELA-TIONSHIP?
FOR HIM
SHE DUMPED HIM BUT HAS SEEN HIM EVERY NIGHT THIS WEEK.
AH. THE THEORETICAL DUMP. VERY POPULAR THIS YEAR.
FOR HIM

The Undump Dump:

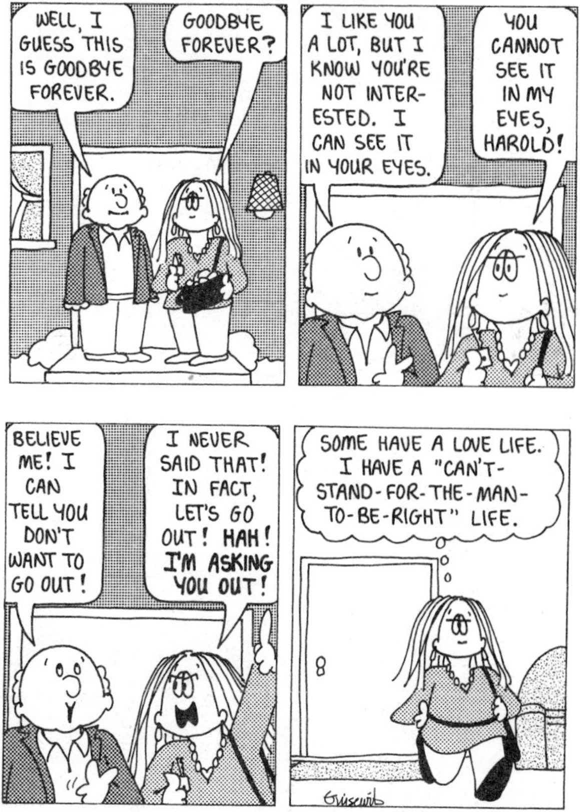
WELL, I GUESS THIS IS GOODBYE FOREVER.
GOODBYE FOREVER?
I LIKE YOU A LOT, BUT I KNOW YOU'RE NOT INTERESTED. I CAN SEE IT IN YOUR EYES.
YOU CANNOT SEE IT IN MY EYES, HAROLD!
BELIEVE ME! I CAN TELL YOU DON'T WANT TO GO OUT!
I NEVER SAID THAT! IN FACT, LET'S GO OUT! HAH! I'M ASKING YOU OUT!
SOME HAVE A LOVE LIFE. I HAVE A "CAN'T-STAND-FOR-THE-MAN-TO-BE-RIGHT" LIFE.
Guisewite

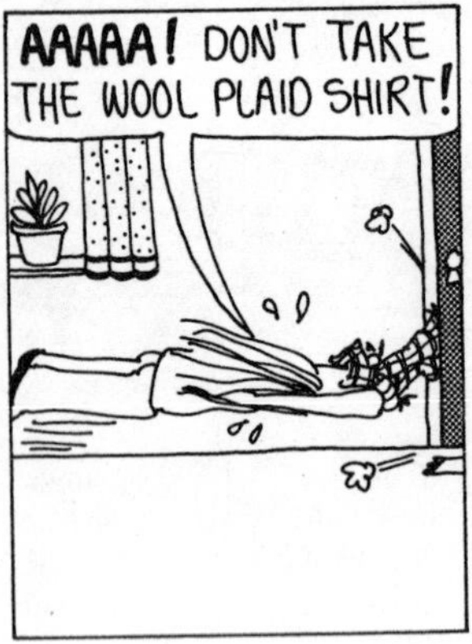
AAAAA! DON'T TAKE THE WOOL PLAID SHIRT!

Happily Ever After

It takes a lot of stamina to find love.

To live a full, meaningful life, but to also always keep a little place open for the chance of meeting someone new . . .

To commit to working, studying, volunteering, traveling, reading, working out, cooking, creating, entertaining, and remodeling . . . and then, when your schedule is booked solid for the next year, to try to find an hour to go out with someone's neighbor's nephew . . .

To give everyone a real chance, in spite of the fact that you have nine minutes left on your biological clock and only eight free minutes a week . . .

To believe the next person will be different even though the last 400 have been exactly the same . . .

To satisfy the fantasies of all girlfriends, mothers, fathers, and relatives . . .

To keep an open, flirtatious, loving heart at the exact same time you're disgusted with all members of the opposite sex . . .

To create a real home for yourself because you're "not waiting for love to let real life begin," and then be willing to share your closet space. . .

To be a complete, confident, capable human being while emanating a constant aura of availability . . .

To put on makeup every single time you go into the 7-Eleven just in case this is The Day you meet The One . . .

To not give into the temptation of getting married just so you can move to the other side of The Line . . .

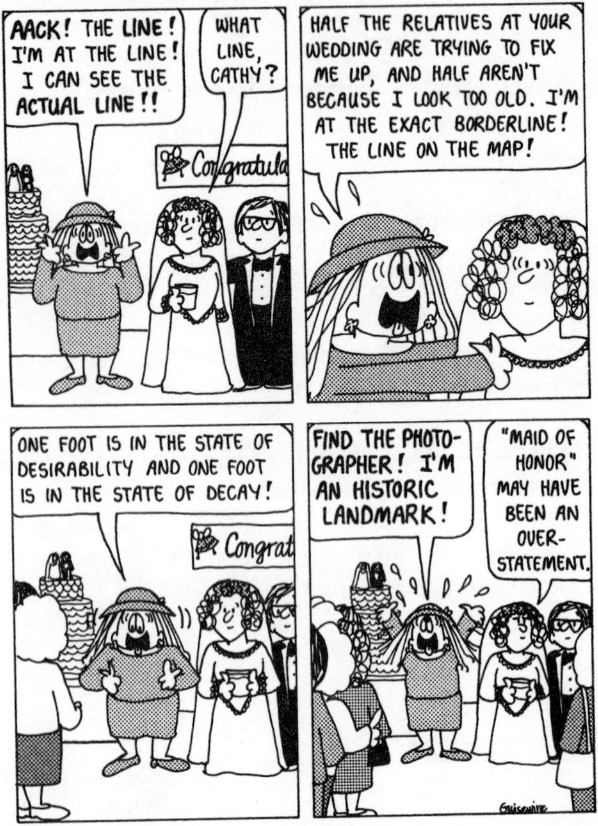
AACK! THE LINE! I'M AT THE LINE! I CAN SEE THE ACTUAL LINE!!
WHAT LINE, CATHY?
Congratula
HALF THE RELATIVES AT YOUR WEDDING ARE TRYING TO FIX ME UP, AND HALF AREN'T BECAUSE I LOOK TOO OLD. I'M AT THE EXACT BORDERLINE! THE LINE ON THE MAP!
ONE FOOT IS IN THE STATE OF DESIRABILITY AND ONE FOOT IS IN THE STATE OF DECAY!
Congrat
FIND THE PHOTOGRAPHER! I'M AN HISTORIC LANDMARK!
"MAID OF HONOR" MAY HAVE BEEN AN OVERSTATEMENT.
Guisewite

In the last 25 years we've proven how how happy we can be on our own, and we've also proven how much we need each other.

We've approached the classic quest of life with new standards, new demands, new values, new goals, new impatience, and new names.

We survived the revolution between the sexes, and still want to hold each other's hand.

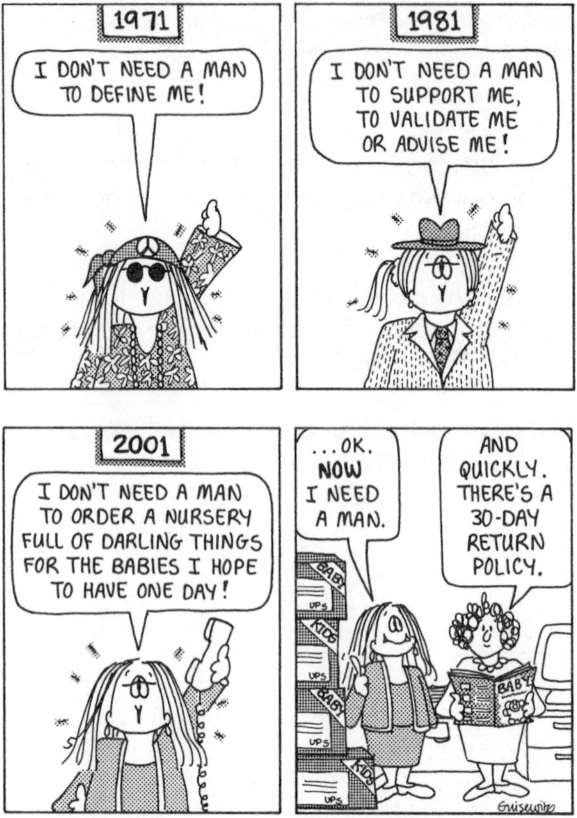
1971
I DON'T NEED A MAN TO DEFINE ME!
1981
I DON'T NEED A MAN TO SUPPORT ME, TO VALIDATE ME OR ADVISE ME!
2001
I DON'T NEED A MAN TO ORDER A NURSERY FULL OF DARLING THINGS FOR THE BABIES I HOPE TO HAVE ONE DAY!
...OK. NOW I NEED A MAN.
AND QUICKLY. THERE'S A 30-DAY RETURN POLICY.
BABY
UPS
KIDS
BABY
Guisewite

We've set new boundaries.

We've asked the hard questions.

We've enlightened.

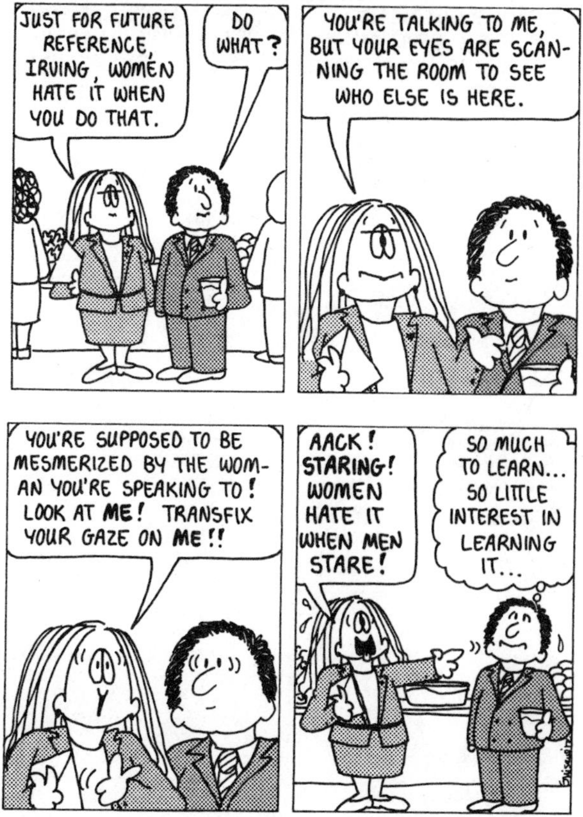
JUST FOR FUTURE REFERENCE, IRVING, WOMEN HATE IT WHEN YOU DO THAT.
DO WHAT?
YOU'RE TALKING TO ME, BUT YOUR EYES ARE SCANNING THE ROOM TO SEE WHO ELSE IS HERE.
YOU'RE SUPPOSED TO BE MESMERIZED BY THE WOMAN YOU'RE SPEAKING TO! LOOK AT **ME**! TRANSFIX YOUR GAZE ON **ME**!!
AACK! **STARING**! WOMEN HATE IT WHEN MEN STARE!
SO MUCH TO LEARN... SO LITTLE INTEREST IN LEARNING IT...

We've radiated.

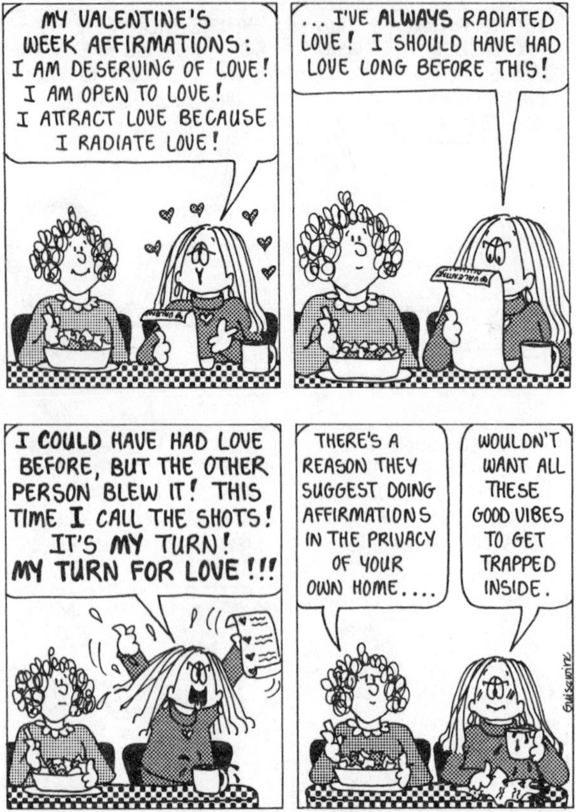
MY VALENTINE'S WEEK AFFIRMATIONS: I AM DESERVING OF LOVE! I AM OPEN TO LOVE! I ATTRACT LOVE BECAUSE I RADIATE LOVE!
... I'VE ALWAYS RADIATED LOVE! I SHOULD HAVE HAD LOVE LONG BEFORE THIS!
I COULD HAVE HAD LOVE BEFORE, BUT THE OTHER PERSON BLEW IT! THIS TIME I CALL THE SHOTS! IT'S MY TURN! MY TURN FOR LOVE!!!
THERE'S A REASON THEY SUGGEST DOING AFFIRMATIONS IN THE PRIVACY OF YOUR OWN HOME....
WOULDN'T WANT ALL THESE GOOD VIBES TO GET TRAPPED INSIDE.
Guisewite

We've played by the rules.

We've screamed to the universe.

I'M READY TO MEET SOMEONE, CHARLENE. THERE. I SAID IT. I PUT IT OUT TO THE UNIVERSE.

YOU MUMBLED IT TO THE UNIVERSE, CATHY. DOESN'T COUNT.

IF YOU WANT THE UNIVERSE TO LISTEN, YOU HAVE TO SCREAM IT WITH ALL YOUR HEART!

I'M READY TO MEET SOMEONE!!

EXCEPT YOU HAVE TO SIMULTANEOUSLY ACT DISINTERESTED SO THE UNIVERSE WON'T THINK YOU'RE DESPERATE.

IS THERE NOTHING LEFT IN LIFE THAT ISN'T A MULTI-TASK?

We've primped.

We've pouted.

We've won.

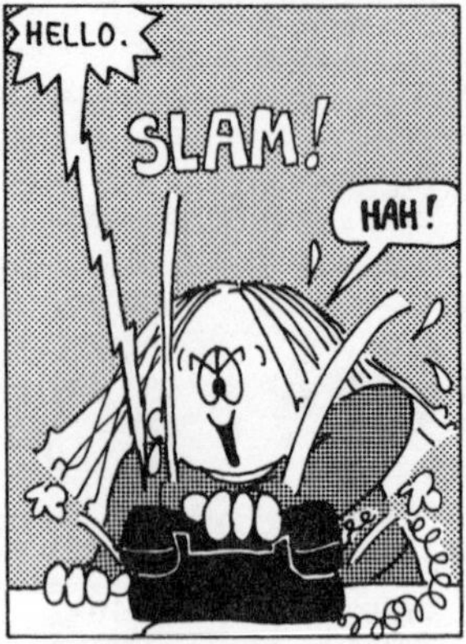
HELLO.
SLAM!
HAH!

We've run.

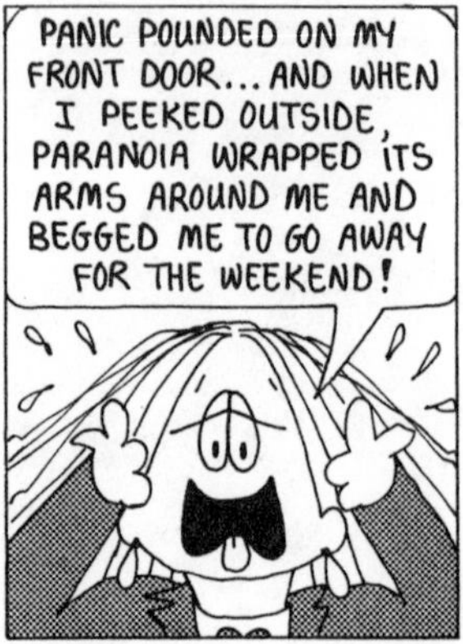
PANIC POUNDED ON MY FRONT DOOR... AND WHEN I PEEKED OUTSIDE, PARANOIA WRAPPED ITS ARMS AROUND ME AND BEGGED ME TO GO AWAY FOR THE WEEKEND!

We've agreed.

We've believed.

We've wallowed.

We've freaked.

We've tried and tried and tried and tried.

The clothes are different, the hair is different, the conversations are different, the rules are different, and the world is different, but the goal is just the same.

It's the one thing we knew we wanted from the first minute of life. We saw it in the first eyes we looked at, heard it in the first voice, felt it in those first strong arms. We've been looking ever since.

Love is always worth one more try.